About Island Press

Island Press is the only nonprofit organization in the United States whose principal purpose is the publication of books on environmental issues and natural resource management. We provide solutions-oriented information to professionals, public officials, business and community leaders, and concerned citizens who are shaping responses to environmental problems.

In 1994, Island Press celebrated its tenth anniversary as the leading provider of timely and practical books that take a multidisciplinary approach to critical environmental concerns. Our growing list of titles reflects our commitment to bringing the best of an expanding body of literature to the environmental community throughout North America and the world.

Support for Island Press is provided by Apple Computer, Inc., The Bullitt Foundation, The Geraldine R. Dodge Foundation, The Energy Foundation, The Ford Foundation, The W. Alton Jones Foundation, The Lyndhurst Foundation, The John D. and Catherine T. MacArthur Foundation, The Andrew W. Mellon Foundation, The Joyce Mertz-Gilmore Foundation, The National Fish and Wildlife Foundation, The Pew Charitable Trusts, The Pew Global Stewardship Initiative, The Philanthropic Collaborative, Inc., and individual donors.

Laurance S.
Rockefeller

Laurance S. Rockefeller

Catalyst for Conservation

ROBIN W. WINKS

ISLAND PRESS
Washington, D.C. ● Covelo, California

Library of Congress Cataloging-in-Publication Data

Winks, Robin W.
    Laurance S. Rockefeller: catalyst for conservation / Robin W. Winks.
        p.   cm.
    Includes bibliographical references and index.
    ISBN 1-55963-547-9 (cloth)
        1. Rockefeller, Laurance Spelman. 2. Conservationists—United States—Biography.   I. Title.
    QH31.R56W55   1997
    333.7´2´092—dc21
    [B]   97-20447
                                                                  CIP

Printed on recycled, acid-free paper ⊕

Manufactured in the United States of America

10 9 8 7 6 5 4 3 2 1

Contents

Acknowledgments

This book is the product of a larger study of what I call "the rise of the national park ethic." I believe there to have been five distinct stages by which the present definition of national parks was reached in the United States. As I did my research I realized that cutting through these stages there was a consistent pattern of private philanthropy that helped to define and create national parks. At first I intended to describe this philanthropy in a single chapter; soon I realized that a single philanthropic family, over four generations, had contributed far more than any other philanthropists to the national parks movement. The contributions of the first two generations of this family had been explored through biographies; the third had not. Thus, I set aside my larger project to examine the impact of the Rockefeller family on the rise of the national park ethic. John D. Rockefeller and his only son, JDR, Jr., have been the subjects of much research; JDR, Jr.'s third son, Laurance, who most consciously sought to follow in his father's footsteps, and who did even more than his father to diversify the definition of a national park, has not been the subject of sustained study. Hence this short biography, which focuses on Laurance S. Rockefeller's work as a catalyst for conservation. For a chapter of a book-in-progress to become a separate study is not unusual; for what began as only a portion of a chapter to become a book is much more unusual; but then, the subject of this biography is an unusual man.

At the beginning of my study of the rise of the national park ethic, I received grants from the National Park Foundation and the Eastern National Parks and Monuments Association, and I am most grateful to both for the timely way in which they primed the pump. I also received assistance with research expenses from Laurance S. Rockefeller, the Woodstock Foundation, and Yale University. Though this book was in some measure initially a by-product of my larger inquiry, which begins with the National Park Service Act of 1916, it also stands alone, for it has grown, changed, and taken on a central life of its own. I thank all those who have assisted me along this journey.

To be near many of the sources I was provided with work space at Room 5600 of the Rockefeller corporate headquarters, for which I am thankful, though I did not use it. Instead, I sought out the drier elevation of Santa Fe, New Mexico, where Douglas Schwartz, president of the School of American Research, gave me office space, and the slopes of Totoket Mountain in Connecticut to write.

I am grateful to the late M. Frederik Smith for many conversations, for giving me unlimited access to his materials, and for his friendship over the years. His two useful manuscript biographies of Laurance S. Rockefeller helped inform this assessment of LSR's activities in the field of conservation. Clayton W. Frye, Jr., Ellen R.C. Pomeroy, and Fraser Seitel helped me to define and redefine my task and assisted in rooting out errors of fact. They never interfered with the product. Fraser Seitel also generously gave me transcripts of his seven lengthy interviews with LSR. Henry L. Diamond provided a sweeping critique of an early draft of the manuscript. Nash Castro's close readings helped detect errors of omission and commission and his thoughtful suggestions were important at several points. Ruth Fowler provided me with a steady flow of encouragement and data, especially on illustrations. Carol S. LeBrecht and Jane Bedford supplied copies of speeches, citations, testimony, and other primary materials. Peter O. Crisp helped me to grasp the concept of venture capital, and Donal C. O'Brien, Jr., lead counsel and senior partner of Millbank, Tweed, Hadley, and McCloy, untangled the legal complexities of the story of Kykuit for me. Charles Granquist provided administrative clarifications. At Marsh–Billings National Historical Park, David Donath and Janet Houghton reacted to relevant portions of my manuscript. The staff of the Rockefeller Archive Center in North Tarrytown, New York (and in particular Darwin Stapleton and Thomas Rosenbaum), produced every file I requested in a quick and friendly order. Fraser Seitel coordinated the photographs.

William Conway, president and general director of the Wildlife Conservation Society, and Stephen Johnson, also of the Society, opened the archives and the library of the New York Zoological Society, commonly called the Bronx Zoo, to me. Robert O. Binnewies, executive director of the Palisades Interstate Park, let me read the minutes of the Interstate Park Commission, and his assistant, Kathryn Brown, copied many extracts from the documents for me. Robert

Cahn, a noted environmental writer, gave me records and correspondence relating to Horace M. Albright. Paul C. Pritchard, president of the National Parks and Conservation Association, and Alan A. Rubin, president of the National Park Foundation, gave me access to records on Laurance Rockefeller's activities with their respective groups. Benjamin Levy and Barry Macintosh of the National Park Service answered many odd questions.

I thank Yale University Library, and Margaret Powell in particular, for obtaining materials on microfilm and microfiche and for allowing me to carry away great stacks of books to a far-away place. I am grateful to Judy Schiff for access to the papers of Charles Lindbergh and Robert Moses, and to the New York Public Library for help with the large collection of the latter. I thank the Seeley G. Mudd Library at Yale for tracking down all of the volumes of the report of the Outdoor Recreation Resources Review Commission. Joseph A. Miller, librarian of Yale's Forestry Library, ran down many relevant items for me while John P. Wargo of Yale's School of Forestry and Environmental Studies suggested excellent leads.

I am grateful to the staffs at the Truman, Eisenhower, Kennedy, Johnson, Ford, and Carter presidential libraries, the Nixon Papers Project, the National Archives, the Library of Congress, the state archives, libraries, and historical societies of New York and Vermont, and the Adirondack Museum for their efficiency and help. The staffs of the University Research Library of the University of California, Los Angeles, and Clemson University Library were also most helpful. Roger G. Panetta of Marymount College, Laura Kline of Marist College, Clara Lee of Scenic Hudson, Inc., Norman Van Valkenburgh, formerly of the New York State Conservation Department, Frances F. Dunwell and Alfred H. Marks of New Paltz, New York, and David H. Gibson of the Association for the Protection of the Adirondacks answered questions or gave me access to materials. I wish especially to acknowledge the courtesy of Mrs. Lyndon B. Johnson for meeting with me at her office in Austin at a time when she was particularly busy and for her gracious hospitality. I thank my research assistant, Ted Bromund, for responding to every call for help. I thank Jim Jordan, formerly of Island Press, a meticulous editor. I thank my wife, Avril, for her patience during a cranky time.

Above all, I thank Laurance and Mary Rockefeller for their interest in my work, for their willingness to let me read documentation that might have been taken as an invasion of their privacy, and for extended interviews. LSR is sometimes said to be a shy man, but this is scarcely the case. He is, rather, perhaps pensive: a person who thinks before he speaks and takes the time to find the right word (often accompanied by a self-deprecating and often humorous aside). He is introspective, persistent, and determined, all qualities that came through in interviews. In the 1990s his interests have grown rather than narrowed, even as his business activities have drawn in to a tighter compass, and thus this account is in no measure a definitive or an academic statement. It could not be, for such statements cannot be written of the living, who still have major contributions to make in the years to come; nor are all the essential written records fully available for the historian's scrutiny. What follows is a beginning, an appreciation, a preliminary inquiry that may, in time, form part of a much larger, deeper study of the one Rockefeller brother yet to be the focus of a major biography. The author of such a study will need a formidable understanding of the complexities of modern business and, if not of medicine, at least of the organization of philanthropy in relation to it. I hope that this book, limited as it is to conservation issues, will contribute an important portion to that larger study when it is attempted.

Mary Rockefeller read an intermediate draft of the manuscript and took a particular interest in the story of the Marsh–Billings estate in Vermont. I regret that she did not live to see the book in its final form. The partnership she and her husband formed was markedly close and compassionate, and their interest in this project was joint.

I should note for the record that I was given full cooperation in the writing of this extended essay and was left free to research where and as I wished, to conclude as I would, and to write as I have. Whenever I asked to see documents, they were promptly supplied to me. At no time did anyone suggest what my conclusions should be, and they are my own, as are any errors found here.

I

Mr. Conservation

The president of the United States came rather abruptly through the door to the right of the audience, apologizing as he walked for being late and keeping so distinguished a group waiting. Here, in the elegance of the White House's Roosevelt Room, serenely federal, clearly historical, George Bush began to read. There was a sense of intimacy to the room, and with cameramen lined up against the back wall, it seemed a bit crowded: the podium was only a few feet from the audience, who listened attentively as the president explained how the Congress of the United States had ordered the unique gold medal he carried in its blue plush case awarded less than a hundred times in the history of the nation. The first recipient was George Washington in 1777. This day the Congressional Gold Medal was being given for the first time for contributions to conservation and historic preservation.[1]

President Bush said that young Americans appeared to know little of the medal's recipient, who now stood quietly to the president's right, listening. The award, the president suggested, ought to help remedy this, for the recipient was "a hidden national treasure," a person who had loved and nurtured and by example taught about conservation nationwide, who had in his work on behalf of New York City shown how parks and boulevards were also part of the "great outdoors." He was a "champion of natural and human values"; he was the "foremost trailblazer in venture capitalism" as well. His life and works would, the president hoped, stand in summary of a century in which Americans had come to appreciate the very real problems of their environment, indeed of the world's environment. The president turned toward the recipient, who was listening with respect, erectly attentive: it was September 27, 1991, in the nation's capital, and in the presence of his wife, members of his family, of his staff, of senators and others, Laurance Spelman Rockefeller moved forward to receive the official recognition that he was, in fact, Mr. Conservation, the man who had done more than any other living American to place outdoor issues—recreation, beauty, national and state parks, environmental education, a responsible combination of development and conservation—clearly on the public agenda.

Laurance S. Rockefeller, or LSR as he was known to many who worked with him, was brief and gracious in "gratefully and humbly" accepting the Gold Medal. He cited his grandfather, father, his brother Nelson, his wife Mary, and his son Larry for what they too had contributed, invoking four generations of "labors of love for our great country." He accepted the medal not primarily as an individual but because it honored all those who had taken part and would in the future take part in saving the nation's heritage. With this ceremony in the Roosevelt Room, chosen as the site in part because an earlier president, Theodore Roosevelt, had done so much to launch the conservation movement in America, the nation honored one of its environmental leaders. The environmental movement, LSR said, was "central to the welfare of people," and it would remain so for as long as "this piece of gold glistens." Nothing was more important to him, he noted, than the "creation of a conservation ethic in America." Though he praised the president for the new Clean Air Act, LSR was looking to the future rather than to the past, and perhaps he hoped that even this joyous occasion might serve to move the man who had promised to be the nation's conservation president (but so far had not fulfilled this promise) to more vigorous action. Much remained to be done, LSR noted: a forthcoming world environmental summit, to be held in Brazil, which the president had shown notable reluctance to attend, was the moment when concern for the environment would find its highest, worldwide expression. Looking across the crowded room, toward the secretary of the interior, the head of the Environmental Protection Agency, and the cameras, the recipient concluded that "the nation's needs demanded that environmental quality must be high on the national agenda." Even at this moment of honor and recognition, Laurance Rockefeller was looking patiently and with his usual stubborn persistence to the future, seeking as he had always done to be a catalyst for change.

The short ceremony concluded, the president and the recipient shook hands, the president quipping that his staff had told him that he might look at the medal but couldn't touch it. The assemblage politely laughed, perhaps a little disproportionately. Mary French Rockefeller, LSR's wife, in electric blue, rose to be greeted by the president, after which he sought out each person in the room, to shake a hand, exchange a quick word, at least to wave, and after a final murmur of congratulations, to leave for his next affair of state. LSR, receiving the warm congratulations of others, no doubt already was thinking about the next step by which he could further the environmental agenda to which he had committed so much effort. The Congressional Gold Medal did not make him Mr. Conservation; he had been that for many years. Rather, it affirmed the significance of his contributions and provided a form of national validation for them.

As the president had noted in his brief allusion to Rockefeller's pioneering in venture capital, conservation was not, of course, the only significant matter on LSR's mental map. When asked by an interviewer what motivated him, he had replied, "I profoundly feel that the art of living is the art of giving. You're fulfilled in the moment of giving, of doing something beyond yourself. That's the moment of truth.... The act of giving, the act of creating, the act of doing—[by these] you're alive and fulfilled."[2] He had been a pioneer in aviation, in environmentally compatible resorts; his philanthropic contributions to medical research, especially on cancer, were extensive. When philanthropy relates to the conquest of disease or the healing of a shattered environment, it is a subject for the long haul, as LSR would remind people over and over. Everything, he told another interviewer, is related. What was required, in business, medical research, or conservation, was to "think newness and to see connections."[3]

II
The Quieter Path

There are over 200 books on the Rockefeller family. They figure significantly in at least 400 more. Many of these books are about the third generation, the children of John D. Rockefeller, Jr.: Abby, John D. 3rd, Nelson, Laurance, Winthrop, and David, in the order of their birth. One may read all these books, some friendly, some angry, to discover that there is one Rockefeller who is barely present in most of them. This is Laurance, who moves in and out for a page or so and is then gone, neglected by an author who sometimes is in search of scandal or the stuff of headlines, or whose interests are in politics, high finance, or international affairs.[1]

As a result, most of these books have neglected the Rockefeller who, in the tradition of grandfather and father, arguably has moved and shaken to the most long-range purpose—the preservation of the nation's natural heritage, of great historic landscapes. That preservation and the resulting creation of a conservation ethic that is endurable, bipartisan, and rooted in a consistent sense of values is a quieter but far more significant achievement than much that is done in politics, education, or business. Laurance Rockefeller chose this quieter path early in life.

This book is about a person who is still alive. This welcome fact poses problems for any biographer. There is no attempt here to tell LSR's whole story. Rather, the book is an effort to catch the intensity of the subject's most con-

sistent concern and to relate in some detail why and how this concern will outlast him. There are people who have no sense of place, who neither know nor
care whether a mountain range in Wyoming, a run of hills in Vermont, or a
tidal marsh in New York endures over time for others to share. But some care
deeply. There are those who have no sense of time—a rather American failing—and who appear to believe that their meaning rests almost entirely
between the parentheses of their birth and death dates. Other people plant,
build, and protect for a distant future long beyond their own mortality. Some
people contemplate both place and time and are content in reflection without
action. Some act on their reflections. This is an account of one such person.

Not all judgments on the Rockefellers as a family, or on LSR as an individual, are as favorable as will be argued here. Some commentators have noted that
he has been a shrewd and careful investor, and though such a judgment would
be taken as praise in business circles, have turned this conclusion against him.
Others have observed that his philanthropies, extensive as they are, have not
reduced him to poverty, as they might a Christian monk. With respect to conservation, some critics have suggested that Laurance Rockefeller was, at best,
inconsistent, and at the harsher edge of judgment, insufficiently purist in his
approach to environmental issues.

With all rich men and women there is, of course, a substantial body of pop-
ulist literature that concludes that their riches were won from the labor of others, or that the structure of capitalist society ensured that the rich would grow
richer as the poor grew poorer, or that riches are *prima facie* evidence of uneth-
ical behavior. There is little that can be said to refute this generic argument,
which is simply unexamined ideology. The historian's argument—that all individuals must be understood in the context of their time, place, and background—is dismissed by the simplistic argument (sometimes Marxist, but
often lacking even the rigor of thought a Marxist scholar brings to analysis)
that wealth in itself both corrupts and is a sign of corruption. A historian who
argues that capitalism has, on the whole, been a motor for human progress, and
that success in a capitalist society is the product of a dozen or more traits,
many of them desirable and all of them quite human, may be accused of being
equally ideological. All wealthy men will have their critics, for wealth is believed
to carry great responsibilities; the proper evaluation of a life is in the deeds
done with that wealth.

There have always been those who do good for others, as there have been
those who think only of themselves. But organized philanthropy, the giving of
great sums of money to improve society by searching for the cure to a disease,
or building a great library, or creating a major recreational or educational

resource, is a product of the nineteenth century, and even more of the twentieth century. The best known philanthropists have been men of moral conviction, generally rooted in an organized religion but not satisfied with the way in which their church, any church, dealt with systemic problems. They were individuals like Andrew Carnegie, generally said to be the first modern philanthropist, who did not think that giving a dime to one beggar would bring significant change to society, or the life of the beggar, while giving millions of dimes for libraries, hospitals, and research institutes to protect clean air and promote a healthy environment might change a harmful societal trajectory into a better one. Philanthropy tends to be most generous and most noticeable during times of rising crime, social disorder, and violence, when thoughtful reflection leads to the desire to mitigate poverty and ignorance. This desire was underpinned in the nineteenth century by the doctrine of progress, in the early twentieth century by belief in the power of the individual, and in the late twentieth century by a conviction that neither churches nor governments could, alone, ensure people of the exercise of their natural rights.

Andrew Carnegie had written that "those who would administer [their wealth] wisely must indeed be wise." He opposed "indiscriminate charity," which often encouraged "the slothful, the drunken, the unworthy." He wished to benefit the community, and the individual only as a member of that community: to use private wealth "to place within [the community's] reach the ladders upon which the aspiring can rise—free libraries, parks, and means of recreation, by which men are helped in body and mind; works of art, certain to give pleasure and improve the general condition of the people. . . ."[2]

These remarks, from Carnegie's famous essay on "Wealth," published in 1889, were much satirized by the 1930s, and even more so after World War II, for Carnegie appeared to be embracing a Darwinian "survival of the fittest" doctrine while clothing it in moral rhetoric. He did not admit that the slothful, drunken, and unworthy might be so because of systemic patterns of greed, abuse of power, and denial of access to education and good health. His suggestion that he was wise and others were not did not go down well in a time of increasing democratization of education. Carnegie's particular interest, free public libraries across the United States (and in his native Scotland), depended upon the belief that education would lift the potentially worthy out of the mud, a belief based upon the notion of the improving society. With access to knowledge, natural selection would bring the most intelligent and hard-working men to the top, thereby improving the community at large. Wealth more than nobility obliged one to help the unfortunate. Many of the great philanthropists of the twentieth century have been more sophisticated in their language while sharing Carnegie's basic assumptions. They have believed that philanthropy, unfettered by the compromises of the political arena, might attack the root causes of poverty—disease, illiteracy, racism, dependency on drugs, a lack of beauty in one's life, despair—more directly than government. John D. Rockefeller 3rd could devote his philanthropic energies to population studies, to research and the distribution of information on birth control or, later, abortion (from which, he wrote in 1976, there must be "no retreat" if women were to take control of their lives and assert their inherent right to freedom)[3] because he did not need to win voters to his cause. Individuals of great wealth could pursue their dreams while governments could hardly hope to dream at all.

Charity work was allied to and often based in a generalized religiosity in the nineteenth and early twentieth centuries, but by the 1920s and 1930s religion was less important than the social work ethic that sought to ameliorate for the weak the impact of *laissez faire* capitalism. The 1930s saw a rapid growth in fact-finding commissions, the use of statistics, the application of sociology and social psychology to the welfare of individuals and communities. Bureaucracies, in government and in charitable organizations, turned to science to supply answers to society's problems.

But science did not supply answers; rather, by multiplying factual data, it complicated, refined, and redirected the search for answers. It asked new questions. Science combated racism but there was a countervailing scientific racism. Science quantified the numbers in population growth, identified the vectors of diseases, supplied cures. Yet, a scientific rationalism was not what many of the great philanthropists sought from their gifts. Most held to a belief that there was something higher, beyond science, upon which communities must draw. They generally believed in people; they believed that individuals, if exposed to education, to art and to music, to the sublimity of great landscapes, and to the complexity and beauty of the natural world, would blossom. These individuals would form a community of spirit and intellect, and would, through a sense of stewardship passed to them by their experiences, tithe themselves financially and intellectually to help the next generation.

Such ideas may seem simple. In practice they are anything but. John D. Rockefeller, a so-called robber baron, found nothing contradictory in pouring much of his vast wealth into activities he believed would benefit society. Unlike Carnegie, he did not focus on a single activity, however: he took up Carnegie's list, as it were (and he began before Carnegie wrote), to create parks, colleges, universities, and hospitals and to enhance nature's natural beauty by the standards of his time. He had one son, John D. Rockefeller, Jr., who did even more,

more extensively, broadly, deeply, and imaginatively, in education, medical research, and conservation. All of John D., Jr.'s children would also be philanthropists, some more than others, each specializing to some extent. His son Laurance would most directly carry on the wide-ranging work of father and grandfather in education, conservation, and medicine, while being closely identified with issues of the environment, to which improving education and medicine contributed.[4]

Many commentators employ pseudo-psychology to explain the extensive philanthropy of a Carnegie, Ford, Mellon, Annenberg, or Rockefeller, by suggesting that their gifts arise from some form of guilt. This is an argument that cannot be refuted by a historian, though no more can it be proven by those who favor it. Still, the suggestion that individuals who have been highly intelligent, diligent, shrewd, and prescient in the accumulation of their fortunes should suddenly, after years of the most rational thoughts and acts, become the victims of emotional decisions ought to be highly suspect. It may be, as some social psychologists argue, that the competitive urge to gain more is in time replaced by an equally competitive urge to win fame and favor through public benefactions, but even were this true it is poor cause for condemning actions that bring the same extent of public good whatever the motives. Further, common sense would suggest that it is seldom true.

Common sense suggests, and history supports it, that individuals change across time: they learn, reflect, and are different people from one decade to another, sometimes dramatically and quickly so and sometimes only very slowly so. To blame a subsequent generation for the sins of the fathers is quite unhistorical, akin to blaming the twentieth century for eighteenth century slavery, or bad medicine or superstition. To suggest that an intelligent person is acting thirty years on in life from precisely the same motives acted on earlier is to maintain that one has led an unexamined life. Perhaps some people do lead such lives, but most do not.

The Rockefeller family fortune was created by John D. Rockefeller, who was born in humble circumstances near Richford, New York, in 1839, and who was, when he died in 1937, probably the richest man in America. His parents, and especially his mother, provided a stern and moral upbringing: one should lead a life of thrift, piety, hard work, and good deeds. As Baptists, the Rockefellers viewed alcohol, tobacco, and all frivolous and time-wasting activities (such as card-playing and dancing) as sinful. (Since there were neither tennis courts nor golf courses in the Rockefellers' world, his mother, Eliza Davison Rockefeller, did not indict them as well, though she likely would have done so. Much later in life John D. Rockefeller freed himself sufficiently of these definitions of wasted time to enjoy the golf course.) As the oldest son, John D. had particular reason to observe his mother's expectations.

His father, William Avery Rockefeller, was a salesman, largely of herbal medicines. He saw more humor in life, and he often was away for long periods of time. During these absences, John D. was the man of the house. In 1853 the family moved to a small town near Cleveland, Ohio, a city in the midst of pre–Civil War growth, where John D. attended high school and briefly a commercial college. When he was sixteen he became a bookkeeper clerk for a commission merchant's firm, and in due course he began his own firm with a partner. During the Civil War they thrived, for Cleveland was an important supply base for the war in the West.

During this time, and especially in the face of the war's impact, John D. Rockefeller became a philanthropist, even though income was modest. This was unusual though not truly rare, for there were many people making money and conscious that it was the circumstances of the times that helped them to do so, and who felt it appropriate to pay something back to society. But most people gave within a limited circle, to their church, to their immediate neighborhood, to causes that friends supported. While Rockefeller gave generously to his Baptist church, he also gave to a Swedish mission in Illinois, to an industrial school, to a society for blacks who were blind, and to a Catholic orphanage. Rockefeller was interested in the impact of his generosity and the likelihood of it being well used, and he often gave discreetly, wanting little or no publicity for doing so. He effectively tithed himself for causes he thought sound rather than those causes most supported by the social elite.

During the Civil War, John D. Rockefeller also became a rich man. His commission house handled the oil that came in from western Pennsylvania—the first successful oil well was drilled in 1859—and he quickly realized how important oil was going to become. In 1863 he and his partners built a refinery in Cleveland to produce kerosene in commercial amounts, and the "illumination revolution" had begun. Rockefeller's reputation for hard work, efficiency, and honesty soon paid off, and the refinery became the largest in the world. The oil industry suffered from frequent overproduction, wide price fluctuations, and chronic instability, and Rockefeller was determined to bring order into this chaos. In 1870 he and others incorporated the Standard Oil Company and transformed it into a near monopoly, a trust that could to a large degree control supply, influence demand, and stabilize prices. Though trusts would become illegal and the target of Progressive political reformers, trust-busting their cry, there was nothing illegal at the time in trying to control the chaotic industry. In particular, Rockefeller had the wisdom to avoid the oil fields, where individualism was most rampant, in favor of dominating the refining, distribution, and marketing of oil. By 1879 the Standard Oil Company had attained unquestioned monopolistic power, through careful control over costs, quick dominance of the export market, excellent and prudent management, ruthless acquisition of competitors, ever-growing volume, and market control.

John D. Rockefeller had never expected to become so rich. He took his pleasure from playing what he called the Great Game, from the sense of accomplishment in being more energetic, intelligent, and daring and for having a greater eye for detail combined with a greater sense of the connectedness of things than his competitors. Even his most famous critic, the muckraking writer Ida Tarbell, never accused Rockefeller of dishonesty, praised his abilities, and complained only of his pressing the law to its limits in his favor. She thought the company was greedy, but she did not make this charge of Rockefeller himself.[5]

When Rockefeller was forty-nine years old, he began to consider how he might devote more attention to giving large portions of his money away. He had diversified his investments intelligently, and these investments required his attention. Standard Oil was in good hands, and as the largest share holder he could expect to continue to make a great deal of money from the company; but he knew that it was easier to make money than to use it well. His rate of giving had declined, though he continued to make many relatively small donations to a variety of good causes, and he now wanted to be as systematic and influential in his philanthropies as he had been in his business activities. As will happen with most rich men, he was receiving hundreds of requests for assistance, and he could not personally hope to sort out the deserving from the fraudulent, the system-affecting from the merely palliative.[6]

Further, John D. Rockefeller now had a son. After his wife gave birth to four daughters, the first in 1866, she produced a boy, John D. Rockefeller, Jr., in 1874. John D., Sr., wanted to teach the boy both good business practices and sound philanthropic principles, and he needed to set an example for him. His first truly large philanthropic undertaking was the founding of a new University of Chicago, nominally Baptist though largely independent, which he hoped to see become the greatest center of learning in the Midwest. He began in 1889 with a gift of $600,000, a large sum for the time. He already had an able and imaginative assistant to help channel his gifts to productive causes. This man, Frederick T. Gates, would become the precursor of similar figures for each male member of the next two generations of Rockefellers, for John D., Sr., knew how to seek out the best-informed advice, to reject flattery when it had no basis in knowledge or dedication, and to pass on to his son and grandchildren his ability to surround himself with able lieutenants.

John D. Rockefeller, Sr., felt no guilt about his vast wealth. He did not believe that he was responsible for the Ludlow Massacre, the single blackest mark against him in public eyes, when in September 1913, National Guardsmen burned a miners' camp at Ludlow, Colorado, causing the death of two women and eleven children who had tried to hide in a cellar above which a flaming tent suffocated them. The miners were striking against the Colorado Fuel and Iron Company, demanding recognition for their union. Rockefeller owned a controlling interest in CFI. The public blamed John D., Sr., and John D., Jr. (who was on the CFI board of directors) for the massacre, and both were vulnerable to the charge that they were so opposed to socialists, anarchists, and union organizers who advocated violence as to have encouraged a climate of repression.

By 1911, or perhaps earlier, John D. Rockefeller, Jr., had become interested in the problem of industrial violence, and he had a more progressive view than his father did of what comprised fairness to workers. He felt some guilt about Ludlow, and he wanted to consult with experts and find a scientific solution to the growing problem of polarized labor-management relations. To this end he hired Ivy L. Lee to handle public relations for the family and William Lyon Mackenzie King, a dynamic Canadian (and later, prime minister of Canada) who had studied economics at the University of Chicago, to move the new Rockefeller Foundation, which was chartered in May 1913, into the arena of industrial relations. These men helped reshape the Rockefeller image. Far more important, they confirmed to John D., Jr., what he most powerfully believed: that he should "tell the truth in all matters," should change his policies to make them more closely in line with public opinion, and must be open in his dealings and about his intentions. At a time when wealthy Americans were afraid there would be revolutionary violence across the land, and when many were hunkering down until the storm had passed, Rockefeller, Jr., committed himself to a policy of openness. He, Ivy, and King then carried his father with him.

John D. Rockefeller, Jr., far exceeded his father in the extent of his philanthropies. Having wealth at the outset, and having seen the value of organized philanthropy, he gave away greater sums to more targeted purposes. Shy and somewhat withdrawn, an only son, and sheltered even when he tried not to be, he took good advice when he knew he had heard it, he made the giving away of his money his chief business, and he became perhaps the greatest philanthropist in American history. He opened up the world of modern philanthropy more dramatically than any American had ever done, into medicine, education, conservation, and improved race relations, and cast the Rockefeller philanthropic net worldwide. His first son, JDR 3rd, born in 1906, followed in this tradition, as did his other sons, Nelson, Laurance, Winthrop, and David. Laurance would focus on medicine and conservation as his philanthropic interests.

Like his grandfather, Laurance Rockefeller would have a fundamental influence at a crucial moment on two of the century's most important technological and cultural breakthroughs, taking the wealth he inherited to greater heights. The first of these was commercial air transport. As a major stockholder in Eastern Airlines and a tireless supporter of the airline's founder, Captain Eddie Rickenbacker, LSR cast his lot with one of the most rapidly growing, most dramatically affective, and romantic business endeavors of the immediate post–World War II years. Although LSR had inherited a fortune, and at thirty came into even more, he did not rest on his inheritance; rather, he "grew his money" by committing himself to culturally significant innovative enterprises where venture capital could have the greatest influence. He also embraced the revolution that computers would bring to the application of human abilities, their relationship to artificial intelligence, and the quantum leap in business efficiency and capacity that would result.

In philanthropy, as in business, Laurance Rockefeller wanted to plant seed money where it would have the greatest effect. He knew that the catalytic influence of hundreds of thousands of dollars strategically placed at the right moment could have the impact of hundreds of millions that came too soon or too late. Further, one must continue to galvanize any enterprise by helping to create new openings and to stimulate new initiatives. Memorial Sloan-Kettering Hospital (as it is now known) had been particularly important to JDR, Jr., and LSR made it the focus of his own benefactions for medicine. As Vice President George Bush remarked at the ground-breaking ceremony for the new Rockefeller Research Laboratories in 1986, the "greatest and most enduring legacy" JDR, Jr., left to Sloan-Kettering may have been "his son Laurance."[7]

Laurance Rockefeller's commitment to conservation must be understood in these contexts. He understood the power of being a catalyst in business and in giving. He honored his father by pursuing some of the same goals and his grandfather by use of some of the same methods. He wished to stand firmly within the family tradition but also to be his own person, separate from the two preceding generations and from his brothers. He did not doubt the integrity of his grandfather, though he knew some did (none questioned his father's integrity, though some questioned his judgment), and he wanted always to do the right, honorable thing. He believed in "the healing power" of compromise, to follow the paths of patience to a shared goal, especially when the issue was conservation and, later, the environment, on which opinions were so polarized. He would, of course, have his critics, in part simply because he was a Rockefeller, in part because some conservationists and environmentalists opposed all compromise, and in part because, unlike many men of great wealth, he was willing to listen and to change his mind, so that he seemed open to the charge of inconsistency.

The history of thought on conservation and the environment is particularly prone to misplaced hindsight. We know today of the risks posed by a wide range of pesticides, for Rachel Carson and others alerted the public to those risks in the 1960s. To denounce a nineteenth century farmer, geneticist, or environmentalist—a term not yet invented—for using pesticides is simply to be foolish, since they not only lacked the knowledge and the vocabulary of the 1990s, but they were not yet even asking the same questions. Conservation, viewed until the 1950s as protecting the nation's forests and streams in order to encourage responsible hunting and fishing and to assure continued health to the recreation and forest industries, had not yet been displaced by environmentalism, which at the least means protecting the nation's natural resources and natural beauty for posterity, and during the transition from one to the other, views of sound practice changed dramatically.

Conservation and environmentalism are not the same thing, of course. The first was a response to the destruction of the bison, the extinction of the passenger pigeon, the transformation of a once abundant land into barren and sterile soil through harmful farming practices. Conservation was based on observation, common sense, and pride in the unique North American environment. Its supporters included lumber men, sportsmen, the great fishing clubs of the Adirondacks, and the urban-based clubs that encouraged trophy hunting. Conservation began with wildlife and moved on to soils. Theodore Roosevelt, hunter, outdoorsman, scholar, and president of the United States, was a conservationist. New York City's Boone and Crockett Club sought to promote "manly sport with the rifle"; it, and hundreds of naturalists, taught natural history, founded museums, collected specimens, and promoted rules about fairness in the pursuit of wildlife. Conservationists established the first national park in the United States, Yellowstone, in 1872. They restocked streams, rivers, and lakes with fish. They argued for the protection of forests as habitats for wildlife, for the creation of wildlife refuges along the seasonal migration paths of game birds, and for the study of breeding patterns and mating calls. Conservationists believed that nature should be protected in order to be useful, or uplifting, indeed ennobling, to mankind.

Later, as we will see, environmentalists went much further. Rachel Carson argued that DDT, a pesticide, was used against only those insects defined by farmers and ranchers as pests. But this was to define an insect solely in terms of the most obvious and immediate human needs and knowledge. Insecticides did not stop their destruction within the food chain. Animals that ate poisoned insects grew ill. Dead insects could neither pollinate nor contribute to the food chain of amphibians, fish, or bats and birds. The very term *pesticide* was anthropocentric—concerned only with immediacy and man. When Carson published *Silent Spring* in 1962, the developing study of ecology moved ahead of the insights of the work of the first ecologist, George Perkins Marsh, whose *Man and Nature*, published in 1864, had showed the connection between the degradation of the landscape and the elimination of spawning grounds. Environmentalism came to mean leaving the natural landscape alone as much as possible rather than reshaping it to man's definitions of beauty; to building no roads, planting no alien trees, letting nature take its course in so far as possible. Environmentalism recognized that human beings are part of the natural order and that they must learn to live within it rather than seeking to transform it. Environmentalism demanded hundreds of decisions as to what constituted moral behavior. It also demanded practical decisions: did one put out a fire in a great national park because tourists wished to see the animal life that would, if the fire destroyed ground cover, retreat far away from the highways? Or should one put out only those fires that were caused by man, letting those caused by natural forces take their course? But if man was part of nature, should not the fires of man also be left to burn? The environmental debate would become, by the 1980s, intense, acutely difficult, and deeply confusing. It was apparent to all that environmentalism was different from conservation, that it required more education, more planning, and therefore more interference with traditional lifestyles than conservationists would tolerate.

Yet, environmentalists also tended toward the anthropocentric. An ecosystem might be seen as an innocent product of the interconnectedness of all organisms. But to speak of a "healthy ecosystem" or of the "stability" of an ecosystem meant one ascribed goals—of health, or balance, or even biodiversity—to nature. If nature is innocent, it is also random. Science was, conservationists argued, value-free or at least value-neutral. The very notion of an ecosystem suggested a systematic evolution of interdependent organisms rather than the random application of natural selection. Critics argued by the 1990s that this assumption would lead to biocentrism: the idea that all organisms have equal value. But to whom and for what? How could this be so if one believed in traditional Christianity? How is it possible to argue that the Bill of Rights, created by human beings, did not appropriately accord special rights to people as opposed to insects? What would the basis for civil government be in the future if biocentrism were carried to its logical conclusions?[8]

Laurance Rockefeller was a conservationist like his father for much of his life. By the late 1960s he moved closer to an environmentalist position. He was one of the most influential individuals in America to make that journey, from conservation to a muted environmentalism. He had the capacity to put his money into that journey, to educate teachers, politicians, and policy analysts. He was a product of his times and a shaper of those times. LSR was, by the 1990s, willing to at least consider the possibility of life in outer space, to consider the efficacy of holistic and alternative medicines, to consider the implications of biocentrism, to consider a trajectory for the successor Rockefeller generation that would carry his children, and his brothers' children, away from business and organized religion entirely. As he remarked, he remained open to influence.

In turn, LSR was an influence himself: on the international as well as national park movement, on outdoor recreation, national beautification, historical preservation, and on what constitutes the public good. Through his interventions and his generally well-placed insertions of seed money he reshaped the hotel industry, promoted better zoos and more extensive greenways, and raised expectations and performance on the part of travelers, conservationists, and environmentalists. Throughout most of his life LSR believed in the possibility of combining conservation with development, in the management principles of multiple use, in a mutually beneficial alliance between commerce and conservation. His views shifted and his understanding grew but he remained largely consistent from the time he first visited great national parks in the American West in the 1920s until he created and gave to the nation new national parks.

The national park system of the United States developed in fits and starts, the ethic that underlay the system evolving through experience and heightened awareness of what national parks could be. When John D. Rockefeller, Jr., first took an interest in the national parks, there were relatively few of them and clear standards for designating areas as national parks were still being developed. There was much emphasis on "the nation's playgrounds," on currying and cutting the forests and roadside areas to a standard of neatness that was more European than American. The parks were places to visit, to stay in clean if somewhat spartan hotels, to camp out under the stars, and to "experience nature." They existed as pleasuring grounds for the people, as places where great scenic landscapes could be protected, where even the ravages of nature might be repaired in order to assure a splendid view. Wilderness was not seen as valuable for itself. The great western parks were cathedrals of stone, testimony to God's handiwork, sources of inspiration, scientific marvels, exhibits of curious geological phenomena, and preserves of ancient and mysterious Native American ruins.

By the 1930s the national parks included "patriotic shrines"—scenes of Revolutionary and Civil War battles and historic remnants of early colonial settlement. Historical and cultural parks promoted a sense of national identity, pride, and patriotism. The park ethic evolved further as more and more antiquities were placed under the protection of the National Park Service. Increasingly the parks were seen as a source of education as well as wonder. Not until the 1980s did the ethic evolve to the point that there was general recognition that national parks were not tourist attractions or money earners, but that they were an important component of a national system of preservation and environmental protection and insufficient to such a sweeping goal.

Most individuals who wanted to create the great system of national parks that grew from the Organic Act of 1916 through the burst of creativity of the late 1930s believed that it was essential to strike an alliance between the forces of commerce and of conservation. Certainly the national parks were meant to be protected against extensive development, the resources within them held in perpetuity for the enjoyment of future generations. But this language was not taken as being so pure as to prevent the building of access roads to the parks, or hotels within them, or the opening up of well-groomed trails so that a person from the city might walk safely through them. Further, it was widely believed that the parks would best be protected by creating a constituency that would defend them, and this constituency would consist for the most part of the American traveling public. Figures associated with the early evolution of the national park ethic—such men as Stephen T. Mather, the first director of the National Park Service, or Horace M. Albright, perhaps the most influential person in the history of it—sought to find a balance. That they were taken as having successfully done so is a judgment of their times. Today both are criticized for making compromises with the park ethic, a logically indefensible charge since at the time the ethic itself was in evolution and thus was not a stable position open to some fatal compromise.

Though individuals who are knowledgeable about America's national park movement are well aware of Laurance Rockefeller's contributions to the country's system, they often are far less aware of what may well be his greater contribution—the evolution of an understanding of the nation's recreational needs. In the 1950s recreation and national parks were not seen as in conflict; in the 1960s and 1970s, the National Park Service actively sought out new additions to make to its National Recreation Areas, while accepting that though such areas were units of the world's premier National Park System, they were to be held to a lower standard of quality, significance, and protection. But beginning in the mid-1950s, when the U.S. Bureau of Reclamation sought to build a dam at Echo Park in Dinosaur National Monument, the evolution of the national park ethic moved rapidly to a more all-embracing position that any unit of the Park System, however designated, should be accorded the same protection. This would come into conflict with new views of the desirability, or not, of organized recreation in parks. Many American historians of both conservation and environmentalism trace to the Echo Park Dam controversy the widening rift between recreationists and environmentalists. A conservationist was increasingly defined as a person who wished to see the nation's land and water protected in order to make possible continued habitat that would afford recreational hunting and fishing opportunities for a very long time to come. Environmentalists increasingly saw resource protection as an end rather than as a means. They wanted to protect resources in perpetuity, for all future generations; they sought to educate the public and politicians about the values of biodiversity; and often they were opposed to hunting and fishing, even when biologists maintained that culling was essential to the survival of a species. Some thought that the sacredness of life itself—all life, not just human life—was at stake. Between these positions, recreationists were courted, divided, and at times misrepresented.

In this context Laurance Rockefeller played a significant role as chairman of the nation's first, and by far most sweeping, review of future recreational needs. He would contribute in important ways to the protection of both natural and historic values along the Hudson River and elsewhere in his home state of New York and to the study of species survival at the New York Zoological Society. But he also built resorts, and though most lay outside the boundaries of national parks and nature preserves, the way in which he built and promoted these hotels represented a corporate statement about his views on recreation, conservation, and the environment. Thus his actions as a businessman, philanthropist, and conservationist brought him into the midst of the evolving ethic over national parks and other preserves.

LSR's philosophy, which he described as encompassing conservation *and* use, contributed significantly to this evolving ethic. Context was all. He strongly believed in balance, and this meant at times that he favored compromise between what he viewed as untenable extremes; at other times, and depending on the matter in question, he would stand unyielding. Most often, he was quietly persistent, returning even two decades later to try once again to accomplish a task that he still felt worth doing. In May 1995, in remarks prepared for the occasion on which LSR received the first Theodore Roosevelt National Park Medal of Honor from the hands of President Bill Clinton, he made it clear that he opposed a bill then in committee in the House of Representatives. This bill, artfully (and misleadingly) entitled the National Park System Reform Act, called for a re-examination (and justification) of the boundaries of all the units of the National Park System (by then 368 in number) and for the dropping of entire units found lacking in national significance, unworthy of national park status as defined by decades-old statutes, unmindful of the evolution of a park ethic over the years. Under the act, some of the national parks might be turned over to the states for administration, and some might be passed into the hands of private enterprise, if they could be made to pay for themselves through greater emphasis on their recreational, perhaps even their entertainment, values. A few might be abandoned entirely. Rockefeller had thought long and hard about how to combine recreational and conservation values, and he increasingly had come down on the side of the latter if there was incontestable conflict between them. He understood that contexts change and that actions must be judged in their contexts. In accepting the Medal of Honor he spoke out in opposition to the prospective de-accessioning of park units, this defrocking of sacred sights, urging that a hasty Congress not damage a system that had grown across the years to worldwide leadership.

Laurance Rockefeller, no less than any other intelligent observer of the last fifty years, is of the Age of Ecology, and it should come as no surprise that his thought on matters of conservation has changed as the history of ecological thought evolved. One may, of course, date the beginning of this "Age" at any of several points. One of the usual benchmarks is the publication in 1864 of George Perkins Marsh's *Man and Nature* (in its revised edition subtitled *The Earth as Modified by Human Action*), a book which, in the critic Lewis Mumford's words, was "the fountainhead of the conservation movement." Other dates may also serve, since in any evolutionary process, there will be many points in time that in hindsight are arguably basic to the development of an ethic: Perhaps Gifford Pinchot's taking up leadership of the National Conservation Association in 1910, the year of Laurance Rockefeller's birth? Perhaps the establishment of the first academically based study of the relationship between man and nature in 1915 at the Yale School of Forestry? Perhaps the creation of Acadia National Park in 1919, the first such park to combine natural landscape and a built environment? Perhaps even, as the historian Donald Worster has argued in *Nature's*

Economy,[9] the Age of Ecology did not begin until the dropping of the first atomic bomb. Whatever date one chooses, one finds the Rockefeller name woven into it.

Rockefeller's own introspection reflects the separate streams found in the American ecological movement. One body of thought is concerned with how to use resources wisely, for profit, for the benefit of mankind, and for economic growth: here one finds LSR's venture capitalism, and in particular the remarkable success (and achievements) of his resorts. A second strain of thought is concerned with an arcadian view, which finds an organic, spiritual bond between the land and humanity, in which one is steward to the other, and through stewardship, people learn about themselves, their creativity, limitations, and strengths. A third strain is experiential: what one learns from contact with nature, from the simplest forms of feeling and learning—feeding squirrels in a park, enhancing the view of a lake or tree by approaching it differently on foot or by road—to the most complex, as when living in the midst of a vast, growing, explosive metropolitan mass. These three strains of thought come together in a series of actions that fully validate the reverse aphorism that "action *is* thought." This is "the quieter path."

III

Growing Up: Toward Self-Reliance

Laurance Rockefeller was, of course, initially taught by his parents, his father, John D. Rockefeller, Jr., and his mother, Abby Aldrich Rockefeller. His grandfather and his siblings were very important to him, and as the fourth child of six, he was never out of touch with any of them. His earliest memories are of the out-of-doors, of such simple matters as a visit to Central Park, then curried and combed in the way its principal designer, Frederick Law Olmsted, and his partner, Calbert Vaux, intended. His education at the Lincoln School in New York City and the Olmstead School in Lakewood, New Jersey, was unconventional, experimental, and liberating, but not very sound in what was then called "the fundamentals." His travels with his parents and brothers to the Rocky Mountains, the West Coast, and Europe left deep impressions on him, as did his summers on Mount Desert in Maine. His higher education at Princeton and the Harvard Law School strengthened and confirmed his interest in philosophy and moral studies.

All children gain, though usually not in equal measure, many of their most fundamental qualities from their parents. In Laurance's case, his mother, daughter of Nelson Aldrich, Senator from Rhode Island and a leading light of the Republican Party, was particularly influential, and many of the characteristics associated with him were also hers. She lived graciously with those who worked for her in the several households in which the children grew up—

at Pocantico, the family estate, near Tarrytown in New York's Westchester County; at Seal Harbor, the family's summer home on Mount Desert Island in Maine, just outside the boundary of Acadia (until 1929, Lafayette) National Park; in Williamsburg, Virginia, where John D., Jr., was engaged in historical restoration work; and at their townhouse on West 54th Street in New York City. As one observer remarked (who might well have been speaking of Laurance in later years), she had a genius for making people feel they worked with her rather than for her. Perhaps because of this, she also treasured loyalty—in those she worked with as well as those who worked for her—and felt that disloyalty was the most difficult offense to forgive. Years later, when her sons were independent and highly successful in their own right, Laurance would demonstrate the particular qualities of forgiveness and loyalty that marked his childhood experience.

Abby Aldrich was twenty-seven when she married John D. Rockefeller, Jr., though she had met him when he was in his second year at Brown University and she was only twenty-one. She bore him six children between 1903 and 1915, a daughter and five sons—Laurance, the fourth child, was born on May 26, 1910, in New York City. This was not a time of working wives, certainly not amongst the well-to-do, and Abby was very much a presence in her children's day, seeing them off to school, making a point of being at home when they returned, setting aside an hour to read to them, or as they grew older, to listen to one of them reading to her. When the children were away, they wrote her warm and newsy letters. As with all growing boys, the brothers sometimes quarrelled or fought, though Nelson and Laurance (or Nels and Bill, as they called each other) almost never between them, for they became particularly close and loyal through adulthood. She gave them responsibility for their own decisions, encouraged them to save and to account for their allowances as their father wished, nurtured an interest in nature, wild flowers, birds, and later, art. She spoke often of being a good neighbor, wherever they were, and reminded them that objects, of which they could accumulate a goodly number if they wished to use their financial resources in that way, ought to have a point, a purpose, and some inherent worth and attractiveness. She disliked any hint of racial discrimination and told her sons that they must show respect to all people.[1]

Though outgoing, vivacious, and high spirited, Abby Rockefeller disliked publicity, even favorable publicity, for she knew how easily it could distort. She was generous, happily accepting of the wealth her father, and then her husband, represented, but equally concerned that people with money should "do good things with it" lest they become selfish and inward. She believed that a sense of duty should be the leading emotion in her children's lives, and she thought that duty was a pleasure and not a burden. She treasured solitude "in order to learn to know oneself and to get a grasp on things," and while she loved a party and meeting interesting people, she knew when to draw back and savor her own thoughts. Her interest in modern art, in American folk art, and in sharing her husband's concerns, especially his philanthropies, was deep, sincere, and well informed, and though all of her sons showed the same concern for art, Nelson, Laurance, and David went beyond accumulation and collecting. In time, objects associated with his mother would come to fill LSR's apartment, and her portrait hangs in his dining room.

To be sure, the Rockefeller brothers did not grow up like other American boys. They traveled widely, they attended an exciting experimental school, they dressed well, they had their portraits painted for the walls of their New York townhouse, and they knew the pleasures of moving from one home to another as the seasons, their activities, and their ages changed. But the famed thrift of their grandfather, their parents' sense that they ought to know what a dollar could and could not buy, JDR, Jr.'s stern insistence that they account for every penny of their allowance or of what they earned, and his firm control over family finances and their inheritances until he deemed them ready to handle large sums, gave each the sense of value, of wanting a dollar's worth of good for a dollar's worth of labor, that marked America as it grew into the industrial and financial giant of the world. They did not feel the anxiety those who must fear a catastrophic loss felt, for in an emergency there was an amplitude of support within the family, both financial and human. They nonetheless had their own anxieties: about doing well, pleasing their father, finding something of worth to contribute to life, even about such then common matters as being forcefully trained to give up a natural left-handedness for the right hand. They were the products of their time, and that time's ethics, medical conventions, spiritual commitments and yearnings, and perhaps above all, of the strong sense of duty that scholars would later diminish by using labels, such as "the Protestant ethic," "the achieving society," "the upwardly mobile demands of capitalism," and other phrases that may explain group but seldom individual behavior. In adulthood, each of the children, though sharing many common characteristics, was quite different.

Laurance Rockefeller was tutored at home for his first year of school and in 1917, with his brother Nelson, was sent to the Lincoln School, an experimental "learning environment" run by the Teachers' College of Columbia University according to the principles of John Dewey, advocate of "learning by doing." At the school the curriculum grew out of the "immediate interests of children," and according to the school's prospectus, it emphasized "meanings, insights, understandings, and broad techniques."[2] This meant history, science, and contemporary studies, not Latin or the classics. The school's founders had wanted to call it simply The Modern School, or The Experimental School, or even The People's School, but in the end they chose Abraham Lincoln by default. The school had no examinations, imposed no formal expectations and—unusual for the time—was co-educational. It emphasized, in addition to subject matter, the cultivation of self-control and self-direction and how to work cooperatively with others.

LSR attended the Lincoln School for eleven years. As he and Nelson walked (or on occasion roller-skated) to class, followed at a distance by the family limousine, they chattered about the built environment around them, learning as LSR later recalled "to see rather than merely to look." By its third year the school was in such demand, a new building, massive and granitic, was built near the Teachers' College. By then LSR understood that in attending the school he was fulfilling a Rockefeller expectation that went well beyond simply acquiring an "education for democracy," and that even at school he could not escape from his family and the awareness of the duty that being a Rockefeller placed upon him.

The school was, in fact, a product of the General Education Board, which organized and financed it. The Board was in effect a Rockefeller foundation set up in 1902 largely to help stimulate education for women and for African-American children in the South. The teachers at the school taught self-reliance and personal empowerment, and to this end they recruited children from all walks of life, mixing the sons and daughters of the rich with scholarship students from the slums. Graduates later declared that no one could tell who was rich and poor, and though this is quite unlikely, everyone tried hard to make it seem to be true in their interactions. For LSR the school was an "antidote" to life in the family, with an often authoritarian father, for it meant an open, almost unscheduled freedom in "a magnificently progressive social environment." Teachers were friends. From this non-authoritarian environment, LSR learned to be comfortable with older men as mentors and partners. Since there were no examinations there was no hierarchy of performance, which meant that one could work with others rather than in competition against them.

Years later LSR could not recall all of his teachers, but he remembered well their guiding principle: no memorization, no rigidity, all emphasis being "on *doing.* The prevailing philosophy was that in order to do, students had to learn to think, to solve problems, to create.... To think was to plan." The purpose of such an education was "to inculcate in students ... the importance of

assuming responsibility." The "youngsters assimilated the mechanics of cooperation . . . [and] developed a passion to be a catalyst with sufficient confidence
and influence to tackle almost anything that seemed worth doing."[3]

But if LSR did not remember every teacher over seven decades later, no matter. He had respected and learned from them then. Gordon Mirick was "better and better" (this was 1927) in math, Mr. Stolper (English) was "a good
teacher" and besides, "very nice," and Jerome Kuderna (physics) had "recognized ability," a cool judgment that. He attended "good, short" sermons, listened to brother Nelson's advice about life, lost at basketball, survived more
than one gymkhana, and when asked to read some poetry, chose two poems
on the illusions of war.[4] School and family records suggest that LSR was as
happy as he later remembered himself to be. He took a leading role in a Shake-
spearean pageant, played a dapper marquis in another, was business manager
of the school's annual publication, sang in the glee club, served on the student
council in his final year, and played varsity basketball (his height already sin-
gling him out), in which he twice lettered.

These years at Lincoln were interrupted in 1921 when LSR and John D. 3rd
were boarded at the tiny Olmstead School in New Jersey. The two boys suffered from severe colds every winter, and the school, which took only ten
pupils, emphasized outdoor activities, which LSR's parents felt were essential
for him if he was to grow strong. Olmstead had a stable of horses, and LSR,
who already enjoyed riding, spent much of his time there in a saddle. In the
spring, he and his mount, Nancy, won several prizes in the annual gymkhana.
His penchant for catching colds in the city was much lessened by his year in the
country, and in 1922 LSR returned to the Lincoln school, strengthened in self-
confidence by having been on his own for a time.

While the openness of the Lincoln School was a basic influence on LSR
and how he learned, three summer trips west during these years undoubtedly
taught him much about the subject that would become his life's preoccupation.
The first visit, in 1920, was the shortest: his father and he and his brothers visited Denver and other western cities, stayed in good hotels, and traveled in a
private railroad car, as the rich customarily did during the great age of rail. It
was at the end of this summer that JDR, Jr., decided to send LSR to the Olmstead School, in order that he grow in health and to give him a greater identification with the outdoors. In 1924 JDR, Jr., took Laurance and his two older
brothers, John D. 3rd and Nelson, on an extended trip to Taos, to Mesa Verde,
Yellowstone and Glacier National Parks, and to Jackson Lake, in Wyoming,
and the fourteen-year-old boy responded with pleasure and excitement to
everything they saw and did. Two years later, in 1926, JDR, Jr., took Laurance

and his two younger brothers, Winthrop and David, on a camping trip to Yellowstone, Jackson Hole, the Grand Canyon, and the California redwoods country. LSR was the common denominator among these three trips, the only child present on all of them, for perhaps already his father had recognized his intense response to the natural landscape. In this manner JDR, Jr., passed his philanthropic interest in conservation to his son, these trips and others to Williamsburg, Virginia, and other historic sites being a kind of laying on of hands, a passing of a torch in the interests of conservation and historical preservation.

LSR was especially influenced by his 1924 journey. The trip may have been intended to bring the father closer to his sons, but it was not entirely successful in this regard, though Laurance, who combined a sense of mischief with an observant compassion, understood his father fairly well and knew that he had stern responsibilities to the family name. JDR, Jr., traveled in a large motor car supplied by the Colorado Fuel and Iron Company while the boys, following behind in a second, were always brought forward by their father to be introduced and on occasion to lend a hand with minor chores. At Taos pueblo, the most dramatic of the several Native American villages along the Rio Grande River in New Mexico, they were introduced to Native American leaders, officials from the Bureau of Indian Affairs, and others, enjoyed a picnic under a vast cottonwood tree on the pueblo grounds, and observed traditional ceremonial dances performed for their benefit. LSR helped in the distribution of candy to the Indian children and was impressed by the dancers' clothing and their stately courtesy. LSR was only vaguely aware at the time that his father was being besieged by various groups who wanted to see him take a position with respect to Indian education and religious training, between officials and missionaries who wanted Native Americans to abandon their ceremonies as symbols of a pagan or animistic past and embrace fully the ways of the Christian white man and others who believed in the equality of Native Americans, respected their spiritual practices, and were trying to revive their traditional arts. LSR responded positively to the dances and their chants, to the pottery, jewelry, and blankets, and over the years he would add many objects to his collections that attested to his sense of appreciation for those who created such beauty. JDR, Jr., purchased Navajo blankets, silver, and rugs when "primitive art" was the term most who professed an appreciation for such objects used, but LSR would sustain an interest longest. Stops at Santa Clara and San Ildefonso pueblos, and in Santa Fe, confirmed that interest. He and his brothers had been taken to Williamsburg earlier that summer, and the contrast was striking.

During this trip the group met the superintendent of Mesa Verde National Park, Jesse L. Nusbaum. Mesa Verde was an early park, established in 1906 before there was a Park Service, and Nusbaum was an old-style park superintendent, which is to say something of a character. He was also a trained archaeologist who explained the significance of the resource—the "story" of Mesa Verde—so well to the father and his sons that they talked about how lucky they had been to have him show the great cliff dwellings to them and how much other visitors who did not have Nusbaum as a guide would miss. JDR, Jr., suggested that he would contribute funds to help create a facility for interpretation, not only at Mesa Verde but as a pilot project for other parks. He insisted that the "interpretation service," or exhibit, or whatever resulted, should not be called an "educational service" or center, for he believed the public would respond well to the first and less so to the second, a point on which he was surely correct. (As a result, Nusbaum set the pattern for an amenity and a service that would be basic to the Park System, and today one encounters an "interpretive center" or exhibit in virtually every unit.)

Nusbaum knew that other forms of "interpretation" were occurring elsewhere, through information offices, nature guides, tent museums, and the like. The Park Service's Educational Division had built portable working models of Yellowstone's geysers earlier that year. Nusbaum had, in fact, approached a San Franciscan philanthropist, Stella M. Leviston, for $5,000 for a museum at Mesa Verde three years earlier. But it most assuredly was JDR, Jr., with his offer of another $5,000—it is not clear from the record whether Nusbaum revealed that he already had a like sum in hand—and his prescient sense that what the parks needed was interpretation rather than education, who set his stamp upon a now venerable and highly successful National Park Service institution: the Branch of Interpretation, as formally and finally institutionalized in 1941.

That JDR, Jr., so readily saw the distinction between interpretation and education is important, for few people who are not trained historians do. Education is didactic, and, while not necessarily learned in the classroom or a museum, that is the public perception. Interpretation tells the story of a place in a way to bring it alive for the visitor and to stimulate discussion of the meaning of the site for oneself and for the community at large. At Mesa Verde, JDR, Jr.'s most important gift was less his money than his enthusiasm and insight, for without his and his sons' visit, the Park Service would simply have built another museum (of the kind it did build, for the first time with its own funds, at Crater Lake in 1930). Family tradition credits JDR, Jr., with the concept of the interpretive center, a concept to which LSR frequently would contribute as he grew older, and the family tradition is essentially correct,[5] since the Mesa Verde interpretive center was followed by interpretive exhibits at Grand Canyon and Yellowstone National Parks that were established with the aid of the Laura Spelman Rockefeller Memorial Fund.

Small sums can be crucial at precisely the right moment, a lesson LSR learned on this western trip. His father also donated just enough money in 1924 to make it possible for Nusbaum to excavate a trash heap in the corner of Mesa Verde's Spruce Tree House, providing the proposed interpretive center with solid research data. The next year JDR, Jr., funded the excavation of a Basket-maker site at Step House, and for the next three years he made new excavations at other sites possible. These small gifts were crucial to the emergence of a truly interpretive museum with scientific credibility, one that went beyond the few photographs of Mesa Verde (donated by the Denver & Rio Grande Railroad), unlabeled pot shards, and dried flower specimens that the Rockefeller group had seen Nusbaum display in a converted ranger station.

Identified as "the Davison family," the traveling party moved on to Walsen-burg, Colorado, to Pike's Peak, Denver, and across Wyoming by private rail car, through Billings, to Gardiner, Montana, which was the end of the line for Yel-lowstone National Park. They were greeted by Yellowstone's superintendent, Horace M. Albright, who had been alerted by the acting director of the National Park Service, Arno B. Cammerer, to lay on a fine tour for them. Cam-merer also told Albright that he was under no circumstances to ask the Rock-efellers for any money, even though it was well known that JDR, Jr., had pro-vided generous funds for Lafayette (after 1929, Acadia) National Park and a variety of other park-related projects.[6]

Albright's great hope was to add the Grand Teton Mountains and Jackson Hole to Yellowstone National Park, and he provided JDR, Jr., with an itiner-ary that included a visit to Jackson Lake, from which the Grand Teton and Mount Moran stood out in a particularly spectacular way. He indicated a small hill near the lake where the group would go while designing a tour that omit-ted further venturing into Jackson Hole, where the Rockefellers might hear of opposition to Albright's idea. They returned full of praise for the itinerary and then moved on, again by private train, to Glacier National Park for some extended camping, with a visit to the Blackfoot Indian Reservation on the Canadian border.

A few weeks later JDR, Jr., wrote Albright to thank him for his help and asked about the problem of clutter along the roadsides from fallen trees and discarded brush, suggesting that the roads should be cleared as he had done at Lafayette National Park. He also complained of telephone poles that ran along the west side of the road. Albright replied rather transparently, hinting that he hoped one day to have the funds to clean up the roadside. JDR, Jr., promptly responded with $12,000 for an experimental project, which, when it proved effective, he extended to $50,000 (he declined to pay for the removal of the telephone poles, since the government had put them up and ought to attend to them, an argument Albright was able to make to the Interior Department, which then obtained the necessary funds from Congress). The roadside cleanup program went so well that Congress later appropriated funds for similar work in other national parks. From this small exercise, observed by LSR and spoken of with pleasure by his father, the younger man learned the valuable lesson that, although the Rockefellers had the means to meet the total costs of most projects of this kind, it was more effective to provide a partial incentive and to draw in others who would feel equal responsibility for an initiative so that Rockefeller money could be used to seed other projects elsewhere.

LSR returned to the West again in the late spring of 1926 with his father, mother, and two younger brothers, Nelson being away in France. This time the family spent twelve days in Yellowstone. Albright had been cleared to make a straightforward approach to JDR, Jr., and noting that LSR had a new camera with him, he designed a tour that included many opportunities for photography and again included Jackson Lake and, since he could accompany the group, a tour of Jackson Hole itself. They spent a night in a small lodge on the lake's edge and carried on as far as Jenny Lake, with JDR, Jr., and Abby complaining of the ramshackle buildings, a burned-out gasoline station, billboards and other advertisements, and a dance hall that stood between the road and the mountains. Rockefeller asked Albright to tell him what it would take to clean up the view, and the superintendent replied that much of the disorder was on private land and that it was no simple matter.

On the return trip to Yellowstone, Albright had the driver stop at a hill on the west side of the Snake River, the late afternoon sun providing a dramatic backdrop to the Tetons and the foreground filled with lengthening shadow. LSR never forgot this view. Albright described to the group his dream of a national park (no longer to be part of Yellowstone) for the area, and while the senior Rockefellers were silent, the boys were enthusiastic. The night before the Rockefellers left, they came to Albright's house for dinner. When he was in New York the following November he called on JDR, Jr., with maps and a detailed estimate of what it would cost to acquire 14,000 acres on the west side of the Snake River.

As Albright later recalled the meeting, JDR, Jr., said that he was not interested in anything less than "an ideal project" and this would require buying all the land in upper Jackson Hole. Thus an estimated cost of $397,000 became nearly $2 million. Laurance Rockefeller was not part of these discussions, but he returned to Jackson Hole as often as he could to hike and hunt and, in 1934, on his honeymoon. It became his home in the West, the place of his greatest identification with the mountains, the site of his first major venture into hotel construction, and the symbol of his commitment to continue the work his father had begun.

Much later there was disagreement over precisely where the boys were when the idea of a national park was first discussed, and there were reports that a local spokesman for the national park proposal had visited JDR, Jr.'s office in 1923 and had met with Kenneth Chorley, then his number two man on conservation matters, to discuss the project, suggesting that JDR, Jr., had remained silent on both occasions with Albright because he already was thinking of purchasing the land. The best evidence suggests that Albright stopped at a hill near the old Jackson Lake lodge on the southward trip into the Hole, where the group had lunch, and the boys watched moose browse in the marsh near the river; that they visited dude ranches, including one owned by Struthers Burt, a writer who had been part of a group that had met in 1923 to discuss a possible park; that it was Mrs. Rockefeller who was most disturbed by the unsightly commercialism around Jenny Lake; and that on the return trip north Albright arranged for a stop at Hedricks Point, a bluff above the Snake River, and there spoke of his and others' desires with respect to a park. Whatever the precise sequence, and whomever one should credit for planting the seed in JDR, Jr.'s mind, there is no question that Albright effectively promoted the project and organized a visit that impressed the philanthropist, and that LSR was present and profoundly moved, or that Albright thereafter became a fixture in his and his father's life.

Certainly there had been a small group of local ranchers and others who had met in 1923 to discuss some form of protection for a portion of Jackson Hole and the Teton range. Those first in favor of a preservation plan most often are those closest to the resource. They may rightfully claim that they know and understand it best. Often they seek to protect their own environment and their way of life. The impulse may be pure, or greedy, but it almost always is parochial in its first expression—this spot here, right here, must be protected, for it is beautiful, threatened, dear to us, historic, architecturally significant, the last of its kind, habitat for an endangered species, backdrop to a grand view, foreground to the sublime, whatever—and somewhat exclusivist in its intentions. This was true at Jackson Hole, when the local group met at Maude Noble's cabin to discuss "the Jackson Hole Plan" (as it came to be known). Cattlemen, businessmen, a few naturalists and writers—all wanted a preservation plan of some sort to protect "their" mountain valley without jeopardizing their businesses or life-styles. At the time the Jackson Hole Cattle and Horse Association was happy to endorse the plan. They were not thinking of

a national park—indeed, they disliked the National Park Service, which was
nearby at Yellowstone, and they opposed any extension of the park boundaries
south (as had been proposed by Congressional bills between 1918 and 1923) to
take in the northern part of the Hole. And then, in 1926, when JDR, Jr., began
to purchase private land, even whole ranches, in the upper Hole, apparently
with the intent to make them a gift to the federal government, that is, to preserve this beautiful, threatened, dear, historic, backdrop and foreground, this
habitat, for all the people, they protested. This was not, of course, preservation
as most of the locals saw it; it was surreptitious takeover, interference by an
outsider, even plotting between that outsider and the federal government, and
this was entirely too grand a dream.

By the time Grand Teton National Park was created in 1929, when LSR was
nineteen and no longer a child, he had learned a valuable lesson. Men of great
wealth will often be seen as a possible savior for any number of threatened
dreams; if the men of great wealth broaden and embolden the dream to give
it national or even international scope, by virtue of a larger context for their
vision and greater resources for accomplishing it, they will be seen by many as
destroyers rather than saviors. More important, he glimpsed how grand projects take on a life of their own, how he would have to have his own vision of
what he wished to accomplish and, though open to suggestions, remain clear in
his intent and persistent in his methods lest he be buffeted about by purely
local and limited ideas. Later the Cattle and Horse Association would declare
that they did not share JDR, Jr.'s vision, and in a sense they were right, even as
they endorsed the earlier, rather more selfish and limited desire for federal and
philanthropic assistance in protecting Jackson Hole, perhaps in creating a
national recreational area of some kind, to guarantee to them their ranches,
their game, and their scenery.

Two years later, when he graduated from the Lincoln School, Laurance
Rockefeller was determined to go to Princeton for his college education. Lincoln had prepared him for life, as its head explained to JDR, Jr., when he asked
why his son did not appear to be ready for the entrance examinations—Lincoln was not, the principal said, a prep school at all in the conventional sense,
and he recommended that LSR be sent to just such a school for a year and then
enter a less demanding university. Neither father nor son would have any of
this, and by virtue of a summer of the most intense study in his life, LSR was
admitted to the Princeton class of 1932.

The problem at Princeton was not simply the question of formal academic
preparation. LSR had, as he himself noted, been brought up in a "fundamen-
talist Christian world . . . ." He had been firmly grounded in ideals and values

that told him what he should not do. Now he was surrounded by young men
who behaved in ways he did not and could not approve. For the first two years
at the university he strove to reconcile the world's values with the ones he had
been brought up with, and in the end he did so by concluding that standards
and values must be taken as guidelines rather than absolutes: it was up to the
individual to keep trying to achieve his or her own standards and values and to
play down the conflicts of "racism, religion, sex and moral guilt." As a result,
LSR was a lonely young man who threw himself into drama, the Student
Christian Movement, the Philadelphian Society—a less moralistic version of
the SCM—and through the Society (of which he became the president), a
Princeton Summer Camp where he became a student director.

The first year at Princeton ended with LSR only precariously still enrolled.
Two months into his freshman year he had written to his parents with no hint
of problems to come, though his letter, battered out on a new typewriter,
newsy and affectionate, revealed enough idiosyncrasies of spelling and syntax
to suggest that danger lay around the corner. He was "right on the ball"; he
hadn't "smoked, gotten drunk, gone away from college, cut any classes, played
cards, gone to the movies or wasted time sitting around friends [sic] rooms."
He took a cold shower every morning, joined in a big parade to the football
stadium (Princeton won 50-0), hoped to make the track team, and walked
everywhere, because the campus was "so beautiful." Then in April his father
wrote sternly to him that there were two things LSR was not to fail to do: "go
through your college work this year . . . [while] straining every nerve to lay
foundations that will insure a satisfactory scholastic standing another year
without your living on the brink of a precipice as you have this year," and see
to it that he was on Dr. Grenfell's boat for the summer.[7]

The reference to Dr. Grenfell's boat put in jeopardy an event to which LSR
had been looking forward all year. His father had arranged for LSR and Nelson to spend the summer of 1929 in Newfoundland, working for the well-
known Dr. Wilfred Grenfell, a missionary doctor who wrote an adventure
classic of the time, *Adrift on an Ice-Pan,* and who was bringing both medical
treatment and Christianity to the Inuit along the remote shores of Labrador.
His father chastened LSR for having lost precious time taking part in a play,
and he warned him that he must go to a tutoring school during the summer
and yet meet his agreement to be "the second Rockefeller boy" on Grenfell's
boat, leaving "no possibility of failure" in achieving both.

LSR wrote a note to himself, concluding that the task was impossible, and
then asserted that if his father felt he could do what was demanded of him,
then he could, for his father was a good judge of character. The result was furi-

ous weeks of being tutored followed by the reward of a stimulating adventure in the far north, amidst high mountains and heavy seas. The work was so hard, as the two brothers unloaded and reloaded Grenfell's boat deep into the night, that JDR, Jr., wrote that he thought he might dispense with the servants at home and let LSR and Nelson take over the house and grounds when they returned. At one point Nelson fell ill of food poisoning, while at another Laurance, doubling as a voluntary secretary for Grenfell (who dictated so slowly at times that he appeared to fall asleep over his own words), became quite ill himself, having burnt the candle at both ends one time too often; Nelson insisted that the captain, who seemed unable to act decisively for fear of the enveloping fog, should use his ship's bell to sound the nearness of rising cliffs, and thus find his way quickly to a hospital. Both boys remembered the trip as a great adventure, and it marked LSR's transition into self-confidence and adulthood.[8]

During his teenage years LSR had traveled three times to the West with his father, and in the summer between the Lincoln School and Princeton, JDR, Jr., Abby, and three of the boys went to France, with Laurance given the task of keeping the accounts and settling up the bills, which by all evidence he did immaculately and "on salary." Perhaps for no better reason than this, some thought he might be an economics major, but after his Labrador sailing summer, he became more and more interested in the question of moral guidelines, and as his grades improved, he knew that he wanted to major in philosophy, which he did at the beginning of his junior year, his interest strongly enhanced by his faculty advisor, Robert Scoon, then the head of the philosophy department. LSR did more than major: he took every course in philosophy offered, and he would thereafter remain a good friend to the Princeton philosophy department. As he now wrote to his father, "I am of the opinion that the appreciation and the desire for what is good takes more study and insight than does the understanding and taste for the best music and art." His goal was not just intellectual training: he wished "with my own experience and reasoning . . . to develop an independent and personal philosophy and sense of value as a result of my own intuitions and insight." He was, as he said, studying the differences between right and wrong. When he submitted his senior thesis on "The Concept of Value and Its Relationship to Ethics," for the class of 1932, LSR concluded that, "Ultimately the validity of . . . intuitions must rest on metaphysical grounds, and so are a matter of faith. It is at this dropping off place of facts and values that the basic religious experience is found." Moral values, he said, are based in how to survive. Thus the environment becomes "an inter-personal relationship." Morality and ethics "flow out of the empirical and social experience of man." Rockefeller closed with the words of William James: "Be not afraid of life. Believe that life is worth living, and your belief will help *create* the fact."9

In the 1930s, then as now, bright university graduates who had studied the liberal arts and were uncertain what they wanted to do tended to study law, and LSR followed in this path by enrolling at the Harvard Law School, where he expected to find useful ways to apply his sense of values and his interest in philosophy. In the fall he had a recurrence of the bronchial problems he had so often experienced at the Lincoln School, and with the onset of pneumonia he had to spend the year recuperating at his grandfather's home in Florida. The next summer, after attending a conference run by the Institute of Pacific Relations, since he had become interested in that region of the world, and impressed by the conference site, Banff National Park in Canada, he prepared again for law school. But near the end of a second year, as he prepared for the first-year examinations he had been unable to take the year before, he realized he did not want to be a lawyer. The training seemed rooted in past precedents while his own interests were increasingly in present social causes and in conservation. He was also in love and wanted to marry.

LSR and his father spent two days alone together at Seal Harbor, discussing the future, and while they did not agree on how best to attain the goals the younger Rockefeller wished to set himself, they found themselves in happy agreement over the goals themselves. The law was of fundamental importance. But one could hire highly intelligent and well-trained lawyers, while conservationists who tried to think in global terms were then in far shorter supply. The nation was locked in the Great Depression, the government had begun a New Deal that would reshape society, and both these national upheavals spoke more to values than to economics, the law, or even business. LSR wanted to continue his education by learning from people rather than in classrooms and to apply what he learned in the most practical of ways.

During these years and after, LSR thought a good bit about his formal education. He had never learned to spell really well and he never would. He had managed, despite the Lincoln School, to get good grades in college mathematics; more important, because of the Lincoln School, he knew how to ask good questions, an art many never mastered. His values were intimately connected to his experiences with nature: early walks in Central Park, where he fed squirrels and identified birds, a time with his mother when all the boys looked after pet rabbits, his college summers in the Princeton camp at Blairstown, near the Delaware River, when he learned about the natural sources of energy, even his experience of driving back one summer—fifteen years old and licensed in

Maine—from Seal Harbor, Maine, to New York, watching the trees appear and disappear in the headlamps of his car. One summer he had taken a course in geology, and though the science did not greatly interest him, it showed him how to examine a landscape.

Years later, when describing how he came to look at landscapes so closely, Rockefeller gave particular credit to two of his childhood interests. The first was his fondness for horseback riding. He encountered much of nature from the back of a horse, and anyone accustomed to horses knows that they, their sense of footing, the lowering branch, and the view from the saddle intensify one's awareness of the parts that go to make up a scene. By the time he was sixteen he was quite skilled with a horse.

The second interest was photography. With money earned from raking leaves, LSR bought a camera for his second trip to the West, and he became the unofficial photographer for family travels, to the point that, in order to get him to focus on quality rather than quantity, his father offered to pay him a small sum of money for each particularly good picture. LSR quickly realized that the camera was a shield against his initial diffidence, for one can remain behind the black box, framing a scene, without having to converse. He saw how the camera gave one distance and perspective and how a photograph required a sense of composition, an awareness of one detail in relation to another. He so enjoyed taking photographs, he had a complex filing system created for them, and thousands would be taken, and preserved, over the years. To see a landscape as a photograph was false, of course, but to add the photographic dimension to seeing by asking oneself what story one wanted to tell sharpened one's perceptions.

Many young men of the time also came to see nature through the sights of a gun. JDR, Jr., had little interest in hunting, though he moved among many men who did, and he did not personally disapprove. Nonetheless, he was quite surprised one day when Horace Albright was visiting, and the conversation turned to rifles, to discover that LSR had purchased one and taken a police course to learn to use it. Though father and son also fished on occasion (the older man with little pleasure, the younger with much more), neither hunting nor fishing played an important role in LSR's perceptions of conservation and of nature. Rather, his early experiences with sailing, perhaps next to photography, would become another important avocation and would influence how he looked at land and seascape. Years later he would sail the Caribbean and Hawaiian coasts, taking countless photographs, examining the shores with a view to the ideal beach, the perfect backdrop, the most beautiful places where he might build a resort hotel.

Some writers have suggested that all the Rockefeller brothers were interested in conservation, and that each was in competition with the others and with the memory of their father and grandfather regarding conservation. This seems a groundless suggestion. To be sure, JDR, Jr., implanted a deep regard for the land in his sons and his actions in quietly buying up property in Jackson Hole so that in time the foreground to the cloud-piercing Grand Teton Mountains might become part of one of the nation's most beautiful national parks no doubt had something of the force of the biblical injunction "go forth and do likewise" attached to it. Still, the actual conservation measures of the brothers differed considerably. Brother Winthrop, for instance, included language in his Statements of Beliefs prepared for his 1964 campaign for the governorship of Arkansas about his desire to "conserve and manage" natural resources, and he initially endorsed the National Park Service's desire to turn a lengthy part of the Buffalo River into a National River under NPS management. But the Buffalo River proved to be one of the Park Service's most poorly managed units, and Winthrop would fall afoul of claims that his Winrock Farm, built on Petit Jean Mountain in the Arkansas Ozarks, had done serious damage to what was widely regarded as the best state park in the Arkansas system. Though JDR 3rd made significant contributions to environmental matters through his interest in population control, and David maintained the family interest in Acadia, the conservation mantle of JDR, Jr., fell more fully to Nelson, who through political action as governor of New York attempted much, and even more to Laurance, whose activities were for a long time more in the private sphere.

It is quite clear that, through personality and inclination and as the middle boy of the five, Laurance was the moderator between the brothers, and that this had an influence on his character and his strategy when pursuing conservation goals. He was extremely close to Nelson, the next older brother, and was always supportive of him; he was the brother most likely to be the peacemaker if there were squabbles, and who always made a point of being on hand when needed. Despite childhood differences, he was the brother Winthrop chose to be his best man when he entered into a marriage that all might well have guessed would lead to disaster, as it did in just eighteen months. Nelson and Laurance were the only brothers at their father's bedside when he succumbed to pneumonia in May 1960. Nelson's marriage to Margaretta (Happy) Murphy, his second wife, which came immediately after his divorce from his first wife and at a time that was politically most undesirable, took place in Laurance's Pocantico Hills home, and Laurance was the only brother in attendance. Laurance and his wife Mary were the only family present at Lenox Hill Hospital when Nelson was declared dead from a massive heart attack one cold night in January 1979.

Time and again LSR was there, showing that the family was important to him. This is not to say that the other brothers did not care, for they clearly did, but it was Laurance who, whatever else might be pressing upon him for attention, found the time to provide a shoulder to lean on when it was needed. The death of four siblings in just six years, two of them within six months of each other—Winthrop, of cancer, in 1973; sister Abby in 1976, also of cancer; JDR 3rd in an auto accident in the summer of 1978; and then Nelson in January of 1979—must have tried him sorely. Now he was the oldest, and he would have need of his contemplative ability to see matters whole and long, to believe that there was a plan in nature to which individuals must respond.

In this he was helped by his independence of thought. His grandfather, maker of the great family fortune, devout Baptist, man of hard work, thrift, a flinty sense of humor, and a compelling sense of privacy, handed out shiny dimes to passing poor children and required that barrel bungs (or stoppers) be cut a quarter-inch shorter both to save on the bung and to allow the barrel to accommodate more oil. In most character sketches, these stories are used to illustrate his eye for detail, his thrift, or other values, which, depending on the author, are interpreted as diminishing.

Such stories miss the point. The shiny dimes and shorter barrel bungs were about independence, for debt tests self-reliance, and self-reliance, JDR thought, is the most important quality from which a person can act with confidence. When he thought of the industry by which he made his millions, his mind generally went to the larger aspects of it: to men, method, organization, and policies. His philanthropies were more often systemic than individual. He did in fact have a grand vision. What he wished to see nurtured through philanthropy, or sound organization of the oil industry, or in his son were the virtues of self-reliance, independence, and confidence. John D., Jr., who had graduated Phi Beta Kappa from college, understood this; for him, efficient giving was essential to achieving the greatest impact with his philanthropy. He encouraged his own sons to account for their actions; he wanted all to work to some productive end within the family as they were growing up. When he enhanced his son's interest in photography by offering to pay a small sum for each good picture, assuring that his son would take his time and apply his mind rather than snap and run, he felt he was playing a central role in his moral development. Each of his sons responded in their own ways to their upbringing, Laurance with an air of self-reliance that too often was interpreted as withdrawn or reserved.

Laurance Rockefeller's independence was, throughout his adult life, helped by a happy and secure marriage. When he was seventeen he met Mary Billings French, the sister of brother Nelson's Dartmouth College roommate. He later recalled having a "sort of first crush on her."[10] Though they moved in similar circles, nothing came of this until LSR was in his second year at the Harvard Law School and Mary was studying sculpture in Cambridge, where their friendship grew to courtship. When LSR decided to leave law school, and told his father that he wanted to marry, JDR, Jr., gave his warm approval. The wedding was held in Woodstock, Vermont, where the Frenches had a summer home, on August 15, 1934. Nelson was best man.

Mary shared Laurance's interest in nature in a personal and direct way. While her principal philanthropy and activity was the Young Women's Christian Association, for which, with LSR, she undertook a round-the-world trip in 1963, she encouraged him in his conservation interests, seeing nature somewhat differently, enjoying it through early morning walks with her dogs, sailing in the Caribbean, accompanying her husband on three world trips for *The National Geographic* magazine, and reminding him in subtle ways of the presence of a direct and personal God at work within nature.[11] They had "parallel careers," as LSR stated when speaking at Princeton University in 1991 during the ceremonies at which he received the University's Woodrow Wilson Award, by supporting each other and participating in what each was doing. There was, he said, a wonderful "feeling of partnership" in his marriage. They believed in each other and shared a taste for an unostentatious life-style, even amidst their wealth and privilege.[12]

In 1976, when putting the "Case for a Simpler Life-Style" in a widely reprinted essay for *The Reader's Digest*, Laurance Rockefeller wrote of "the emerging ecological ethic" in America. He believed that more and more people were "coming to understand that man must live in harmony with nature and not as its adversary." The notion, he wrote, "that we have boundless resources of materials, manpower and spirit, and therefore can afford waste, clearly no longer is true." The discovery that "a simpler life-style provides greater satisfaction than relentless pursuit of materialism" would provide Americans with "a major new moral and spiritual resource," he concluded. A return to the old virtues of "simplicity, self-reliance and thrift," the virtues of his childhood, might prove to be the key to national survival. Achieving this would mark the nation's maturity.[13]

Of course, there is an irony in a man of great wealth advocating a simpler life-style. LSR meant what he said, and he personally avoided anything that was ostentatious or smacked of consumerism, but remarking on the pleasures he took from chopping his own wood when in the country no doubt struck some readers of the *Digest* as unrealistic. LSR would not deviate from the message this article contained, however, and he remained pleased with it, for it summarized what he felt he had learned, despite their wealth, from his grandfather and father, from his childhood and his family, and from his wife and his environment. He fully understood that he was the product of privilege; he believed this gave him a great responsibility; his boyhood experiences, accounting for his allowance, earning his pay, and being rewarded for a particularly careful photograph ironically made him more aware of the value of the dollar than many boys less fortunate than he and his brothers. He was more interested in preservation than in acquisition, in the beauty of natural places than in the grandeur of baronial palaces, and in stewardship and socially responsible behavior than in the high life. These are the values he felt he had taken from his childhood. For him, "a simpler life-style" was a description of self-reliance.

Long after, his adventures in formal education recollected in tranquility, Rockefeller reflected on all these influences, on the expectations of parents and teachers, and on how a person becomes what he is:

> Every living thing seeks to fulfill itself according to its own potential. Creative fulfillment is a basic need of all people. With my brothers and myself, there was a difference in scale but the problems we faced in seeking self-fulfillment were not so different from those encountered by every man.
>
> If you think of the artist in every man seeking creative fulfillment and his life given to him as a canvas, then you see that we were given more materials and a larger canvas to work with than other men. And more was expected of us. But the search for creative fulfillment was not so different from that of other men. How we painted on our canvas and what the final pictures came to be is for others to judge.

IV

Mentors and Partners

Reflecting upon how he came to hold the convictions he did at various points in his life, especially about conservation, Laurance Rockefeller has often singled out a small handful of individuals as his mentors. He also had many partners and friends who influenced him, and helped him think a problem through, providing him with the background material that would move him toward a decision. Mentors did more than this, however: they influenced character, his and others. Mentors were individuals he greatly admired.

These mentors had certain characteristics in common. All were men. All were older than Rockefeller, generally about twenty years older. All showed him the warmth he felt his father seldom did. All were concerned with the environment in some way. Generally they had only one or no son of their own. They were all people whose memory he held in respect and affection long after they were gone. He called each a "trail blazer," someone who had helped him find his way.

LSR met some of these mentors through his father. This was especially true of Fairfield Osborn and Horace M. Albright, who in the 1990s he recollected as perhaps the most important influences on his thinking about conservation, the former broadly theoretical, able to find precisely the right expression for an illuminating generalization that embraced the world, the latter highly practical, certain that commerce and conservation could cohabitate, dedicated to pro-

tection through an expanding national park system. There were other significant mentors, of course, and many people whom LSR met without the mediation of his father, but Osborn and Albright most often recurred in his
thoughts.

Fairfield (or "Fair," as his friends called him) Osborn was a breath of fresh
air in sometimes stuffy boardrooms. He was curious about many things, roam-
ing from one subject to another, as LSR described him, like "a rogue elephant."
Rockefeller felt they shared an "interrelated energy field"; years after they met,
Osborn recognized the younger man's similar curiosity, sending him a portrait
inscribed, "from one rogue to another." Osborn and his English wife Marjorie
were often in JDR, Jr.'s home, and the young LSR learned from him quite early
about the world's growing problem with overpopulation—an interest shared
with JDR 3rd—and in particular about population problems in the Pacific
Islands, a subject on which Osborn and a co-worker, Leonard Outhwaite, carried out early research, through which LSR became interested in island life,
especially in the Caribbean and Hawaii. Above all, LSR recalled, Osborn
helped him to understand "participating in doing," not simply standing back
and observing, or reading, or even engaging in passive philanthropy, but in playing an active role within his philanthropic interests.

In 1972 Rockefeller was invited by *The Reader's Digest* to write on "The Most
Unforgettable Person I Ever Met" for a continuing and highly popular essay
series. He hardly thought twice about it, partly because he was worried that the
general public would hardly know who Osborn, who had retired in 1968, was.
Rockefeller felt he could help to make Osborn's work live after him—work that
the two men had done together since LSR became a member of the board of
the New York Zoological Society in 1935—by commending him to the attention of the readers of America's then most popular magazine. When LSR
wrote the article he emphasized Osborn's dynamism, his innovative work to
make zoo habitats more realistic and attractive, his writings on the post-war
population explosion, and his sense of global responsibility.[1]

Osborn's prophetic masterpiece, *Our Plundered Planet*, published in 1948,[2]
when he was sixty-one, is one of the rightful claimants to being the first widely
popular environmental book. Within the year of its appearance, *Our Plundered
Planet* was reprinted eight times and it was soon translated into thirteen lan-
guages. Osborn argued that if America accepted its role as the leader of the
free world, thrust upon it by the Cold War, it must reconsider the "silent war"
that all industrial societies, with the United States in the lead, waged on the
environment. Mankind's "persistent and worldwide conflict with nature"
would, if not curbed, destroy civilization as it was known. Osborn's book drew
on the insights of earlier theorists such as George Perkins Marsh and Ernst

Haeckel, a German biologist who in 1867 had coined the term *ecology*. In reading these and other theorists, Osborn understood that conservation was something far more than assuring hunters and fishers of a supply of game and of assuring foresters and farmers of continued productivity and fertility of the soil. Osborn related the movement to urban realities; he argued that schools must begin to teach about ecology; he saw that it was impossible to consider the environment in a nationalistic and isolated way, telling his readers (especially in a second important book, *The Limits of the Earth*, published in 1953) that sustainable natural resources could be achieved only in an international context. To achieve his goals, Osborn built institutions—the Bronx Zoo, the Conservation Foundation, which he initiated with help from Rockefeller and others in 1948, and Resources for the Future, an environmental and economic think tank in which LSR also was involved—which would outlast him. He viewed society much as Carnegie and JDR had done: an organism best reached through organized institutional change (as with Carnegie's libraries) and best helped through centralized, efficient sources of information and philanthropy (as with JDR's gifts to universities and hospitals). Thus LSR learned from Osborn and gravitated to him almost intuitively, since they shared a desire to make a difference, to do so through institutional organization, and to do what they did with a view to the international dimensions of the problems they tackled.

Osborn and LSR were optimists. Other contemporary writers on the population explosion argued from a dour Malthusian reductionism. William Vogt, author of *Road to Survival*, also published in 1948, high-handedly told everyone that birth control must be practiced by all or they would die, giving little thought to how any radical change in society must emerge from that society's customs rather than be imposed upon it. Paul Ehrlich, whose *The Population Bomb* (1968) most dramatically set the tone of debate, suggested that coercion would be necessary to end the population explosion. Osborn shared the sense of alarm Vogt and Ehrlich and others projected while remaining convinced that education might bring change without brutal government intervention, and LSR agreed that this was the path to take.

Over the years Osborn and LSR worked together on many projects, from the goals of Save-the-Redwoods to the development of the Bronx Zoo into a Wildlife Conservation Society. Their close collaboration began when the New York Zoological Society decided to have its own exhibit at the 1939 New York World's Fair. The Society's exhibit at the fair was to be a prototype for a new type of zoo, which featured natural habitats and made education rather than recreation its primary goal.

Their collaboration culminated in the creation of The Conservation Foundation by Osborn, Samuel Ordway, George Brewer, and others, with LSR as a firm supporter of the foundation's goals long after Osborn stepped down in 1962. It was through his work with the foundation that LSR became most aware of the importance of scientific data in support of environmental arguments. Russell Train, Osborn's successor, also ranked high on LSR's list of mentors and friends—indeed, he would argue that only Train was entitled to be called "Mr. Conservation" after Train became the founding chairman of the national Council on Environmental Quality—and kept Rockefeller closely focused on the foundation's work. Osborn and his successors, including Train and William Reilly, were instrumental in shaping Rockefeller's larger view.[3]

Horace M. Albright, the park professional first met at Yellowstone and later the second director of the National Park Service, was an advisor and mentor to John D. Rockefeller, Jr., and after him, to all of the Rockefeller brothers, but most particularly to Laurance Rockefeller, as he increasingly made national parks a particular interest. After Albright's retirement in 1933, he served as an advisor on a wide range of conservation issues, would sit on the boards of Jackson Hole Preserve, Inc. and Resources for the Future, work closely with the Palisades Interstate Park Commission and Colonial Williamsburg, all Rockefeller interests, and would represent the Rockefellers at dozens of conferences and on dozens more committees. When LSR became President of Jackson Hole Preserve, Inc. in 1940, when he was thirty years old, Albright was always available to provide sage advice, to help LSR overcome his timidity about public speaking, and to remind him that people were part of the environment too.

Albright was a Californian who had left the pursuit of a law degree with a year to go, very much as LSR would do years later, to go east to work with Adolph C. Miller, a professor of economics from the University of California who was picked by Woodrow Wilson's Secretary of the Interior, Franklin K. Lane, early in 1913 to help develop the nation's national parks and monuments. Thus he was on the scene in Washington when the National Park Service was created in 1916, and he contributed for nearly two decades to the evolution of the national park ethic.

Albright's conservation ideas were well ahead of his time. He was bitterly unhappy later in 1913 when John Muir, the spiritual founder of the national park movement, lost his battle to save the Hetch Hetchy Valley in Yosemite National Park from being dammed, and he deeply wanted to see a professional and elite service created to manage the existing parks and to extend the idea of a series of national reserves intended to protect in perpetuity the nation's great landscapes. He worked closely with the first director of the National Park Service, Stephen Mather, and succeeded Mather in January 1929, when Mather was incapacitated by a stroke.

As we have seen, the friendship between Albright and LSR originated in the relationship between Albright and JDR, Jr., and it was under Albright's guidance that LSR's father undertook the most extensive series of benefactions to the nation's national park system ever carried out by a single individual. When LSR took over the national park mantle from his father, Albright guided him. Albright, who shared LSR's belief that public access to the national parks was possible without doing serious damage to the resources the parks were created to protect, a premise possible in the uncrowded years before World War II, and clearly decreasingly so in the years after the war, helped devise guidelines for sound management practices in privately owned Rockefeller enterprises within or adjacent to the parks. The two men remained in frequent and warm correspondence until Albright's death in 1987.

Mather was a rich man, a philanthropist, and self-made millionaire involved in the mining of borax. Albright was, by temperament and experience, a park professional who, like Mather, saw no inherent contradiction between the taking of borax out of a national park area and protecting the hot, dry desert lands of the Death Valley, from which the extraction was occurring. Upon his retirement, Albright became executive director of the United States Potash Company, then president and general manager, and in 1962 a director of the United States Borax and Chemical Corporation, and he would have an office in Rockefeller Center, always within easy reach of the Rockefeller brothers.

Mather and Albright shared a desire to "conserve unimpaired for future generations" the growing system of parks that came under their direction. Yet they saw no oddity in the notion of development of the parks, for they believed that good roads, trails, comfortable hotels, well laid out campgrounds, the infrastructure of what some voices of a later generation would denounce as "industrial tourism," was essential to public appreciation of the parks. They recognized that some portion of the park's resource would be compromised by the infrastructure, but they believed this compromise was justified by the growing constituency that light use of the land would create. They were directors when there was far less awareness than there is today of the dangers of "loving the parks to death," of growing waves of visitors who would hardly leave their cars as they circled through Yellowstone's developing figure-eight highway system or drove their campers deep into the Yosemite Valley, directors who saw the parks as national pleasuring grounds for an upwardly mobile and middle class people. Mather and Albright are not heroes to many students of the national parks movement in the 1990s, and yet, without their sense of compromise and their urge to bring people to the parks, there might well not have been the great growth in the system or the rise of a distinctive public affection for the Service that is so noteworthy and nationally distinctive a feature of the national parks of the United States, surely—for all the complaints that would be made, and legitimately, over the years, about that Service and that system—the most extensive, best managed, diverse, intellectually elegant in conception, and consistently interesting national park system in the world.

In 1986 LSR was given a second opportunity to write a "most unforgettable" article for *The Reader's Digest*, and he immediately decided it must be on Albright. In the end he did not write it, for two people could not be the "most unforgettable," but he hoped to have such a piece written by a conservation writer who had not previously committed himself in print to a choice. Though there was to be no article, LSR's correspondence concerning the possibility made it clear that Albright stood second only to Osborn in his regard.[4] Instead, LSR did something far more beneficial to honor Albright than write an article about him. Later in 1986 he established the Horace M. Albright Employee Development Fund, through a personal gift and through Jackson Hole Preserve, Inc., to make grants to National Park Service employees so that they could "pursue endeavors that increase their personal growth and enhance professional skills." This fund, administered through the National Park Foundation, would keep Albright's name green long after a magazine article had been relegated to the library stacks.

Another man besides Fairfield Osborn with whom LSR worked during preparations for the 1939 New York World's Fair was Robert Moses, the powerful urban planner who would remake New York City, its harbor, bridges, and highways and parks, who shaped how the city felt about itself. At the height of his powers, Moses was one of the best-known and most influential people in the city, a figure who, Rockefeller later said, was unparalleled for his dynamism. Moses, Osborn, and LSR collaborated in 1939 to bring from western China the first panda ever exhibited in the United States, and as a result they helped to change the Chinese sense of responsibility toward the panda. Moses was not precisely a role model—when he visited LSR in Pocantico he would engage in "friendly" games of water polo and win by pushing his opponents' heads under water—but he showed LSR how to telescope a problem to reach a solution more quickly, how to break through (or sometimes simply ride over) constraining red tape. Moses helped LSR realize that he had no interest in going into politics; LSR's admiration for Moses was mixed, for he knew that Moses was arrogant and headstrong; yet, above all, Moses showed him how to become a nonconformist in the best sense, how to defeat a bureaucracy to get a necessary job done, how to go beyond LSR's upbringing—during which he had been taught to be thrifty, correct, and careful, and to do what people expected of him—to become his own person. Some people were so intelligent,

Rockefeller observed, they had no need to be original; Moses demonstrated how originality was more important than merely being quick, and how originality was a form of power. Three decades after LSR learned these lessons from Moses, he would succeed him as chairman of New York State's Council of Parks.[5]

There was one other important mentor: LSR's brother Nelson, two years his senior, always full of energy, determined to get things done, the politician in the family. Though Laurance had no interest in pursuing a political path himself, he knew he needed to understand those who did, and watching Robert Moses and Nelson Rockefeller clash when Nelson became governor of New York in 1958 was a "learning experience." Nelson and Moses expanded his sense of style; both, LSR said, were "invigorating." Nelson, however, had a vision of how the synergism of local, state, and federal governments, working together, yet each playing a distinct role in a federal nation, could transform society, a vision that Moses, with his narrower focus on New York City, lacked.

Partners were not the same as mentors, but they also were important. LSR's trusted partner in conservation and many other areas was his wife, Mary French Rockefeller. Mary not only was supportive of LSR's many initiatives, she was an active participant in many of his wide-ranging interests and activities. When Mary died on April 17, 1997, at the age of eighty-six, LSR lost not only his wife of sixty-three years but a constructive critic, clear-eyed observer, and attentive listener. The enduring influence of Mary's warmth, generosity, and quiet faith on those closest to her became apparent during her memorial service at New York City's Brick Presbyterian Church in May 1997. All four of Mary and LSR's children—Laura, Marion, Lucy, and Larry—reflected poignantly on what their mother had meant to them and to their father. Other partners included conservationists like Conrad L. Wirth and Nash Castro of the National Park Service, and Kenneth Chorley of Jackson Hole and Colonial Williamsburg. There were figures like Nancy Hanks of the National Endowment for the Arts, who "resonated to the arts like a tuning fork," or individuals who helped LSR to truly see Native American and Asian art. There were people who were much more than partners if not precisely mentors, persons with whom Laurance felt he "shared energy fields": these included Charles Lindbergh, the Last American Hero (as one biographer called him), a man who understood "it is heroic to be oneself"[6]; Captain Eddie Rickenbacker, another daring aviator; and Lady Bird Johnson, First Lady of the land from 1963 until 1969.

The young Laurance Rockefeller first met Lucky Lindy when his father had him to dinner in New York the year after Lindbergh's famed solo flight across the Atlantic in *The Spirit of St. Louis* in 1927. Laurance specifically asked to

meet him, and years later, when they met again, he would remind him of the
day.[7] As he later came to know him, LSR realized that Lindbergh, like himself,
had worked at overcoming his intense sense of privacy in order to have wider
influence. He felt a close spiritual relationship with Lindbergh, especially when
Lindy accepted service on one of LSR's environmental committees in the 1960s
and became an important spokesman for the environment, working for the
World Wildlife Fund, the International Union for the Conservation of Nature,
the Friends of the Earth Society, and The Nature Conservancy, striving to save
whales, monkeys, bald eagles, the Hawaiian coast, and entire tribes of people.
In Lindbergh's autobiography, put together after his death, he spoke of his fear
of an uncontrolled technology and concluded that "preserving the environment is inseparable from maintaining our heredity itself."[8] By the 1960s Lindbergh had come to believe that the technology to which he had contributed, the
airplane, was destroying the environment: "If I had to choose," he wrote, "I
would rather have birds than airplanes." LSR admired the man, his work,
many of his ideas, and his heroism, and saw him as almost a spiritual leader,
a position Lindbergh shared with his wife Anne Morrow Lindbergh, whose
best-selling 1955 book, *A Gift From the Sea*, spoke of the need for a solitary dis-
tancing from one's routine for a time to rethink one's relationship with nature
and oneself.[9]

Captain Edward V. Rickenbacker was a national hero too. Born in Columbus, Ohio, in 1890, Rickenbacker had been a fighter pilot ace in World War I,
shooting down twenty-two enemy planes. He was the first winner of the Congressional Medal of Honor whom Rockefeller came to know well, and they
worked closely together when Rickenbacker was president of Eastern Airlines.
LSR found Eddie Rickenbacker to be a "profoundly spiritual" individual and
a "great American," and Rickenbacker reciprocated the feeling, never allowing
Laurance's birthday to pass without a warm letter of greeting, and taking pleasure from the confidence Rockefeller displayed in him as he built the airline.
Though Rickenbacker moved increasingly to the political right in the years
after World War II, while LSR held to his liberal Republic convictions, they
remained firm allies, often exchanging views on the "potentials for good (and
evil)" represented by the air age.[10]

No doubt these men of the sky appealed to Rockefeller because he too was
interested in flying. During World War II he was a naval lieutenant, beginning
as a procurement officer in the Bureau of Aeronautics and then playing a larger
role in fighter development and production. He followed the war closely, fascinated with the question of air power, looking toward the time when it could
be applied fruitfully in peaceful pursuits. He also was quick to see how the airplane would change the nature of government as well as business. But the more

powerful link, most particularly to Lindbergh, was through environmental issues.

Lady Bird Johnson shared LSR's enthusiasm for travel, for beauty and quiet places, and his concern for how society must re-create and re-educate itself every generation. They would work closely together on the beautification of the nation's capital and other places, on the creation of new parks, and on issues of public education, and as we shall see, it would be through his work with Mrs. Johnson that LSR would most clearly show how much he favored a bipartisan approach to conservation and all matters affecting the environment. Indeed, there was no one he quite so much enjoyed working with, and his pleasure in the partnership he and the First Lady formed was almost unbounded.

Though this partnership began over the question of the beautification of the nation's capital, it grew to embrace a far wider range of concerns, long outlasting the Johnson presidency. LSR and Lady Bird took four trips together (see chapter VIII) to see how best to promote the cause of national beautification, and LSR made his private airplane available so that the press could follow the First Lady as she set about educating the country. They shared, Rockefeller felt, that "awareness of nature which gradually becomes a religious springboard of faith." She was, he remarked in 1975, "the most disciplined person I have ever seen . . . a woman of great strength and intelligence." Mrs. Johnson reciprocated, admiring LSR's ability to enlist people in his work, his undeviating pursuit of his aims: he had, more than anyone she knew, "diligently pursued a life purpose," and her times with him, when they exchanged ideas and research findings on how to achieve their shared goals, were among the "high peaks" of her life. LSR recognized this affinity of methods and goals by presenting to Mrs. Johnson in 1996 the first Laurance Spelman Rockefeller Conservation Award for Distinguished Service.

LSR sponsored a dizzying array of research, generally indirectly through foundations and other institutions, sometimes quite directly. This research almost always had to do with what would come to be called "the quality of life" debate. Interesting thinkers would pique his curiosity, he would read some of their work, invite them to meet with him, learn more about them and how they thought, often ask them to mull over some problem which intrigued him, and then remain in touch with them for life, his intellectual loyalties being as firm as his social and familial ones. A case in point is the "urbanologist" William H. Whyte.

Whyte is best known for *The Organization Man*, a best seller published in 1956. A Princeton graduate just before World War II, Whyte had gone into advertising, then to journalism, and in 1949 had written an article on the Yale graduating class of that year, a class that, it seemed to him, had produced an inordi-

nate number of privileged university graduates who wanted to take refuge in
the alleged security of the great and growing post-war corporations. *The Organization Man* grew from the article; it was marked by impressive statistical
research and extensive and perceptive interviews; it concluded that the Protestant ethic, with its emphasis on hard work, an honest day for an honest dollar,
and the absence of show, had become an excuse for conformity and a device for
an unending and unimaginative search for security. Here was a book that also
praised self-reliance, and especially for the privileged, though in far more
sophisticated terms than most books of its kind.

LSR provided Whyte with an office in Rockefeller Center and told him to
think widely about the urban environment. Soon Whyte was producing reports
on both technical and aesthetic matters—easements, land trusts, vest pocket
parks, the importance of trees to the city—as "a one-man think tank." "Holly"
Whyte's greatest ability was simply to observe, to truly see how people behaved
in an urban landscape, to spot the significant detail in group behavior that suggested how to make a blank wall less blank and less of a wall. Whyte worked
closely with LSR during his association with Lady Bird Johnson on how to
promote natural beauty in America, he was an influential consultant to the
New York City Planning Commission, and in 1970, with financial support
from LSR and the National Geographic Society, he launched the Street Life
Project, in which he and a group of sociology students from Hunter College
recorded how people actually used the spaces around them, deeply influencing
development guidelines. His most obvious accomplishment was in the recovery
of New York City's Bryant Park, directly behind the New York Public Library,
taking it back from drug dealers and prostitutes and making it a vibrant public space, but his most persistent achievements may still lay ahead, as his books,
The Social Life of Small Urban Spaces, City, and *The Last Landscape,* continue to be
influential statements about city planning. In Whyte's sparsely furnished office
in Rockefeller Center are dozens of reports, drafts, and speculative papers from
his hand, all of them still influential in the thinking of LSR.[11]

There were, of course, others who were influential in Laurance Rockefeller's
life, often like Whyte through their writings. There was Albert Schweitzer,
near-saint, medical missionary of Lambaréné, in Africa, who taught LSR reverence for life and whom he often liked to quote. There was Alan Watts, expo-
nent of bridging the cultures of East and West, who made the ancient knowledge of China, Japan, and India explicable, even usable, to a Western mind.
There was Lewis Thomas, master essayist, doctor and researcher, and head of
the Memorial Sloan-Kettering Institute for Cancer Research who, himself
dying of cancer, had the courage to look squarely at death. From Thomas, LSR
learned that a whole, fulfilled person does not need the stories that are told to

children about dying. At various times LSR would be influenced by Teilhard de Chardin, the metaphysician; by Jan Christian Smuts, the South African leader, whose 1926 book *Holism and Evolution* interested him; by Joseph Campbell, the explorer of the relationship between myth and spirituality in *A Hero of a Thousand Faces*, to whose chair at Sarah Lawrence College LSR contributed handsomely; and by Deepak Chopra, who was a spokesperson for exploring alternative medicine. The link between such writers was the idea that a person becomes responsible for his or her own intellectual and spiritual evolution. The human person might be limited by DNA and by gravity, Rockefeller pondered, but within every individual was unlimited knowledge: the task of life was to plumb one's infinite possibilities, to re-create oneself, to surround oneself with energy fields of creativity, to draw upon "co-creators," who unleashed the self-reliance that so many had within themselves.[12]

Thinking as he did, Laurance Rockefeller did not include many formal leaders of religion in his list of mentors and few among his influences. He respected such men as Harry Emerson Fosdick, the theologically liberal pastor of the Park Avenue Presbyterian Church and later of Riverside Church, and Norman Vincent Peale, who had written a best-selling book, *The Power of Positive Thinking.* He greatly admired the Reverend Billy Graham. While LSR was a mainstream Protestant, he was also resolutely broadminded, dipping into the work of many unconventional writers and taking an interest in less centrist thought. He read widely in moral philosophers from his undergraduate days as a philosophy major at Princeton, and he selected from them what made sense to him, whether from Immanuel Kant or Paul Tillich. He would always strive, he said, to be in touch with himself, for he agreed with the theologian's judgment that sin lay in "self-estrangement."

Some of LSR's mentors and partners were well to the political right, or held views that today would be unacceptable to the great majority of Americans. Charles Lindbergh was a leading voice of America First, the isolationist political movement that, at times, sounded anti-Semitic. Rickenbacker would, after World War II, become increasingly convinced that communists in high places threatened American liberties. At times Albright was a little pressing in seeking preferment for friends. Fairfield Osborn's views on natural selection were undoubtedly elitist and some commentators, then and since, felt that he verged on racism. Many were critical of Peale's writings even when they admired him personally.

But LSR never responded to the negatives of his friends. If he remained unswervingly loyal to his family, his friends, and his associates (even to the point of almost never firing employees but, rather, moving them to some job that was more compatible to their talents and temperament), he also never adopted the worst traits of those friends. Indeed, he appears simply to have ignored these traits. Rickenbacker often referred in his letters to his right-wing views; in his replies Rockefeller said nothing about politics and addressed himself to business and social matters. Lindbergh condemned the airplane, and the destructive nature of commercial society and its impact on native peoples, and LSR agreed, but when Lindbergh wrote or spoke of his isolationism, Rockefeller said nothing, or mildly remonstrated with his friend about the interconnectedness of things and how no one, and certainly no nation, could live in isolation. LSR showed no hint of anti-Semitism, racism, or fascism in his business dealings or his social life, and if some critics of Osborn could read such sentiments in his speeches and books, LSR simply thought they were wrong. He recognized the facile in "feel good" writers but did not think this element in their writing vitiated their basic message. LSR had the ability to take from his mentors what he needed and wanted, without being led or dominated by them; for him, mentorship was a matter of equality and partnership. How could a relationship be otherwise if one would honor the tenets of self-reliance as he had learned them at the Lincoln School?

LSR believed in a "democracy of religions": that all religions should have regard for each other. Too often religion was culture bound. Recognizing spirit at work in different guises, a "democracy of spirit" was the road to ecumenical achievements and to personal spirituality. Thought should be inclusive, not exclusive, ever ready to consider any possibility, to see body, mind, and spirit as a continuum. People are inherently moral, LSR concluded, and did not need a formal religion to make them so; rather, religion was the external expression of that morality. People were incredibly adept at preserving their social environment; if they would but think inclusively, they could become equally good at protecting their physical and ultimately their spiritual environments. Thus he leaned toward thinkers who saw the world whole and who did not extract environmental issues from that whole world. What he must do, he had decided rather early, was develop his ability to surround himself with mentors and partners, with good people—good in both senses of the word—and as he looked back in semi-retirement at what he had done in business, for medicine, for the environment, he concluded that he had generally succeeded. Life was not an ego trip: it was a journey in which one shared the energy, power, and glory of "constantly becoming." Some hard-headed businessmen might think this conclusion "entirely too Zen" for them, he observed, but they were wrong: the thought was "just right."[13]

Laurance S. Rockefeller portrait photo, 1979. (Yousuf Karsh, Ottawa)

President George W. Bush presents LSR with the Congressional Gold Medal for his lifelong contributions to the environment, September 27, 1991. (Official White House photo)

Laurance with (*right to left*) grandfather John D. Rockefeller, mother Abby Aldrich Rockefeller, and father John D. Rockefeller, Jr., at the family estate, Kykuit, Pocantico Hills, Tarrytown, New York, circa 1930. (Rockefeller Archive Center)

Three of the four Rockefeller brothers (*left to right*) Nelson, John D. 3rd, and Laurance with their father on a trip to the western United States, circa 1924.

Two "best friends," Laurance and Nelson, on horseback in the Adirondack Mountains in New York State, mid-1960s.

The Rockefeller siblings (*left to right*) Winthrop, John D. 3rd, Abby, Laurance, David, and Nelson at their summer home, the Eyrie, in Seal Harbor, Maine, mid-1960s. (Ezra Stoller Associates)

LSR and zoological "mentor" and old friend, Fairfield Osborn, at Osborn's retirement party in the staff dining room of the Bronx Zoo, September 1968.

LSR and national parks "mentor," Horace M. Albright, in front of Phelps Lake at LSR's JY Ranch, Jackson, Wyoming, mid-1970s.

Laurance and Mary Rockefeller with friend Charles A. Lindbergh on Tongatapu in the South Pacific, 1974. (*National Geographic* magazine)

Lady Bird Johnson, LSR, and Mary Rockefeller at the Billings Farm, Woodstock, Vermont, 1967. (Personal collection of Laurance S. Rockefeller)

Laurance and Mary Rockefeller with Captain Eddie Rickenbacker, 1948. Rickenbacker was the founder of Eastern Airlines. (PAA photo)

LSR in St. Louis, Missouri, with James S. McDonnell, founder of McDonnell Aircraft Corp., which Rockefeller helped finance, 1948. (McDonnell Douglas Corp. photo)

LSR (*in cockpit*) with Frank N. Piasecki, founder of the Piasecki Helicopter Co., which Rockefeller also helped finance. Photo taken in Bridgeport, Connecticut, 1950.

Laurance and Mary
Rockefeller at Caneel Bay,
a resort that Rockefeller
created on St. John Island
in the Virgin Islands, 1964.
(G. Victor Davis)

LSR escorts Queen Elizabeth II, as Prince Philip and Mary Rockefeller follow,
on the Queen's visit to Little Dix Bay, a Virgin Islands resort that Rockefeller
created, 1966.

LSR, president of Jackson Hole Preserve, Inc., speaking at the formal opening of the Virgin Islands National Park, which he donated to the nation, 1956. (Sam Falk)

Laurance and Mary Rockefeller standing on volcanic lava in front of Mauna Kea Beach Hotel on the occasion of its grand opening in July 1965. Rockefeller created this resort on the Kohala coast of the big island of Hawaii.

V

Conservation and Use

In his adult life Laurance Rockefeller had three compelling interests: his socially responsible venture capitalism, broad philanthropy with an emphasis on medical research, and conservation, also a philanthropic activity. He never saw these interests as residing in compartmentalized worlds, apart from each other or from daily routine. It seemed obvious to him that if one were to engage in philanthropy, one needed to make money in order to do so. Though he grew up amidst wealth, it never occurred to him that he had no obligation to make more, to show himself his father's son. He served on many boards, invested in many companies, which made him large sums of money—his success rate has been very high—though making money was not his first or even his second concern. To be sure, it did not have to be, for he entered business after his marriage adequately financed by his father. If LSR did not organize his life primarily in search of financial gain, he believed financial gain would find him. A primary motive in serving on philanthropic boards was to help generate more philanthropic income. He saw each of his major interests as part of a circle, a wheel of life, with only the thinnest lines of separation between them. Conservation, the creation of areas of tranquility, helped to restore peace of mind and create healthy bodies. He did not chop his own wood at his Wyoming ranch in order to validate "the simple life"; he did it because he enjoyed it, and it was good for him. Medical and especially cancer research contributed to fitness, to improving the ability to enjoy long and happy lives in order to use and benefit from the environment. His venture into resorts was to make money certainly, but those resorts had to be compatible, beautiful, so that they too would contribute to peace of mind. In all these avenues Rockefeller was a pioneer because he was willing to take risks. He leveraged himself by encouraging able persons to devote themselves to interests in which he believed, a capacity by which time and again he demonstrated his leadership ability.

Laurance Rockefeller's most important role in American life would be to take environmentalism as his domain and to carry it from the obscurity of a cultish subject to the highest point in the national agenda. He did this in good measure because of who he was and of how he was, and because of personal qualities of character that made him peculiarly effective in this arena. Before his entry onto the national stage as a conservationist, the subject had largely belonged to solitary men who appeared to be misanthropes or, at the least, who considered human beings interlopers in the wilderness, undesirables on the landscape. Laurance's contribution was to show that human beings were part of the ecology too, that they had a right to the landscape and a place in the wilderness, and that properly informed by education and knowledge and empowered by a democratic society, they would make decisions that helped rather than hurt the environment. He believed in commerce *and* conservation, not in separate compartments but functioning as a whole, together. He thought there could be a balance between conservation and use if the advocates of both were sensitive to each other's needs.

Believing as he did, LSR's contributions to conservation—to national parks, outdoor recreation, historical preservation, protection of local and state parks, promotion of biological knowledge through zoos and wildlife reserves, the enhancement of beauty in the built environment, and environmentally sound resorts—were bound to combine elements that many found contradictory or competing. Nothing better illustrates this than the manner in which Laurance Rockefeller combined his venture capitalism with the promotion of national parks through his Rockresorts. These resorts, built between 1955 and 1969, were precursors to eco-tourism, to the new wave of places developed in the 1970s and 1980s, with far greater sensitivity to the environment. To understand Rockefeller's concept of conservation and use over these years, one must examine Rockresorts. Above all, from 1946, when he formed Rockefeller Brothers, Inc., an early venture capital operation, LSR played a commanding role in this burgeoning new field. Of course he did not work alone, and many people were instrumental to his success, as he was always quick to acknowledge, whether Peter O. Crisp or Harper Woodward, or those later who helped to guide his conservation initiatives.

To be sure, Laurance Rockefeller made money in many different ways. Using the stake provided by his father, he was quick to recognize the importance of the airline industry, providing funds to help Eddie Rickenbacker buy Colonial Air Lines from General Motors, from which came Eastern Airlines. He provided seed capital to J. S. McDonnell to start a St. Louis-based company that produced a single-engine jet-powered military fighter airplane. Both these ventures were well launched by the time of America's entry into World War II and LSR's wartime service in the Navy. After the war, mindful of the major technological innovations developed during the conflict, he turned to their application to commercial transport. He created a lean staff of only three associates, to find and fund small entrepreneurial groups that would address new markets. Thus he put his capital and his growing expertise into Piasecki Helicopter, which eventually became Vertol and was acquired by Boeing; he helped fund the Glenn L. Martin corporation, which produced the Martin 404 for Eastern Airlines; he was central to Reaction Motors, which produced liquid propellant engines for rockets, missiles, and manned aircraft (this company was later acquired by Thiokol); he supported Airborn Instruments Laboratory, which produced aircraft landing systems and avionics equipment; and he backed Aircraft Radio, which produced aviation communications equipment before it was acquired by Cessna. Later, he and his colleagues went into other technologies in their early stages, including the Itek Corporation, which designed and manufactured electronic reconnaissance cameras (including those used on the U-2 surveillance aircraft) and Scantlin Electronics (later Quotron), which designed and built stock quotation terminals.

In July 1969, Venrock Associates, an investment company, was formed. This was a limited partnership funded by members of the Rockefeller family and (usually) nonprofit entities that had enjoyed long-standing relationships with the family, including the Museum of Modern Art, Colonial Williamsburg Foundation, and Rockefeller University. Venrock enjoyed superior performance results and specialized in boosting startup or near-startup level companies. By 1996 Venrock had funded 221 companies, and had been a founding investor in Intel Corporation (microprocessors), Apple Computer (personal computers), Komag, Inc. (computer memory discs), Apollo Computer (workstations), and others. Though LSR had not seen the promise in the world of computer technology as quickly as he had understood how aviation and the aerospace industry would develop, he soon set aside any initial hesitations and, as he gravitated to electronics, computation, and then biotechnology, he increased his personal fortune many times over. From the Fairchild Engine and Airplane Corporation through International Nickel, Olin Mathieson Chemicals, banks, railroads, and mines, he was a major player.

Business historians praise Laurance Rockefeller, possibly more than any other figure in the venture capital industry, for his pioneering in early stage, technology-based enterprises. Though he was fascinated by technology, he also was interested in "the social purposefulness" of the technologies to which he was drawn. No one, save perhaps John Hay Whitney, also heir to a family fortune, and Georges F. Doriot, a French-born Harvard Business School professor who led the American Research and Development Corporation, had as much impact. Yet, with the possible exception of his wisdom in being so early a backer of Rickenbacker and Eastern Airlines, the business initiative LSR most enjoyed and of which he was most proud was his Rockresorts.[1]

Rockresorts came to stand for environmentally sound resort hotels built in areas of exceptional natural beauty and high-risk environmental impact. They served as virtual demonstration projects for his conviction that conservation and use were possible, that natural outdoor resources provided the settings in which people could enhance their own creativity while taking pleasure from their surroundings. He understood that by the twentieth century even the concept of wilderness was a social construct—that when one speaks of "managing wilderness," as the U.S. Forest Service does, one is confessing that wilderness no longer can dependably occur naturally—and that some part of the life-enhancing psychological elements of wilderness could be brought to jaded urban dwellers in at least a small measure by increasing a resort visitor's environmental experience. In the resort hotel business there was no greater catalyst for environmental sensitivity.

Rockefeller began by applying four primary criteria to his resort ventures. First, they should be in settings of natural beauty, while the resorts themselves were to appeal to urban-oriented guests in search of self-renewal. (He also fully understood that self-renewal was individual and meant different things to different people.) Second, the resorts should contribute to the economic and social development of the areas in which they were to be built. Third, there must be the prospect of a profitable return over the long run (which, rare in the world of business, he truly defined as a long run, allowing for at least ten and perhaps twenty years). Fourth, visitors should be offered recreational opportunities of a kind that did not damage the environment. These were goals often publicly stated, though it is clear from his actions and comments that there was a fifth criterion: that he personally should find the place beautiful, and the resulting resort should be an example of the best in sensitive site-planning, landscape design, and architecture compatible with the natural environment.

Rockefeller summarized his views in an address before the 70th Annual Congress of American Industry, sponsored by the National Association of

Manufacturers, in December 1965. "The preservation and enhancement of the environment has become an important factor of modern business. Business can take this development in stride in the same way it has, over the years, taken in stride other steps which seemed at the time to be broad social rather than economic obligations. . . . This will turn out in the end to be just plain good business." He then drew a parallel: business and industry had long understood that providing proper working conditions was a necessity. The "awakening of an appetite for natural beauty is simply an extension into the outdoors of the desirability of good working and living surroundings."[2] This was and is a disputed view, of course: that the value of a landscape contributes economically to a region.

LSR had begun years before in the Grand Teton Mountains of Wyoming, where he and his father had put conservation and use to the test. There LSR managed his first lodges. They were not Rockresorts, for he had not coined either concept or name yet, but they were the precursor.

After JDR, Jr., began buying land in Jackson Hole in 1926, he quietly accumulated nearly 34,000 acres. He then offered this land through his Snake River Land Company to the National Park Service to become part of Grand Teton National Park, created in 1929. Foes of the original park, ranchers in the valley, hunters, loggers, the U.S. Forest Service, even the motion picture actor Wallace Beery, professed to find a conspiracy between the federal government—and after Franklin D. Roosevelt became president, in particular with his "socialistic" New Deal—and Wall Street capital to lock up the land and drive ranchers off it. Perhaps the most intense feud over a national park issue in the nation's history ensued, until in 1943 FDR proclaimed Jackson Hole a national monument, knowing the day would come when the monument would be absorbed into the park, as it was in 1950.[3] It was LSR who signed over the land the year before, as president of Jackson Hole Preserve, Inc., a Rockefeller nonprofit corporation established in 1940 to succeed the Snake River Land Company with LSR at the helm. In all JDR, Jr., spent $17.5 million to make possible one of the "crown jewel" national parks.[4]

Because there are hotels in the national park, some regard Grand Teton as "an area of violated naturalness,"[5] which to an extent is true. But no national park is without its violations, since one of the usual criteria for establishment is access. Still, because of the history of the Teton area, and of Jackson Hole when added to the park, there are some significant departures within the park boundaries from general Park Service principles. Jackson Lake is no longer a natural lake, having been dammed, and it functions as a reservoir, the Bureau of Reclamation using it to provide irrigation water to eastern Idaho. Elk hunting is permitted each year, though hunting is not allowed in other national parks (except in Alaska, and then for subsistence only). Fish are stocked in the lakes and streams. Visitors may reach the park by air, for part of Jackson Airport is within the park boundaries, a problem to which LSR would direct much attention, trying to find some compromise by which the runways could be located outside the park or the landing field moved to an entirely different location. Grazing continues in major portions of Jackson Hole, within the park. The highway configurations had, for the most part, been established before the enlarged national park was created. They were, in fact, improved by LSR, who helped persuade Conrad Wirth, the director of the National Park Service, to re-route the main north-south road away from Jackson Lake and to the east of his lodge, out of moose habitat. In short, the Park Service inherited an area that was rather more like Acadia and Shenandoah National Parks in the East than like the other great national parks in the West. In any case, given the history of the region comprised by the park, no one suggests this charge of violated naturalness be laid at the door of the Rockefellers.

These variations from park norms in Jackson Hole bothered many "purists" and others who feared that even more infringements against the emerging park ethos lay in the future. They wanted to apply a "melt back" principle, as it would be called later, leaving the many ranch structures that dotted Jackson Hole to benign neglect, so that over time they would simply decay. Others, mindful of the intense controversy over the park itself, or because they had a different philosophy, argued that the human imprint that already existed should remain, perhaps even be protected, though any additional imprint should be approached with the greatest circumspection. JDR, Jr., and LSR were of this view. Recognizing that the human imprint was an important aspect of the natural history of the region, they favored a carefully developed plan of conservation and use, actually employing the phrase for the first time in this context. Further, they reasoned that the larger national parks required campground facilities, a restaurant or two, and lodges for those who preferred not to camp. After all, this already was the practice in many national parks, including Grand Canyon, Yellowstone, Yosemite, Sequoia, Glacier, Zion, and Acadia. Lodges enhanced visitor enjoyment, built enlarged constituencies for the parks, and by lessening the need for long drives to and from the parks, were calculated in any case to be a worthwhile trade-off reducing overall environmental impact.

There are legitimate arguments to be made on both sides of the question of park development, though clearly the Park Service is charged with preserving the resource and protecting the environment for future generations in preference to favoring public access. Even so, not all agree on what "preserving the resource" means. JDR, Jr., and LSR after him quite properly could quote no less an authority than Stephen T. Mather, who concluded that "scenery is a hollow enjoyment to a tourist who sets out in the morning after an indigestible breakfast and a fitful sleep on an impossible bed."[6]

By 1950, travel was changing, and the small town of Jackson would be the beneficiary or victim, depending upon the point of view, of two major developments: greatly expanded air travel and the rapid rise of skiing as a leisure activity. Once gasoline rationing had ended and a generation of Americans who had endured overseas warfare between 1941 and 1945 had returned, there was a heavy increase in visits to national parks by motorists who wanted to see the country they had fought for and who could at last afford to do so. Grand Teton was especially hard hit, with reports of thousands of visitors having to sleep in their cars, often driving off-road to find a suitable place. LSR was fully alert to the changes, as a major investor in airlines and owner of ski lifts in Vermont. He personally knew the Grand Teton area well, having walked many of its trails since his early visits and his honeymoon at his father's JY Ranch in Jackson Hole in 1934. The Tetons became the early focus of his desire to work out a compromise position between conservation and use in such a way as to enhance visitors' pleasure and, perhaps, their sense of themselves within or at least near a wilderness environment.[7]

Looking back, Laurance Rockefeller felt that he went into the Grand Teton lodge business virtually by default. Though he and his father considered hotels necessary, concessionaires were not coming forward to build them, for the summer season was at best four months long.[8] While skiing was taking hold outside the park, clearly it would not be permitted within, so that there would be only a small winter clientele, or at least so the various concessionaire groups reasoned. Accordingly, in 1951 LSR entertained the secretary of the interior, Oscar Chapman, at the JY Ranch, and explained to him what he and his father hoped to do. Chapman was pleased, for he shared the Rockefellers' conviction that accommodations could only benefit the park.[9]

JDR, Jr., and his associate, Kenneth Chorley, a naturalized citizen from England who was now his principal assistant in conservation matters, proposed an accommodations plan at three levels. There was to be a substantial lodge above the shores of Jackson Lake with three hundred rooms for the middle-class visitor; a small semi-luxury lodge to be fashioned from a former dude ranch, thus not to add structures to the landscape, in the forest not far from Jenny Lake; and a "village" of log cabins, with cafeteria, general store, launderette, showers, and boat marina at Colter Bay. Thirteen million dollars was spent on these enterprises through Jackson Hole Preserve, Inc., which would give the money to its own subsidiary, the Grand Teton Lodge Company, to build and operate the services at Jackson and Jenny lakes and Colter Bay. The lodge company paid local taxes; though initially profits were not anticipated, any there were went back to Jackson Hole Preserve for general conservation work. This last proviso meant that money could be passed to the National Park Service to continue to remove downed trees from near roadways and to clean up the foreshore of Jackson Lake, activities originated with gifts from JDR, Jr., years before.[10]

The situation was filled with ironies. Subsequent commentators who opposed lodges in parks were inclined to attack Rockefeller both for building the Jackson Lake Lodge and for placing it at the base of a low wooded mountain, well back from the lake at a site known as Lunch Tree Hill, so named because JDR, Jr., his sons, and Albright had discussed the future of the valley while having their picnic there in 1926. But surely these critics would not have preferred the lodge to be on the lake's edge, and surely, too, they knew that there already were three rather ramshackle and certainly unsightly small ranch hotels along the lake's shore that JDR, Jr.'s more isolated lodge replaced. Often these same commentators argued that all structures in Jackson Hole should have been removed, from historic ranches to the offending lakeside accommodations, so that the land could revert to its "natural splendor." However, natural grasses were already vastly different than they were during the time of the nineteenth-century fur trader rendezvous, and decades of Park Service efforts to "restore" wildlife to Yellowstone had proved how ineffectual reversion was. When it was built there were those who found the exterior of the Jackson Lake Lodge ugly and obtrusive, and castigated its use of poured concrete rather than rustic timbers, though this had been done because the architect had believed concrete would make it less obtrusive. Still, by the 1970s virtually no one in Jackson Hole country would deny that the Rockefellers had brought great benefits to the economy and to the protection of the larger resource on which it was based.

President Roosevelt declared Jackson Hole a national monument by using the only tool available to him, the Antiquities Act of 1906. This act gave presidents the authority to proclaim and reserve "historic landmarks, historic and prehistoric structures, and other objects of historic or scientific interest." The Act generally had been used to protect "scientific curiosities" (as when Theodore Roosevelt proclaimed Devil's Tower, also in Wyoming, a national monument in 1906) or archaeological sites associated with Native American cultures (the first being Casa Grande Ruins in Arizona in 1918). Still, the intent of the legislation was clear, and for the outdoors lobby to attack the protection or recycling of historic structures within Jackson Hole when FDR had used an act that called for precisely such protection was at the least ironic.

The hotels were immediately successful. Opened in 1955, Jackson Lake Lodge usually was booked to near capacity. Jenny Lake Lodge was virtually impossible to get into. Colter Bay—to which a fine interpretive center for Native American arts was added in 1972, its contents a gift from LSR and Jackson Hole Preserve, Inc.—proved so popular, it had to be expanded and a trailer village of some one hundred sites was appended. Also in 1972, on the occasion of the bicentennial of Yellowstone National Park, the highway between the two national parks was dedicated as a Memorial Parkway to John D. Rockefeller, Jr., with substantial acreage on both sides of the road, 24,000 in all, establishing a billboard-free visual corridor and, within Grand Teton, a bypass for nonvisitors to the park.

In 1957, two years after the Jackson Lake Lodge was opened, Laurance Rockefeller received the first Horace Marden Albright Scenic Preservation Medal awarded by the American Scenic and Historic Preservation Society for what he had done at Grand Teton. LSR took special pleasure from this, because in a sense it had been Albright, as superintendent of Yellowstone National Park, who had initiated the entire process. From his beginning in 1940 as president, and later as chair, of Jackson Hole Preserve, Inc., until 1996, when he stepped aside to become chairman emeritus, LSR would personally implement Albright's philosophy, not only in Jackson Hole but by using JHPI to project its work elsewhere, from the California redwoods to the Hudson River highlands.

Not all of LSR's initiatives were successes. Working with Fairfield Osborn and the New York Zoological Society, of which he was then the chairman, LSR set up a wildlife preserve in Jackson Hole. The wildlife park was a bone of contention from the start. It suffered from poor management decisions, budget cuts, and changing migration patterns by the wildlife it was designed to protect. The Park Service was unenthusiastic since the wildlife park was located at Oxbow Bend on the Snake River, on land that was assumed to be coming to the park. Olaus Murie, the leading wildlife biologist in the region and a board member of JHPI, bitterly opposed penning up wild animals and resigned from the board over the matter. The buffalo suffered from Bang's disease and the moose became dependent on the food that was supplied to them rather than foraging for themselves. LSR concluded that he had been a bit naive, perhaps wanting to offer visitors photo opportunities so that wildlife elsewhere in Grand Teton and Yellowstone would be unmolested, rather than having thought the problem through. Stockmen and the governor of Wyoming, in part because they were inclined to support anything the Park Service opposed, were in favor of the wildlife park. Still, even to Murie it seemed, as he wrote to Osborn, that only Laurance Rockefeller had held to "the big inclusive dream and grasped the entire picture at Jackson Hole," and Murie did not blame him for the failed experiment.[11]

By the time Rockefeller received the Albright Award in 1957, he already had applied the principles worked out in Grand Teton National Park to Rockresorts, his publicly best known venture. All but two of these resorts were on the seashore; they were innovative projects in which he was swimming against the tide; they were built in relatively remote places and provided little or no entertainment[12]; where practical they were open to the wind and rain; and they often included relevant fine art meant to inspire and educate. They were designed to meet his four "primary criteria." Though many financial advisors warned him that such resorts would fail, he hoped for a sound return over the long run and he had a relaxed view of what was a necessary market share.

The concept that grew out of JDR, Jr.'s and Laurance's work at Grand Teton blossomed in the Caribbean, where LSR built his next resort, Caneel Bay. It too was attached to a national park, though one that did not exist until LSR created it. Beginning in 1949 he and Mary cruised the Caribbean, moving from island to island in their boat, *Dauntless.* Over the years they explored virtually every island in the Caribbean north of Trinidad (much later, LSR would, with regret, note that they did not get to the Cayman Islands). There was little or no development on most of the islands at the time and he found their isolation and beauty emotionally and psychologically very "healing." He did not romanticize the life of unemployment so often burdening the islanders, even as he understood the risks that development would pose for traditional societies. He would stop at bays that attracted him, walk the beaches, swim with an aqualung, check out the coral, and write careful notes about each stop, always using his camera to record, frame, change, and provide deeper perspective on a place.[13]

The Crow Indians have a phrase about their lands being "exactly the right place," by which they mean that they are precisely where the Great Spirit intended, whatever human circumstances may have moved them. LSR may have found Caneel Bay because he and Mary met up with some friends there by accident and saw the possibilities in a small hotel fashioned out of an abandoned sugar plantation on St. John's shore. Or perhaps the fact that Laurance had one of the few frights of his life while swimming nearby—he was followed toward shore by a barracuda that he took to be a shark—helped him to focus on the secluded beach. Or it may simply have been because the bay was beautiful, the island hardly developed, that he could get the land inexpensively, and his dream of creating a national park entirely of his own making was a clear possibility. Whatever the reasons, he felt he had found "exactly the right place" for his first entirely independent resort hotel venture.

Laurance and Mary first put in at Caneel Bay in 1952. The combination of historic old sugar plantation and island that was still largely in bush, virtually without roads, electricity, or fresh water, and yet close to Charlotte Amalie, the sleepy capital of the American Virgin Islands, appealed to both. Here was a place to test whether there truly could be a modern alliance between commerce and conservation, whether man could, as his father had done at Acadia, still aesthetically improve upon nature's views. From Textron, Inc., the owner of the land around Cruz Bay, LSR bought 600 acres for $350,000, with twelve beach front lots and six cottages that dated from the pre-1917 Danish period on the island. (Later, when it was known that Rockefeller was the purchaser, the price of $500–$700 an acre turned into $50,000 for the last two he felt he needed in order to complete a well-rounded property.) Again he projected a ten-year wait for profits—something few developers in the 1950s were content or able to do—and he brought in Henry Beebe, a construction engineer from Colonial Williamsburg, landscape architects and horticulturists, and other people experienced in conservation and the "enhancement" of nature in a variety of ways. He decided that his guests were to swim, snorkel, sleep, eat well but not luxuriously (his own habits being somewhat spartan), and take nature walks. There would be no telephones, no air conditioning, no tipping, no locks on doors, no gaudy patio furniture, and everything built should melt into the landscape. The power cable from St. Thomas was buried under the sea; sewage treatment and water distillation plants were added, in order not to dump directly into the water, as nearly all Caribbean resorts did at the time; the new cottages spoke of LSR's understated taste, as he consulted personally on the furnishings, the fabrics, the carpets, the lamps, the paintings on the walls, so that all would blend and not command attention. One day after the resort opened LSR was observed folding up beach chairs to carry up from the water's edge, for by evening they might block some part of the sunset. Nothing was left to chance.[14]

The Caneel Bay Plantation (the last word was soon dropped) was opened on December 1, 1956. On the same day, Rockefeller spoke at the dedication of his new Virgin Islands National Park.[15] In 1939 there had been a National Park Service study that recommended the creation of a national park or monument on St. John. In 1952 LSR decided to make this old idea a reality, and through a friend, Frank Stick, began to buy options on land, much as his father had done in Jackson Hole. He put the idea to the director of the Park Service, then Conrad Wirth, who responded promptly and in the context of his just-announced Mission 66, which was meant to increase the number of parks, facilities in them, and visitors to them.[16] St. John was famous for its coral, its primitive beaches, and what urbanites liked to call jungle, and Wirth agreed that it was ideal for the first U.S. Caribbean park. Further, there was no reserved area for the protection of forest anywhere in the American Virgin Islands. LSR promptly donated $1.75 million to Jackson Hole Preserve, Inc., which then purchased the 5,000 acres that Stick had optioned (Stick also gave 1,500 acres on the south shore of the island), and the whole was deeded to the National Park Service. Lest he be accused of primarily wishing to create a tourist attraction at the back door to his resort, Rockefeller gave up ownership in the hotel the year before it opened, donating it to the nonprofit JHPI, which nearly doubled the size of the park in 1960 and added half again more acreage a few years later. In 1976 the national park was designated a World Biosphere Reserve as well.

The park would test the proposition that protection was assured by making the area a unit of the National Park System. Some felt that LSR had drawn too much attention to St. John by making it a national park. Others felt that the NPS mismanaged the park. Certainly, the mere existence of a park attracted far more visitors than would have come to St. John at the time. By 1991, when this writer first visited the park, there was little coral to see along its innovative Trunk Bay underwater nature trail. Indeed, realizing that the park's resources had been inadequately monitored, the Park Service had moved as early as 1961 to create another Caribbean unit, Buck Island Reef National Monument, off another of the American Virgin Islands, St. Croix, to protect what was identified as the finest marine garden in the American Caribbean, where the NPS worked to avoid the undoubted mistakes it made in the St. John national park. Still, Virgin Islands National Park grew to nearly 16,000 acres and, despite damage to its offshore coral, remains an outstanding unit in an ever-expanding system.

Though the national park on St. John often is singled out as an example of what happens when people "love a park to death"—that is, when a park has too many visitors precisely because the area has been designated a national park, implying that a resource might be better protected by having less attention drawn to it, and by some other administrative designation or, perhaps, by being owned and managed by a nongovernmental conservation organization—this argument seems unsound when one contrasts Virgin Islands National Park with what happened during the same period of time on nearby St. Thomas, the largest of the American Virgin Islands. There an endless skyline of high-rise and fat-spread hotels occupies nearly all of the land, spilling out into the surrounding sea. No natural beaches remain. A clutter of commercial landscapes, advertising, billboards, overhead wires, fast food outlets, and car rental agencies greet the eye. The only national park unit on St. Thomas, a crumbling administrative building from the Danish period that had high potential for interpreting the islands' colonial history, had to be abandoned as it became surrounded by urban blight and was victimized by a lack of interest on the part of local politicians. In short, there is every reason to believe that St. John would have suffered the fate of St. Thomas had it not been for Rockefeller's timely intervention.

Subsequent Rockefeller hotels were not related to national parks in so close a way, but LSR's work at Caneel Bay led quickly to other environmentally alert projects. These resorts were, he admitted, obtained "under most fortuitous circumstances," and none better demonstrated the desirable qualities he sought— low cost, scenic natural beauty, favorable environmental circumstances, welcoming political conditions, and the potential for contributing to the local economy—than his next hotel, the Dorado Beach in Puerto Rico. Built along another stretch of remarkable shore staked out by LSR, with an old coconut plantation into which the hotel could be inserted, and where the sound of the sea would reach every room, the Dorado Beach Hotel and Resort opened in December 1958, two years to the day after the dedication of Caneel Bay.

The Puerto Rican opportunity was brought to Rockefeller's attention by Adolf Berle and Beardsley Rummel, then economic advisors to the dynamic governor of Puerto Rico, Luis Muñoz Marín. In 1948 the governor had launched Operation Bootstrap, designed to raise the island's low standard of living by granting tax benefits to U.S. business and manufacturing interests. LSR admired him—indeed, he would come to feel that, with the possible exception of Ramon Magsaysay, president of the Philippines from 1953 until 1957, when he lost his life in an airplane crash, Muñoz Marín was one of the most distinguished democratic leaders of his time. LSR already had formed a vision of what he wanted when he began to look in Puerto Rico, echoing the title of Antoine de St. Exupéry's famed book, *Wind, Sand and Stars*, which he thought one of the best accounts of the spiritual dimension of flying he had ever read: he wanted "sea, sand, sun and serenity." This last goal mirrored a second program of Muñoz Marín's, Operation Serenity, begun in 1955 to help Puerto Ricans educationally and spiritually—an effort that was rather less successful than Bootstrap was in its early years.

The Dorado beach area was owned by Clara Livingston, whose father had developed the plantation. She had turned government negotiators, who wanted her property, away with a shot gun in hand, and was rumored to be difficult.

But she was head of Air Civil Defense for Puerto Rico and flew back and forth to San Juan from her own air strip; recognizing a fellow flying fan, Rockefeller asked his friend and golfing partner, Eddie Rickenbacker, who Clara Livingston idolized, to talk with her, and she agreed to sell. The Puerto Rican legislature gave Rockefeller's company exclusive rights over a mile of beachfront, and Harmon Goldstone, LSR's best friend from Lincoln school days and an able architect, designed another fine hotel. As at his other hotels, Rockefeller expanded slowly, emphasizing decentralization and incremental development, learning from experience and actual occupancy, an approach that also reduced environmental damage. When Muñoz Marín attended the opening night dinner at the Dorado Beach, he remarked upon the beauty of the site, which had not been impaired: it was, the governor said, like putting lipstick on the Mona Lisa and getting away with it.[17]

Success came almost instantly, for the Dorado Beach benefitted from a Cold War reality. Cuba, which had the best hotels and service in the Caribbean, was transformed into a communist state by Fidel Castro in January of 1959, and the North American travel market, in turmoil, sought out new Caribbean destinations. That jet airplanes began shortly thereafter to make non-stop flights to San Juan and St. Thomas helped enormously, especially since the flights were by Eastern Airlines. The Dorado Beach went from a projected four-month to a year-round season within six weeks.

When Muñoz Marín launched Operación Manos de la Obra, he had the co-operation of American businesses eager to expand into new markets and to find new sources of post-war labor. Initially advised by Rexford Guy Tugwell, a member of Franklin D. Roosevelt's original Brain Trust and as the last colonial governor a proponent of self-government for Puerto Rico, and working closely with the principal architect of Operation Bootstrap, Teodoro Moscoso, Muñoz set out to augment the number of industries on the island: more manufacturers of petrochemicals, medicines, electrical goods, the making of scientific instruments, more forms of labor that did not exploit workers in the manner of the traditional sweatshop trades. Muñoz worked to improve the standards of public education, health, transportation, nutrition, and recreation, to produce cheaper electricity, build more and better roads, sewers, hospitals, and schools, to carry out basic land reforms, to create new port facilities and airports, and to design government agencies to promote these changes.

Tourism would grow, Muñoz reasoned, only as Puerto Ricans themselves became better educated, better able to work in the service sector, and as Norteamericanos felt more secure about visiting a land they imagined to hold health risks for them. Thus he favored American hoteliers, and above all, Conrad Hilton and Laurance Rockefeller, whose ideas about hotels differed but who both believed in greatly improved incentives for employees and in better working conditions. Hilton had arrived first, signing a contract to build a luxury hotel in 1947, the Caribe Hilton, which opened in 1949. LSR liked the dapper, buoyant Puerto Rican leader from their first meeting, and he especially liked the way in which, as the success of Operation Bootstrap raised living conditions but also threatened traditional Puerto Rican values, Muñoz moved to Operation Serenity, in an attempt to help Puerto Ricans avoid the worst aspects of rampant consumerism. Between 1949 and 1959 tourism increased from 60,000 to 350,000 annually and tourist spending from $5.5 million to $53 million.[18]

During the years LSR was on the board of Eastern Airlines, he worked to promote profitable routes, and though he did not expect Castro to triumph in Cuba, or if he did, to sweep the dictatorship of President Fulgencio Batista aside so quickly, he knew that if Cuba were to fall to communism, alternative playgrounds in the sun would be needed. At times after his hotels became successful, he would imply that he had ridden to success on a wave of good luck, but his pursuit of Caribbean travel—both the means and the destinations— was shrewdly linked to his sense of international trends in leisure activities and his reading of political realities. Brother Nelson was deeply involved in Latin America, especially in Venezuela and Brazil, and brother David's banking interests gave him unparalleled access in the region. Both kept LSR well informed. The success of Rockresorts, especially in the Caribbean, was a combination of interest, convictions, and opportunity.

Though LSR had not focused on the West Indies until after World War II, many of the elements were in place before he began his explorations by sail. LSR was the first of JDR, Jr.'s five sons to go beyond the family's focus on oil, to begin cautious diversification, when in 1938 he joined the syndicate Rickenbacker organized. An initial investment of $10,000 grew until LSR was the airline's largest stockholder. In 1941, LSR toured Central and South America by air, and he quickly saw that British capital was being drained from the region by the war in Europe, and that Germany was a threat to American interests in the area. LSR purchased a controlling interest in a vast ranch in Colombia, raising cattle and harvesting mahogany, and he considered building a hotel at a crucial point on the planned Pan-American Highway.

LSR's 1941 trip around Latin America was sponsored by the Inter-American Escadrille. It had its roots in a meeting in 1939 between the young LSR and Robert W. Johnson, the founder of Johnson & Johnson drug company, who was concerned about the operations of German businesses in South America, especially Argentina and Brazil, the two most economically promising nations, both of which possessed vast natural resources of great potential value to an expanding Third Reich. Hitler was boasting of the triumphs of German technology, winning propaganda points, while increasing German aircraft production through Latin American sales. The Escadrille already existed but was moribund; Johnson asked Rockefeller to persuade Eastern Airlines to support a revived Escadrille that would promote American aircraft and American airlines, which would be simultaneously good for the United States and bad for Germany.

Rockefeller obliged, and he also joined the Escadrille board of directors and helped turn it into a lobby that successfully persuaded Brazil and other South American countries to replace German with American airlines. Though LSR resigned from the board when the United States entered the war against Germany in 1941 to take a commission in the U.S. Navy and work on America's aviation buildup—and later on aircraft production in California—he did not forget what he had learned, and as soon as the war was over, and even before the onset of the Cold War, he was urging Eastern Airlines to expand into Puerto Rico, Mexico, and elsewhere. Thus any suggestion that the decision to open hotels in the Caribbean in the 1950s was purely good luck is to miss the point: Rockefeller was an astute observer of the region, he favored American business over European (and in the late 1940s and early 1950s there were few European investors from a war-torn continent), and he believed that his type of resort would do more for local employment while also doing less against the environment than anyone else's.

Puerto Rico had elected its own governor for the first time in 1948, when the people chose Luis Muñoz Marín. He opposed independence or statehood for Puerto Rico, promoting a "special status," that of Commonwealth, which he hoped would give Puerto Ricans many of the advantages of statehood while shielding them from taxation and helping them to maintain their distinct culture. LSR agreed with this middle-of-the-road approach; just as his mother had never tolerated any notions about "lesser peoples," he wished to see Puerto Ricans not only dealt with as equals but by economic progress made financially so, and he believed that the continuation of Operation Bootstrap, coupled with the spiritual dimension Operation Serenity was designed to invoke, could do this. Further, he felt akin to Muñoz for his integrity, for not using his position to enrich himself, for his simple life-style and for running "the cleanest" election campaigns in the island's history. Muñoz remained a powerful force in Puerto Rican politics and in Rockefeller's life until his death, at eighty-two, in 1980, long after the high hopes of Operation Bootstrap, which so lifted Puerto

Rico in the 1940s and 1950s, were forgotten, Puerto Rico becoming ever more dependent on federal transfers, other ambitious economies having displaced its early leadership, emerging Asian states driving Puerto Rico toward a potentially permanent recession.

By then LSR had looked elsewhere, to Hawaii. Impressed by the Dorado Beach Resort, William Quinn, the governor of Hawaii, which became the fiftieth state in August 1959, six months after Castro's victory in Cuba, invited LSR to give thought to building one of his resorts in the new state somewhere beyond already well-known Oahu. Rockefeller toured the islands as a guest of the government, repeating his by now customary process: approaching beaches from the water, swimming, walking the shore, taking many photographs. In July 1960, as LSR spoke of it later, he came upon that spot that exceeded everything to date: the Kohala Coast, on the west side of the Big Island, Hawaii. Here was ocean, arid rather than humid warmth, yet cool rain forests, with snow-capped mountains behind, running up to Mauna Kea, the highest peak in all the islands, and across to Mauna Loa, the great volcano at the core of what was then Hawaii National Park (and is now Hawaii Volcanoes National Park), an area of such drama it would in time be designated both a World Biosphere Reserve and a World Heritage Site.

So Mauna Kea Beach Hotel was built. The problem was, there was a great lava desert running down to the beach. But when the lava was broken up and mixed with top soil, it proved miraculously fertile. Extensive landscaping, subtle external lighting, intelligent use of the site, the incorporation of native Hawaiian motifs in the designs and cultural objects in the decor, and a central structure modeled on traditional Hawaiian religious platforms then being studied at City of Refuge National Historical Park down the coast, created the most dramatic and beautiful hotel in the state. The resort looked, LSR once remarked, like a great ship when viewed from the sea, at least until the landscaping matured; it was a green oasis when seen from the air; and it opened in 1965 to 97 percent capacity, another success where many had predicted failure.

Laurance Rockefeller did not accept these predictions of failure, for he considered them ill-informed and unimaginative. While he subordinated his hotel facilities to the environment in order to make the guest experience as much a part of the natural surroundings as possible, he did not mistake business for philanthropy. He expected the resorts to become self-sustaining and profitable operations and to contribute to the local economy, though he understood that he would have to underwrite them for some time, until they matured. One of the points of venture capitalism was that it required "patience and commitment."[19]

LSR always resonated to the spiritual dimension of place, especially those of significance to traditional cultures. On the Big Island he observed that the "majesty and beauty and glory of God" were close at hand, "old problems were solved and new questions asked." When he spoke at the dedication of Mauna Kea in 1965, he began with a prayer: "May we all find inspiration in the majesty of the sea and the beauty of the surrounding mountains. May we learn again the joy of living and that good will is the key to brotherly love. May we recognize anew that material goods are but the means—stepping stones to the spiritual meaning and purpose of life." In the spirit of ecumenical values, he restored an ancient *heiau*, or temple—Puukohola Heiau, the Temple on the Hill of the Whale—that had been built by Hawaii's King Kamehameha the Great in 1791, and presented the result to the National Park Service as Puukohola Heiau National Historic Site.

Predictably, some cynics said that Rockefeller had restored the *heiau* to placate local Hawaiians, so that they would work more happily and dependably in his resort. Others said that he was creating a tourist attraction as protection against the possibility that the lava bed from which the hotel arose would— despite a golf course built by Robert Trent Jones, the most famous designer in the business—not prove sufficiently interesting to hold guests. Most likely such results did flow from his actions, but there is no reason to doubt his own expressed conviction, that on Hawaii's serene and beautiful Kohala Coast visitors would find "greater awareness, faith, and belief in the oneness, eternal unity of God, man and nature."[20]

For the Mauna Kea Beach Hotel, Rockefeller assembled an exceptional collection of Asian and Pacific arts, and working with the architectural firm of Skidmore, Owings, and Merrill, he saw to it that these objects were incorporated into the structures and on the grounds with greater sensitivity than had been brought to virtually any hotel project elsewhere in the country at that time, thus helping to promote a practice now commonplace in so-called luxury resorts. Just months before the hotel opened, LSR would be appointed chairman of the first White House Conference on Natural Beauty, and he was immersed in the question, How does one make casual travelers, persons not insensitive to but nonetheless often unheeding of the way in which man-made and naturally made beauty interacted, sit up and take notice of their surrounds? He had become increasingly interested in what the ancient East could teach the West, and he realized that at Mauna Kea he had an unusual opportunity to see that "art could become, just as the elements of nature would become, a constant influence." A remarkable seventh century Pallava Buddha from Nagapattinam in the south of India, carved from granite in the Gupta style, was placed on the grounds. (Later LSR would recall the consternation when in shipment the historic figure's nose was damaged, and the exquisite care that was exercised in repair, so that today no one would ever know.) Working through the Reverend Abraham Akaka of the Kawsaiaha Church in Honolulu (the traditional site for marriages and funerals for Hawaiian royalty from the 1840s), and one of the members of its congregation, Meali'i Kalama, Rockefeller commissioned thirty Hawaiian quilts to be displayed in the hotel, creating the largest exhibit of this medium in Hawaii. Following an extension in 1968 and some redesign in 1973, more art was added. Eventually, as LSR had hoped, visitors became so interested in the objects, the resort offered weekly tours and lectures, and in 1990, after the hotel was sold to a Japanese businessman, past and present owners combined to publish, through the East-West Center in Honolulu, a handsome volume on the meaning and creation of each object, written by the curator of the collection.

This hotel led LSR into the enhancement of another national park. Since the fledgling Hawaiian state had hardly any state park authority in 1965, Rockefeller worked with Charles Lindbergh and Samuel Pryor, a senior vice president of Pan-American Airlines, to purchase land for the expansion of Haleakala National Park on the island of Maui. The reserve protected a vast volcanic crater and the endangered flora and fauna that had grown over the centuries on the crater's floor. The original boundaries of Haleakala were, as with so many national parks, quite imperfect. Beyond its borders were seven pools, said to be sacred to the ancient Hawaiian culture, linked by a dashing stream, the `Ohe`o, with waterfalls connecting the pools, and the Waimoku Falls on a small tributary above. The stream flowed into Wailua Cove at an unspoiled point on the Kipahulu coast. Lindbergh described this lush, green area, so different from the near-desert dryness inside the Haleakala crater, as "ruin-monumented, spray-lashed, life-abounding," and he had built a simple cottage nearby. Above the pools and waterfall there was habitat for the endangered Maui parrotbill and Maui nukupuu, and along the `Ohe`o were remnants of another *heiau,* an ancient farm, and other archaeological sites. From Mauna Kea Laurance and Mary Rockefeller flew in a helicopter over the area in 1967, and they readily joined in the effort to save the entire Valley of the Seven Sacred Pools, as they called it. Lindbergh died of cancer in 1974, and he was buried at Kipahulu, just outside the Haleakala park boundary. In Rockefeller's words of dedication of the bust of Charles Lindbergh in the International Building at Rockefeller Center in August 1975, he singled out Lindbergh's achievement at Haleakala for special comment.

There were many projects proposed to Rockefeller for building hotels in or near great national parks, since by the 1960s it was clear that he was, from the National Park Service's point of view, an ideal tenant. But he did not rush in.

For example, in 1965 the Park Service asked LSR to purchase the Yellowstone Park Company in Yellowstone National Park for $5 million. Conrad Wirth hoped to see the alliance between business and environmental interests brought to Yellowstone to solve one of its most intractable problems just in time for the culmination of Mission 66, the ten-year construction plan Wirth had launched in 1955 to provide more facilities for a vastly increased number of visitors to the parks.

The project was Grant Village, on the south shore of Thumb Bay, on Yellowstone Lake, a planned summer community of totally inappropriate size. The Yellowstone Park Company was owned by a Montana ranching family who had become concessionaires at Canyon Village, another fundamentally unnecessary project that was bankrupting them. The Park Service hoped that LSR would take over, constructing the kind of hotel he had built at Jackson Lake as the centerpiece for a vast campground and marina complex. Through Jackson Hole Preserve, Inc., he had a survey of YP, as it was known, carried out across the summer, and he concluded that the facilities were too run down and the price was far too much. Further, he did not think that a hotel at West Thumb would meet his criteria.

There were two other hotels, however: Little Dix Bay on the island of Virgin Gorda in the British Virgin Islands and the Woodstock Inn in central Vermont. Both were very successful, the first especially so. In 1993, eight years after Rockefeller had divested himself of his Rockresorts, he reflected upon his success in venture capital: "If you don't think of [making] money, you make it as a by-product or you don't. But if you don't, you're not aware of it, if you do, it's a surprise." He did not mean this precisely, of course, for he had wanted his hotels and resorts to be profitable; rather, he meant that profit should not come before good taste, a striving for beauty, and a sense of serenity. Until 1992 he revisited each of his hotels every year.

There were many people who helped LSR achieve his goals. Indeed, with the resorts as with all matters, he described himself as a coordinator, first among equals. There were a number of individuals who helped him in quite basic ways: Mary above all, his brother Nelson, his high school friend Harmon Goldstone, Allston Boyer, Robert Barton, Richard Holtzman (who had been president of Sheraton Hotels in Hawaii), the architect Nathaniel Owings, fellow investors Walter Collins and Kenneth Brown, and later LSR's senior associate, Clayton W. Frye, who served as vice chairman of Rockresorts for almost fifteen years. Still, in the end, these hotels were largely his vision, from the incremental design by which, as he said, one could add on like a quilt, through the landscaping, to the eye for detailed, simple, yet impeccable comfort, down to a hook on the back of a bathroom door that would truly hold one's pajamas.[21]

There was one Rockresort that LSR did not sell: the Woodstock Inn. This proved to be his most difficult project as well as his most enduring, and it grew out of his desire to protect Mary's "home town," as they often thought of it, from the unplanned excesses of overexpansion during the post-war building boom. He would bury power lines in the central part of the town, would buy pockets of land to protect views and hill tops, would create a farm museum on the fields that had belonged to Mary's grandfather, Frederick Billings, and would quietly help repair, stabilize, or rehabilitate many structures throughout the community. Most visible of all was his lodge. A clapboard inn built in 1892, it sat on a lozenge-shaped village green; its owner and manager, David Beach, approached Rockefeller for help in modernizing it. When surveys showed that the cost of doing so would far exceed the value of the structure, LSR decided to buy the inn and replace it with another, the first new hotel built in Vermont since before World War II.

The result was somewhat controversial, for Woodstock's residents responded much according to the values for which Laurance Rockefeller admired Vermonters: a rugged independence, an inclination against change, a taciturn manner of expression and doubts about the wisdom of outsiders. LSR did not regard himself, and certainly not Mary, as an outsider—after all, they had been married in Woodstock's Congregational Church, itself a major beneficiary of gifts from her grandfather—and based on an anticipated skiing boom, he believed the new inn would bring prosperity to Woodstock without doing harm to the unusual charm of the town. In 1960 he had purchased the nearby Mount Tom ski area, and he had added another such area, Suicide Six, later: these were historic areas dating back to the nineteenth century, for the first ski run in Vermont had been built on these properties. He had also bought the Woodstock Country Club and installed another golf course designed by Robert Trent Jones, and he had acquired another historic inn to serve as the town's historical society. While some of these initiatives had been his own, more had arisen from approaches by the owners of the properties. But a few well-to-do owners of summer hideaways were unhappy, preferring Woodstock to remain undiscovered. Some people feared that LSR intended a miniature of Colonial Williamsburg in Vermont and believed that the town's future lay with light industry and more popular tourist attractions; neighboring towns, especially White River Junction, worried that the Woodstock LSR envisioned would draw tourists to it and away from the Connecticut River; others professed to fear the potential dominating power of a single person.

Rockefeller was his usual direct and careful self in Woodstock, waiting even more patiently than usual, content to negotiate quietly for a decade if necessary about the right-of-way for a bicycle path from the town center to the country club. His new Woodstock Inn opened in 1969 and became the town's largest employer and one of the premier hotels in the state. With modest meeting facilities and the nearby country club, it did not need either entertainment or in-town recreational facilities, so that it sat well back from the green, its parking attractively hidden by tasteful landscaping, a historic gilded eagle from an earlier Woodstock hotel atop its entrance, and in winter a massive roaring fire awaiting those who arrived in search of comfort. Whether the inn proved profitable or not—and there were years when it did not, as new motorways and improved technology for highway snow removal made it possible for urbanites from Boston or New York to pass higher into Vermont to more trendy ski slopes—LSR appeared determined to continue his protective and, as he saw it, nurturing role in the community, in part through the impact of the inn, in part through continuing quiet efforts with the town council, his neighbors, and a variety of conservation agencies, and in part through the Woodstock Foundation, which he established in 1968.

"We try to be modest," LSR said when interviewed by a reporter from a New Hampshire newspaper in 1983, "and say that everybody has something else better, but nobody has anything as good in so many ways. . . . Woodstock is one of the six most beautiful towns in America. So we can say that anybody can have a better golf course or better skiing, but not better everything." Asked how he would like Woodstock to look a quarter century later, LSR replied, "As near to what it is now as possible."[22] His interest in conservation and use, and in historic preservation, exemplified by his Rockresorts, reflected his stable conservative values and his sense of compromise, both of which would be basic to how he dealt with national park issues.

VI

National Parks

No family is likely to match the collective Rockefeller contribution to the nation's national parks. Four generations have contributed money, time, the brokering of contacts, the sponsoring of studies, of scientific and historical research, and thoughtful concern to the parks. John D. Rockefeller, Jr., gave more than any other Rockefeller, for he was, as it were, in at the creation, already helping to shape Lafayette National Park even before there was a National Park System and, as we have seen, initiator of the growth of Grand Teton National Park from 1926 until his death. All of his sons would play some role in the development of the national parks, but only Laurance followed directly in JDR, Jr.'s footsteps, in helping to expand older parks, creating entirely new ones, and proposing parks that in the end got away, at least for now.

JDR, Jr., was "the most generous philanthropist in the history of conservation,"[1] and he focused his contributions on the national parks as Andrew Carnegie had focused his on libraries, certain that an expanding national park system would be of great benefit to the nation. He was not much interested in abstract studies of just what these benefits might be, especially in quantifiable terms—such an interest would have to wait for the alliance between conservation and science that produced the environmental movement—because, as he said, he had "an eye for nature" and believed that anyone who did so was a kin-

dred spirit. Critics of JDR, Jr., have pointed out, rightly, that his love of nature
was somewhat distant—watching sunsets from his home, journeying into the
great national parks by private railway car and powerful automobile, and walking in well-maintained woods. His was a patrician approach to conservation at
a time when there were neither extensive advocacy organizations nor many
defenders of wilderness for its own sake. In 1910 JDR, Jr., purchased a summer
home on Mount Desert Island and began his building of carriage roads in
what became Acadia National Park, in part to forestall the automobile and in
part because he believed in manicured landscapes, in nature enhanced, nature
brought to order. His first major gift to conservation, $17,500 (a large sum at
the time), was to the proposed national park in 1915; the next year he presented
the park with 2,700 acres. By the time he was finished he had spent over $2 mil-
lion on sixty miles of groomed carriage roads and hand-chiseled bridges. JDR,
Jr., had his opponents, both in Maine, where there was fear that the fastidious
carriage roads implied that only the wealthy could afford to come to the park,
and in Washington, where early advocates of a professional National Park Service hesitated to criticize him, hoping for support in the future, but privately
said that his designs on the land were contrary to the purposes of a national
park. After JDR, Jr.'s death, the carriage roads fell into disrepair, and then,
somewhat ironically, they were lovingly restored in the 1990s, for by then Acadia National Park was beyond hope as a wilderness and the roads were seen to
have great historic and aesthetic appeal. When JDR, Jr., gave his final gift to
Acadia, 3,825 acres in 1935, he had not only provided a major land base for the
national park we know today—only George B. Dorr's original gift was more
significant in this regard—he had also given it the imprint of a historical rather
than a natural national park, representing as it does one approach to landscape
architecture in the pre-war period.

   As we have seen, JDR, Jr., was instrumental in the creation of Grand Teton
National Park by acquiring over 30,000 acres and spending a million and a half
dollars between 1926 and 1933. In 1943 he virtually required the federal government to take the lands he had purchased in Jackson Hole and add them to the
park, which was established in 1929, or lose the land entirely: if the government
did not act, he told Franklin D. Roosevelt's secretary of the interior, Harold
Ickes, he would sell the land to private purchasers. It was this threat that led
Ickes to advise Roosevelt to use the Antiquities Act to create a national monument. When he closed out his gifts to the National Park Service in 1949,
LSR—delivering the deeds to the land personally to Oscar Chapman, the secretary of the interior, on behalf of his father—JDR, Jr., had accounted for the
most crucial portions of the expanded Grand Teton park. Later LSR, who had
watched this process from the beginning, responded to a questioner who

implied that his father was bluffing when he threatened to sell the land that he thought so too. Whatever JDR, Jr.'s actual intent was, his threat worked, and he had put his imprint deeply on a second major national park.

It was also in 1926 that JDR, Jr., committed himself unswervingly to the restoration of the old colonial capital of Virginia, Williamsburg. This became the largest, most influential, and perhaps most controversial exercise in historic preservation, restoration, and interpretation ever undertaken in the United States. Again, LSR was an interested and alert observer, spending portions of his summers in Williamsburg, fascinated with his father's pleasure in the project.

Historians and others concerned with the recovery, interpretation, and physical representation of the past have always differed on the issue of historical restoration. The nineteenth century English aesthete John Ruskin delivered the most extreme judgment against reconstruction in his widely influential *Seven Lamps of Architecture* in 1849: restoration, he wrote, "means the most total destruction which a building can suffer." Others have argued that "purist" views such as Ruskin's are elitist and fail to meet the educational needs of each new generation.

The debate, still central to an understanding of the many ways in which people internalize and use history—a key debate in the eternal struggle over who "owns history"—also has its practical side. Some commentators who favor full-scale reconstruction of historic sites argue that such reconstruction is an act of reverence for history as well as a provision for a tourist attraction of potentially great economic benefit to people living near the reconstruction: a historical counterpart to the conservation and use philosophy. Against those who maintain that any reconstruction is artificial and ahistorical, since it ignores what the forces of history have done, others seek carefully calibrated mid-way positions: that if nothing except a pile of stones remains, one should not attempt reconstruction, but if a substantial vestige of an original site is intact, repair (which is viewed by some as distinct from reconstruction) is acceptable. Both sides to this debate tend to believe that the average tourist will not care about the difference and that issues of strict "historical integrity" are largely of concern only to professional scholars, archaeologists, and some architectural aestheticians. Whatever the relative metaphysical arguments might be, decisions are influenced by economics: to reconstruct is very expensive; not to reconstruct fully might well lessen an anticipated flow of tourists' dollars.

In 1907 an English architect had begun the reconstruction of Fort Ticonderoga, a key post for controlling trade between Canada and the Hudson River Valley in the years before the American Revolution. The architect, Stephen Pell, argued that the ruins on Lake Champlain, while not much more than a pile of rocks, were extensive enough, and were supported by sufficient historical documentation (including eighteenth century maps, charts, and architect's plans), to make a fully authentic reconstruction possible. His aesthetic success and the lack of scholarly complaint about the project at the time—and the fact that by the First World War the fort was a major tourist attraction—led to other projects, of which JDR, Jr.'s decision to underwrite the reconstruction of Williamsburg was the most significant.[2]

Though the Carnegie Foundation took the initiative in this most extensive and perhaps most successful historical reconstruction in the United States, Rockefeller money paid wholly, if not directly, for the restoration of the major colonial buildings, including the Christopher Wren Building at William and Mary College on the edge of the colonial restoration (which was basic to its visual integrity), the old colonial Capitol Building, and many others. The developing example of how to combine restoration and preservation at Colonial Williamsburg had widespread impact within and outside the United States. In particular, the success at Williamsburg emboldened Canadian leaders to undertake their greatest effort, the restoration of the Fortress of Louisburg, a massive eighteenth century French fortification, high on the remote coast of Cape Breton Island in Nova Scotia. Thus in practical terms, Rockefeller generosity carried the day for the reconstructionists.

Colonial Williamsburg is frequently referred to as a unit of the National Park System, an understandable confusion since it is linked directly to an actual unit, Yorktown, and to an affiliated unit, Jamestown, by the twenty-three mile Colonial Parkway. Further, when these units were proclaimed Colonial National Monument in 1931, the proclamation embraced Williamsburg in order to include it in funding for the sesquicentennial of the Battle of Yorktown. Despite protests from JDR, Jr.'s director of the Williamsburg project, Kenneth Chorley, "Colonial" Williamsburg and Colonial National Monument itself (which became Colonial National Historical Park with the incorporation of the Cape Henry Memorial in 1967) continue to merge in the public mind as unyieldingly as the Colonial Parkway that links them. From 1939, Colonial Williamsburg became JDR 3rd's family responsibility, and in 1953, Winthrop Rockefeller's, and thus it continued to be inextricably linked with the Rockefeller name.[3]

After JDR, Jr., committed himself to Williamsburg, he lived at Bassett Hall, one of the reconstructed homes, for two months each year. His sons often accompanied him. In this way LSR had his first experience with historical reconstruction work and, though he was not really aware of them at the time, the controversies such work can bring.

These three projects—Acadia, Grand Teton, and Colonial Williamsburg—
were JDR, Jr.'s best known initiatives in conservation and historic preservation,
but there were many others of significance. He helped defray the costs of various park-related study commissions proposed by Horace Albright, most
notably an examination in 1924 of the possibility of a national park in the
southern Appalachians—the first step toward the creation of the Great Smoky
Mountains National Park in North Carolina and Tennessee ten years later. The
study group, which included the general manager of the Palisades Interstate
Park Commission, Major W. A. Welch, who had worked closely with JDR, Jr.,
on park matters, concluded that the most exploitable and valuable timber in the
Great Smokies was gone from the lower elevations and that the residents of the
small towns and mountain coves would decline economically if an alternative
form of employment were not available, while the forests at the higher elevations would soon come under attack. Parks and parkways were increasingly seen
as desirable for reasons other than the protection of scenery or natural
resources or for access to both, for they would increase employment and when
an infrastructure of roads, campgrounds, bridges, trails, visitor centers, and
perhaps lodges was in place, paying tourists would underwrite the free recreational outlets of those who could not pay. Early in 1928, through the Laura
Spelman Rockefeller Memorial Foundation, JDR, Jr., provided $5 million to
match appropriations by Tennessee and North Carolina, making possible the
purchase of 6,600 separate parcels of land to promote his dual agendas—the
creation of a "conservation landscape" and the promotion of recreational
tourism to lift the region's standard of living. With the development of the
environmental movement in the 1960s, so naked a linkage of the two agendas
would be less palatable to both the conservation and the business communities,
but in the 1930s precisely this linkage best represented the prevailing national
park ethic.

In time the nation would have a continuous national park, celebrating and
protecting Appalachian landscape and culture, running from the Shenandoah
ridges of Virginia via the Black Mountains of North Carolina to the Smokies,
connected by a parkway that offered numerous smaller national park properties for the pleasure and edification of the traveler. JDR, Jr., was instrumental
in the birth of this remarkable continuity of parklands. He provided $5 mil-
lion on a matching basis to create the Shenandoah National Park in Virginia
in much the same way he had supported the Great Smoky Mountains proposal,
and the new park became a reality in 1935. In the same year Congress voted the
initial funds to build the Blue Ridge Parkway along the crest of the mountain
ranges to connect the two national parks, with construction beginning in
North Carolina southward from the Virginia border. The Parkway was built

in fits and starts over the next fifty years, passing down the backbone of the mountains amidst landscaped splendor from which only rarely can one glimpse the workaday world of commerce, 469 miles park to park. Perhaps the most beautiful stop along the highway is at Linville Falls and Gorge, which is reached by a short walk in the woods. This site, threatened by development, was purchased for the National Park Service as a combined recreational and wilderness area by JDR, Jr., in 1951.

There were dozens of smaller projects. JDR, Jr., paid for a study center at Crater Lake National Park; for the purchase of a key grove of redwoods in California with the intent that one day it would become part of a national park; $1.65 million for a stand of yellow and sugar pine at Yosemite; and a large grant for the development of the Museum of Anthropology in Santa Fe, New Mexico, where the study of Native American arts moved forward, and for excavations conducted by the School of American Research, also in Santa Fe, which led to the creation of new archaeological units of the National Park System in New Mexico and Arizona. Nor did he confine his interest in historical reconstruction to Williamsburg, for he donated land adjacent to Wakefield, the reconstructed birthplace of George Washington on the Rappahannock River in Virginia, which was to become a national monument (in 1930), protecting tobacco and wheat fields, rivers and creeks, and a grove of trees, so that visitors might imagine the Popes Creek property as it was when Washington was born there. In 1954, when eighty years old, JDR, Jr., provided $1 million so that the South Calaveras Grove of sequoias could be added to the North Calaveras State Park in California, a resource once considered for inclusion in the National Park System, making possible the present Calaveras Big Trees Park. In 1959, the year before his death, he would try to jump-start a tallgrass prairie national park near Manhattan, Kansas, with a gift of $20,000, acting on a recommendation of the National Park System Advisory Board. (Such a park would not be achieved, without Rockefeller assistance and further south in the Flint Hills, until 1996.)

To make certain that such endeavors would be protected by continuity of leadership, JDR, Jr., and other men who thought as he did spoke out on behalf of the Park Service's relative freedom from political interference at a time when an ethic of independence was not yet clearly established, in particular in persuading Warren G. Harding, the Republican elected to succeed Democrat Woodrow Wilson in 1920, to exempt park superintendencies and other positions from the spoils system. This was a message JDR, Jr., would repeat often.

He with others also encouraged the creation of an Advisory Board on National Parks, Historic Sites, Buildings and Monuments to advise the secretary of the interior. This board, which was established in the 1930s, provided a forum of knowledgeable and well-placed individuals who could buffer the National Park Service from political interference. Members were appointed for indefinite terms, they took their charge seriously and saw themselves as stewards who helped to protect the director of the Park Service from undue pressure by commercial and local interests who promoted unworthy park proposals, and the members often had substantial private means or the capacity to broker private funds to support park projects. JDR, Jr., was never a member of the board (which later became the National Park System Advisory Board), but there almost always was a representative from JDR, Jr., and later from Laurance Rockefeller, in the group. Unhappily this working relationship began to erode in the 1970s.

Seldom has the adage, "Like father like son," applied so directly. LSR took up the work his father had begun while in his twenties and continued it long after his father's death in 1960. As we have seen, he kept a watchful eye on developments at Grand Teton, he created a national park in the Virgin Islands, and he added substantially to Haleakala. He would make signal contributions to historical preservation and interpretation, provide the nation with a National Historical Park, fund dozens of studies, help to underwrite major national park conferences, and advocate the creation of great new national park units in California and New York.

LSR's first independent initiative was at Grand Teton National Park, where he was moving forward with his first hotel (see chapter V). As he worked on his plan for a three-tier approach to accommodations, he asked himself, what ought to be done to convince the residents of Jackson Hole and businessmen who had opposed his father's purchase of land, and the federal government's takeover of that land, that the park was not harmful to them economically, especially in terms of land taken from the local tax base? He concluded that something must be paid in lieu of property taxes, and in 1945 he asked a trustee of Jackson Hole Preserve, Inc., Leslie Miller, who had been governor of Wyoming from 1933 to 1939, to undertake a study of Jackson Hole's economy from 1929, the first inquiry of its kind. Thereafter LSR would propose some *quid pro quo* to set against lost property taxes in all the parks to which he contributed in order to make a park proposal more palatable locally and more feasible politically.

Miller's report provided plenty of data to support LSR's belief that parks were "good business." Jackson's population had trebled, adding to the tax base; the county's only bank had expanded tenfold; town lots had increased 500% in taxable value; the number of cattle had actually increased. Rockefeller investment in infrastructure and the resulting increase in the number of tourists had far offset any loss in the tax base. National parks, LSR concluded, not only helped to protect places of great beauty, they also spurred the local economy.

Of course, this conclusion posed a dilemma, for many conservationists did not want to see an increase in infrastructure, a doubling in the number of tourists, or evidence that parks could be made to pay. The problem, as they saw it, had changed little from the time when JDR, Jr., had helped forge an alliance for the Great Smoky Mountains. Nonetheless, LSR was convinced by Miller's study and by his subsequent experience with Grand Teton National Park that the majority of people would not support conservation goals if they saw the achievement of those goals solely in terms of expense and that there would have to be offsetting economic gains.

This conviction influenced Rockefeller's approach to national park issues where he had no economic interest of his own. He would play a key role in the creation of a national park in the redwoods country of California, with mixed success, and he would fail to achieve the creation of a national park in the Adirondack Mountains of New York (though he may well have accomplished what he actually hoped to despite the appearance of defeat). In California he did not get the national park he wanted or believed the resource warranted and the nation needed, and the park he got was much less than many park advocates had wished to settle for. As a result, a number of players in the game, and most particularly the Sierra Club, were unhappy with him for the compromise, to which he was instrumental, by which Redwood National Park was created in 1968. Other players, and especially the Save-the-Redwoods League, were publicly content with the national park that emerged, hoping that additions could be made in the future, a hope partially dashed by post-park harvesting of timber by aggressive companies. By the 1970s, therefore, LSR had tempered his support for balancing the two horns of the park dilemma, though he never gave up his belief that any new national park must involve some element of demonstrable economic reality.

This belief would lay Rockefeller open to the criticism that he enhanced or created national parks near his environmentally sensitive hotels in order to have a major attraction nearby that was most likely to appeal to the kind of clientele he wanted to attract. There was some truth in the observation, though this practice was openly illustrative of his belief that conservation and use were compatible. However, except at Grand Teton, where he took over his father's initiatives, he never built a commercial enterprise within a national park, so that use occurred outside the park, in a controlled manner that minimized impact on the resources of the park itself and that brought to the park an appreciative and often knowledgeable constituency. In this way he went well beyond his father, using his expertise in venture capital to promote multiple use within a region while reserving to national park lands the goals of passive recreation, education, and preservation.

While Laurance Rockefeller was involved in the Redwood National Park initiative, and promoting an Adirondack National Park for his home state, he was simultaneously contributing to many other conservation and environmental activities, as the next chapters relate. He was also constantly attentive to the problems of the park toward which he felt a steward's obligation, Grand Teton, in such an important measure his father's creation, and to the growth of the park that he himself had created, Virgin Islands. By the late 1960s and early 1970s it was clear that this park required further attention.

When LSR had purchased the land that formed the basis for the Virgin Islands National Park, and built his Caneel Bay resort just outside its boundaries, he had felt, in the spirit of the 1950s, that he could use St. John to demonstrate how parks and economics were favorably linked. He would protect a singular resource before it slipped away to the forces of commerce while at the same time providing employment to the residents of an area that offered few opportunities. At the public ceremony in December 1956, when LSR turned over to the director of the Park Service the deeds to the initial 4,666 acres for the park, he knew that there would have to be significant additions to it.

When the park was created in 1956 the population of St. John was 750, and there were only five registered vehicles on the entire island. Twenty years later the park, the general Caribbean tourist boom, and vigorous promotion by the government of the Virgin Islands of an industrial incentive program on St. Thomas had helped to increase the island's population to nearly three thousand and the tiny village of Cruz Bay faced traffic jams from the island's 814 registered vehicles. Further, there was growing island discontent. Increasingly employment went to off-islanders. Though by the terms of the bill that had been introduced into the Virgin Islands legislature by one of their own, Julius Sprauve, scion of a St. John family, and as stipulated by the individual sale agreements, former land owners were permitted to remain on their land for their and their spouses' lifetimes, they had not understood the restrictions that would be placed on them within the national park. Now they were told they could not cut trees to burn for charcoal, graze cattle and goats, or establish salt pans. Further, North Americans had bought up many of the available lots outside the park and values—and the cost of living—had risen markedly.

In 1962 the U.S. House of Representatives proposed to revise the boundaries of the national park, adding 5,600 acres to it, in order to preserve the coral gar-

dens, marine life, and seascapes of the island. The draft bill authorized the
acquisition of land by purchase, exchange, donation, or by condemnation if
necessary. The bill had originated with Senator Clinton Anderson of New
Mexico, who was believed to be acting on Laurance Rockefeller's suggestion.
Though the bill limited condemnation to private lands within the park boundaries, and made it clear that condemnation would be at fair market value, it
understandably created a furor on the island. When the residents of St. John
learned that LSR was offering a gift of $1.25 million to achieve the purposes of
the bill, they petitioned the House, President John F. Kennedy, and Rockefeller
to delete condemnation as a method of acquiring land.

LSR was disturbed, for he disliked condemnation as a tactic and had not
been aware that it was included in the bill. He quickly sent a representative to
St. John, accompanied by the chair of the House Subcommittee on National
Parks, and made it clear that he opposed the condemnation provision of the
bill. The editor of the Charlotte Amalie *Daily News,* who had consistently supported the national park, also opposed the bill. LSR recognized that a number of the protesters had arrived in St. John after 1956 and that they were determined to force the government to buy their land at prices created by the
existence of the national park they now decried, but there were other protes-
tors, from old island families, whose concerns were far more legitimate. To be
certain that condemnation was not included in the bill, LSR withdrew his offer
to match funds for the purchase of land. An amended bill, with condemnation
removed, was enacted in October 1962, and Rockefeller restored his gift. Other
lands were added to the park in 1974 and 1978, bringing it to its intended size
of 16,000 acres.

In the next decade the population of the island doubled again. A developer
blasted away part of the reef at Cruz Bay, dredging up sand to create a beach,
killing a mangrove swamp, and creating an "underwater desert." The sleepy village was invaded by mini-malls and, at its edge, by hotel developments, making it permanently unsuitable for adding to the park. Compared with nearby
St. Thomas, vigorously, even ruthlessly developed, St. John remained a garden;
without the national park, LSR knew, it would have gone the way of its larger
neighbor. Yet the park undoubtedly altered island life-styles, and while it promoted employment, it was not always the locals who benefitted; further, the
very existence of a park undoubtedly brought more visitors, and while one
might expect them to tread lightly on the land, being imbued with the emerging national park ethic, many in fact knew little about that ethic, or opposed it.
Thus LSR learned, even more acutely, how a national park was a double-edged
sword, even more than he had done at Grand Teton, where he had taken over
leadership of an enterprise already set in its course. Overall, most observers

favored what he had done on St. John, but there were and there remain vocal critics as well.

Unlike the Virgin Islands park, Redwood National Park was the work of many hands and took decades to achieve. Even today the park is by no means secure, and gerrymandered boundaries, insufficient size, inadequate watershed areas, and too much prior damage by logging interests have compromised the park. Nonetheless, Redwood National Park is a World Heritage Site and a Biosphere Reserve and is a unit of remarkable beauty. Rockefeller called it one of the five or six most important units in the entire system. Its importance lay not in its size, however, but in the resource it protected and the battle to establish it, for it was, with the possible exception of Jackson Hole National Monument, the focus of the most acrimonious public debate in the history of America's national parks.

Frequently a national park requires decades from proposal to fruition: very few are created so quickly as Virgin Islands was. Redwood National Park was first discussed in the summer of 1917, over half a century before President Lyndon B. Johnson, who included the creation of such a park in his 1964 conservation message, would sign the bill making it a reality.[4] Horace M. Albright had met with Henry Fairfield Osborn, "Fair" Osborn's father, who was then president of the New York Zoological Society, in the midst of the redwoods that summer of 1917, the year after the creation of the National Park Service. They were joined by Madison Grant, an anthropologist who worked on "the decline of Native American culture," and who would shortly succeed Osborn as president of the Zoological Society, and John C. Merriam, perhaps the first professional ecologist and in time the head of the Carnegie Institution. In short order the group, joined by others, formed a Save-the-Redwoods League and enlisted the support of the director of the National Park Service, Stephen Mather. The leaders of the league immediately thought of John D. Rockefeller, Jr. He did not visit the redwood groves until the long traveling summer of 1926 with David, Laurance, and Winthrop—a photograph taken by Laurance on July 6 survives in the family archive—when they were particularly impressed by Bull Creek Flat. Between 1927 and 1931, JDR, Jr., gave $1 million to the League and in 1929 gave $1.6 million to the U.S. government for half the cost of a giant sequoia grove to the southeast, in Yosemite National Park. Most of the gift to the league was used to purchase land for Humboldt Redwoods State Park, through which the famed Avenue of the Giants, a highway that tunnelled through and under the trees, would pass.

To encourage fund raising, the Save-the-Redwoods League named over two hundred Memorial Groves for or in memory of donors. One of the key groves at Bull Creek Flats was designated in honor of JDR, Jr., to recognize his major financial contributions to the league. In 1941 LSR became a life member of the league, and for years he too made modest contributions to maintain the Rockefeller Forest in the Humboldt Redwoods State Park. As a trustee of The National Geographic Society he was especially supportive of a study sponsored by the Geographic Society in 1963 that "discovered" the tallest known coastal redwood tree on Redwood Creek—more a matter of identification and measurement, since the grove was known—along the Coast Range near Orick. Clearly the coastal redwood, which differs in important respects from the giant sequoia that grows further south and further inland, was not adequately protected despite efforts on the part of the California state park system, and adding a park to the national system had again become a high priority for the National Park Service.[5]

Shortly after the discovery of "the tallest tree," *The National Geographic, Reader's Digest* (both publications with which LSR had close ties), and the Sierra Club launched a new campaign to secure a national park. The Sierra Club published a special appeal, *The Last Redwoods,* which highlighted the nature of the crisis for the giant trees. Once there had been two million acres of these stately wonders, the Club estimated, but by 1960 they were down to 750,000 acres, and the logging companies were taking out a billion board feet a year of this consistently high value timber so that all Americans might dream of having a picnic table in their back yards.

In September 1964, President Lyndon Johnson directed his secretary of the interior, Stewart Udall, to make a redwoods national park his first priority. The American people needed more parks, and especially more that were accessible to the urban public, as a national park in the redwoods, only six hours drive on good highways north of the San Francisco Bay area, would be. But appeals to the government of California to do something about the rapid depletion of the cathedral groves and redwood watersheds were not well received.

When a new, conservative governor of California, Ronald Reagan, took office in 1966, he was quoted as having said, when asked about any plans he might have to give further protection to the redwoods, "You know, a tree is a tree—how many more do you need to look at?" (This was later changed by the San Francisco press to "Once you've seen one redwood tree, you've seen them all.")[6] Apparently Reagan was under the impression that 115,000 acres of redwoods were preserved in California's state parks, though in fact the figure was 50,000 acres, for he was confusing the coastal redwood with the giant sequoia of the inland national parks. Still, as Reagan correctly pointed out, there were twenty-eight state parks, as well as Muir Woods National Monument in Marin County devoted to the giant trees. Reagan did not feel that the state had been derelict in the matter: after all, the first California state park, created in 1902, had been Big Basin Redwoods in an area that many Californians originally had hoped would become a national park.[7] Secretary Udall was determined to get a national park, however, and the president, whose administration would see the addition of forty-eight new units to the park system—second only to Franklin D. Roosevelt's administration, which lasted far longer—was increasingly eager to add national parks in Washington's North Cascades and in redwood country.[8]

Since early in 1964, LSR had been in the White House often,[9] working with Mrs. Johnson's Committee for a More Beautiful Capital and for an expanding program for national beautification. Stewart Udall was high on Rockefeller at the time, and in 1965 was urging the president to approach the New Yorker about being undersecretary of the interior, while others hoped he might take the secretary's position if Udall stepped down. At the same time yet others, especially in the tourist industry, hoped LSR would be national chairman of a See USA program aimed at generating tourist dollars by bringing in more foreign visitors. Some who thought in more narrow political terms suggested that getting Rockefeller aboard the Johnson team would be a shrewd move since his brother Nelson was in hot pursuit of the Republican presidential nomination, and they believed they could divide the Rockefellers and lessen Nelson's chances, since they knew he would be a formidable opponent, while they were confident that if the Republican party moved to the right away from the liberal Nelson, Johnson would win the election handily. Wiser heads understood that LSR would not accept an undersecretaryship and that, however much he might assist the president with a shared conservation agenda, he would never fail to support his brother either in his efforts to gain the nomination or in a presidential campaign.[10]

Having spoken with LSR often during his visits to the White House and on other occasions, President Johnson now asked him to meet with Governor Reagan "as one Republican to another" to learn under what terms, if any, the state would join with the federal government in a cooperative effort to protect at least some large tracts of redwoods that lay outside any of the group of California Redwood State Parks. Rockefeller's role in creating Redwood National Park soon became controversial because of his conviction that one best achieved an important goal by avoiding polarization. He did not agree with the confrontational tactics of the Sierra Club, preferring to work with Richard M. Leonard, the president of the Save-the-Redwoods League, as earlier his father had worked with Newton B. Drury when he was secretary of the league. LSR was convinced that an all-or-nothing approach would lead to a destructive clash with entrenched timber interests and with the conservative governor and would certainly fail. He also believed that some of the timber companies, such as the Weyerhaeusers, were good citizens and had followed sensible cutting practices. Thus LSR worked steadily from behind the scenes to bring the conflicting parties—the timber companies, the environmental organizations, the government of California, and the National Park Service—to some compromise. He began by sending out his most trusted advisor on park matters, M. Frederik Smith.[11]

Fred Smith was a thoughtful and clear-headed individual who had left a successful and varied business career, much of it in public relations, to join LSR's personal staff. What Rockefeller wanted, Smith wanted. He was a member of the National Park System Advisory Board (and later of its Council), well-informed on park matters broadly, and eager to see some kind of redwoods national park. He had proven credentials, having organized a Council of Conservationists composed of the directors of the Sierra Club, the Wilderness Society, the Izaak Walton League, and other groups, and having written the text for the first ever full-page conservation advertisement to run in a major newspaper (the *Denver Post*), a bold statement against a proposal to build a dam at Echo Park in Dinosaur National Monument on the Colorado–Utah border. In 1956 the advertisement was credited in some circles with having killed the dam, which had originally been touted as essential to a plan by the Bureau of Reclamation to develop a massive Upper Colorado River project. Many members of business as well as in the conservation community had liked the tone Smith had taken, for he had not attacked water use or reclamation but had made a distinction between political and economic motivations and had laid out the economic argument against the dam. The prevention of the Echo Park dam was subsequently seen by environmental historians as the first signal victory for the concept of wilderness. Noted for his patience and willingness to shuttle back and forth between opposing sides in a controversy, Smith became LSR's "ambassador without portfolio" in the negotiations that lay ahead.

Shortly after Christmas 1964, Senator Clinton Anderson of New Mexico alerted President Johnson to a "potential hassle" over the redwood park proposal and the president asked Secretary Udall to provide details. Anderson complained that Smith had produced a plan that took Anderson aback; soon Udall and Smith were in "a warm argument," for Smith's proposals seemed to Udall unduly friendly to logging interests. However, the Department of the Interior did not have its own plan ready yet, and Smith believed that more delay might scuttle any park proposal entirely. Udall attacked Smith's suggestions as a sell-out to the timber companies and concluded that Smith had been taken in by Weyerhaeuser's public relations firm. In what Udall described as "an unusual letter," he wrote to Rockefeller to ask whether LSR stood behind Smith's park plan. While Udall did not question Smith's motives or integrity, he believed he had been badly misled by the timber companies.

Rockefeller replied that he favored a national park plan laid out by a study team financed by The National Geographic Society, which had thrust itself into the debate based on its "expedition" to find the "tallest tree," and he trusted the society's president, Melville Grosvenor, to know a viable national park when he saw one. Shortly the Park Service had its own draft proposal ready, and it wanted considerably more land than Smith proposed though less than the Sierra Club advocated. Smith felt that the other redwood timber companies were considerably less trustworthy than Weyerhaeuser had been, but he respected their arguments concerning the loss of jobs in an already beleaguered industry. While he believed a redwood national park was imperative and that it must come in the Johnson administration, he was inclined toward a recommendation made by the American Forestry Association, which had entered the fray, that any national park should be further south, more immediately accessible from San Francisco, and therefore focused on the Mendocino Redwoods and, perhaps, the King Range.

In the spring of 1965 Johnson passed to Rockefeller a request that he personally look into a controversy that was heating up at Woodside, California, just north of Palo Alto, which touched on the issue of "beautification." The Atomic Energy Commission was intent on stringing high tension wires across this attractive town, in order to service Stanford University's Linear Accelerator. LSR advised the president that it was entirely possible to bury high tension wires, and that no agency of the government ought to contribute to the growth of visual ugliness at a time when the administration was promoting highway beautification. He proposed to wait to see what Glenn Seaborg, the chairman of the Atomic Energy Commission, did first. Seaborg was a Californian, and one ought not to mess on his patch until it was clear that action was necessary.

By late June action did seem necessary, and Rockefeller visited Woodside on his way to look at the redwood state parks. LSR took Fred Smith and Henry Diamond, a lawyer who worked with him on environmental issues, with him. They followed the route of the proposed line "pole by pole" (as Smith wrote later), judging the visual impact the line would have, and while they agreed that Woodside was a "well blessed" community, they also noted that there already were many overhead lines in the town. The energy commission was proposing to reduce its poles in height and to string the line by helicopter, and LSR and his group concluded that the result would blend reasonably well. Further, he was inclined to think that Woodside should have buried its lines long before if this were an issue. Typically, he proposed a compromise: that Woodside accept the line, that the federal government research the high voltage issue further, and that the government agree to bury the line within seven years, when fuller information was in hand.

The three men then spent two days touring the redwoods. They understood that touring was insufficient to understand all the issues arising from the national park proposal, but they had been involved with it since its inception. Knowing that the Sierra Club favored a far larger park and that the Save-the-Redwoods League was prepared to accept the smaller proposal, they compared them in some detail. They sought the advice of Horace Albright, who believed that getting the smaller park quickly was a wise move. When they returned to Washington they asked to see the final plan as worked out by the National Park Service team together with other studies that had been made from time to time, and they consulted with George B. Hartzog, who had become director of the National Park Service at the beginning of 1964.

In February 1967, with all sides to the controversy locked in battle, Johnson asked Laurance Rockefeller to talk with Governor Reagan again. Reagan said that LSR should work through Norman (Ike) Livermore, administrator of the state's resource agency, and William Penn Mott, director of California's state parks, and Rockefeller returned to Sacramento to meet with them. A former lumberman and treasurer of the Pacific Lumber Company, Livermore was an old-line conservationist. His credentials were good: he was a member of the Sierra Club and he had opposed the building of a freeway through Prairie Creek Redwoods State Park. Nonetheless, he believed that there was clear distinction between conservation and environmentalism, and though he favored a redwoods national park, he did not want it to come at the expense of the state or its residents.[12] Mott was in favor of vigorously expanding the state park system, bringing parks closer to the metropolitan centers, and adding more historic sites, and he was inclined to add new redwood parks to his system. Both men were well regarded by people who wanted a park, and Rockefeller was confident he could work with them.

The Sierra Club was pressing for a 77,000 acre purchase as a minimum, to include 33,000 acres of virgin redwoods, and to be combined with Prairie Creek Redwoods State Park to form the best obtainable national park. A park based on the Mendocino Redwoods simply would not do. The club's leaders, and especially David Brower, its executive director, and Edgar Wayburn, its president, declared the area already was irretrievably compromised, with a highway through it, tunnels carved through some of its trees, and with over-developed trails and roads. The park represented an outdated approach to protection.

However, the park the Sierra Club favored would put the Arcata Redwood Company out of business. Across northwest California, town meetings were condemning the park proposal: Trinidad, Orick, Hoopa, Eureka, Ferndale, Rio Dell, McKinleyville, and Arcata all angrily denounced those who would "lock up" the trees. Much was made of a study conducted by the Bank of America that concluded employment in the area would be down by 25 percent by 1975 even without a park.[13] A smaller park than was wanted by the Sierra Club or the Park Service, state retention of all state parks that fell within the proposed boundaries, an exchange of state lands for federal lands elsewhere, some swapping between federal agencies, and an expensive buy out of the timber companies were the components of the proposed compromise.

In April 1967, Henry Diamond called on Joseph Califano, President Johnson's chief staff assistant on domestic affairs, with a letter from Laurance Rockefeller proposing a possible solution. The compromise outlined by LSR would require the concurrence of Secretary Udall, of Secretary of Agriculture Orville Freeman, and of the Bureau of Budget. The Forest Service, which came under the Department of Agriculture, was almost invariably opposed to transferring forest lands to the Park Service, as it would now be asked to do. Various organizations and individuals, including the Save-the-Redwoods League, Albright, Smith, and Livermore, were urging that park planners focus on the Mill Creek area, which already was partially protected by the Jedediah Smith State Park, and which contained some of the most spectacular redwood stands. They proposed that Mill Creek be combined with Prairie Creek Redwoods State Park, some land between the two, and Del Norte Coast State Park, to form a coherent unit. The Sierra Club took its stand on the whole of the Redwood Creek watershed. LSR was now convinced that a park based on all the lands the Sierra Club or the National Park Service wanted would destroy jobs and would poison the well for future federal conservation initiatives in California. Thus he committed himself wholeheartedly to the compromise proposal, which was based largely on Mill Creek and the state parks.

Some authors, hostile to the compromise and perhaps to LSR, have argued that it was he alone who persuaded the President to accept the less desirable Mill Creek compromise, while Susan R. Schrepfer, the person who has most deeply researched the intricate story of how the park was finally achieved, has concluded that the flow of advice and influence was much more complex. As she suggests, LSR had begun with an open mind. In 1964 he had paid professional foresters to study how various park proposals would affect the economy of northern California. He agreed that any national park should be distant from the danger of a thruway being built across its lands, mindful of damage done to Humboldt Creek Redwood State Park by the California state highway department when it built a four-lane highway directly through the park. He was eager to find a way to get a park bill through during Johnson's presidency, since earlier efforts had been lost by changes in administration or Congressional sponsors. Even though his own foresters had initially concluded that the Rockefeller Forest and Humboldt redwoods should be the basis for the national park, this would not have added to protected lands, and LSR was convinced that there must be genuinely new additions in any national park. In 1955 the Bull Creek Flats had been seriously damaged by extensive flooding, which demonstrated the vulnerability of that area. Fred Smith had tried to negotiate with lumbermen on the basis of the National Park Service recommendations, which he had accepted at first, and had concluded that the NPS proposal could not be achieved without bitter conflict at a time when American society already was wracked with divisions over war in Southeast Asia and the civil rights movement. The people LSR most trusted on the issue, Richard Leonard and Newton Drury, were in favor of avoiding constant turmoil and wanted quick compromise so as not to lose the entire project. Drury was especially eager for closure, and in the summer of 1965, he had taken LSR and Smith through the redwoods and somewhat disingenuously had showed them the least attractive part of Redwood Creek and the most impressive views in Mill Creek. Albright came out publicly in favor of the Mill Creek site. While most of the industry felt that if there was to be any park at all, it should be on Mill Creek, where two state parks already denied them cutting, even it would not be achieved easily, for one company, Miller Redwood, would lose most of its land, and its president was bitterly opposed and was lobbying fiercely in Washington. Thus when Smith gained from the Weyerhaeusers a sense that they would not fight Mill Creek, he reaffirmed the proposed compromise to LSR and through him to Secretary Udall. Weighing all this advice, Rockefeller told President Johnson that it would be best to get what he could while he could.

In the meantime, the U.S. House of Representatives had passed a bill that called for an unacceptably small park, while the Senate, led by California's Senator Thomas Kuchel, had brought in a more generous bill more nearly coinciding with the Park Service's minimal desires. Congressman Wayne N. Aspinall and Senator Henry M. "Scoop" Jackson of Washington negotiated a compromise that Hartzog found satisfactory. When he learned of its provisions, Newton Drury, both as an officer of the Save-the-Redwoods League and a former director of the National Park Service, publicly expressed intense disappointment.

The language of the bill creating Redwood National Park speaks of the compromise, for the park was set aside "to preserve significant examples of the primeval coastal redwood forests and the streams and seashores with which they are associated for purposes of public inspiration, enjoyment and scientific study." "Significant examples" did not represent an entire forest, and preservation for scientific study left much room for narrowing the range of the park; there was no suggestion that the park encompassed "the finest" resource of its kind. The compromise left many people unhappy, as compromise invariably does. Though LSR believed that national forest lands should not be used as "trading stock" for national parks, he also argued that the redwoods situation was urgent and unique, and that the Forest Service should be required to transfer land to the national park. Governor Reagan insisted that portions of Camp Pendleton and Fort Ord, two large federal military bases in California, be transferred to the state with the beach front of the former slated to become a premier state park, and when LSR countered with the suggestion that the military base lands be leased, Reagan stood firm on his demand for outright ownership. The state retained control over the three state parks within the legislated national park boundary, and though the park bill made it possible for California to donate the parks to the United States if it chose to do so, it did not and has not. The "tallest tree" was protected and reachable only by a narrow corridor a quarter-mile wide on each side of Redwood Creek from which lumbering outside the park boundary could clearly be seen. Much of the federally owned acreage was cutover land that would require vast expenditures to rehabilitate. Compensation was paid to the timber companies and an expensive retraining program was offered to anyone who lost their job as a result of the creation of the park. The legislation limited the park to 58,000 acres, exclusive of submerged lands, and left several legal questions unresolved. The cost of the park was greater than any in the history of the country: $1.5 billion for the land alone, with hundreds of millions more to assist workers and to restore cutover watersheds.

Surely LSR was right on the question of timing. By the date of the signing of the Redwood National Park bill, on October 2, 1968, Lyndon Johnson had long since declared that he would not run for the presidency again. Nelson Rockefeller had unsuccessfully sought the Republican nomination, and the party's nominee, Richard M. Nixon, was not viewed as being sympathetic to national parks. Further, with every passing year any prospective park became even more expensive, and with the threat of a national park hanging over them, most of the logging companies harvested timber all the more vigorously.

Those who are convinced that a larger park could have been attained in 1968 have concluded negatively about the compromise bill. Those who are equally convinced that there would have been no park at all without the Mill Creek compromise, and who point out that the addition of 48,000 acres by President

Jimmy Carter in 1978 brought Redwood Creek far more fully into the park, have concluded that LSR was instrumental to the achievement of an acceptable national park. Few national parks have been so controversial in the making. None has cost so much per acre. Indeed, Redwood National Park's 110,000 acres are the most expensive protected area in the United States, for in its first quarter century Congress spent $1.65 billion on it.[14] (By contrast, Great Smoky Mountains, nearly five times as large, and mainly acquired in the Great Depression, cost $25 an acre.) Nearly every national park created since has been achieved through expensive compromise, and certainly even the additions to Redwood in the Carter administration, during a favorable environmental climate, were not sufficient to create a park that contained all that is needed in order to truly protect the resource. When Ronald Reagan, the conservative governor of California, became president of the United States in 1981, he ushered in the slowest period of growth in the modern history of the nation's national parks, appointed a secretary of the interior who opposed any additions to the system, killed the Advisory Council to the National Park System Advisory Board, progressively politicized the board itself, and made political appointments deeper into the ranks of the National Park Service than any president had done before him.

The battle for the redwoods continues. In the fall of 1996 a proposal to add 7,500 acres to the national park met with the same vigorous opposition. Local communities, apparently unconvinced that visitors to the park were offsetting their economic losses as land was taken out of timber production, strongly opposed the addition. Many environmental groups protested that the proposal was entirely too small. The park had grown, through minor additions and boundary adjustments, to 110,132 acres, and was still smaller than all but sixteen of the fifty-one national parks; yet, it commanded an annual budget (in 1995) of over $5 million, while receiving only 415,000 visitors, fewer than such relatively little-known units as Cedar Breaks or Colorado national monuments. Its budget was nearly as large as that of Denali National Park and Preserve, which was a park of over six million acres. The debate remains: Is it a flawed national park, which does not attract anything like the number of visitors predicted for it, and does not adequately protect the resource after which it is named, or the best park with the best protection plan that could be obtained in the face of an obdurate governor, entrenched special interests, and a divided and preoccupied nation?

Fred Smith represented LSR on a variety of conservation groups until his retirement in the early 1990s, his last major project being an all-out effort to get the airport at Jackson, Wyoming, removed from Grand Teton National Park.

Since a mere boundary adjustment would not eliminate the growing problem of over-flights, or the demand for lengthened runways that bit deeply into the park, Smith proposed moving the airport well away from Jackson Hole, to Pinedale, Wyoming, or across Teton Pass to Driggs, Idaho. These efforts were so persistent that they led Wyoming's Senator Alan Simpson half-jokingly to tell LSR that Smith was "the most dangerous man in America."

At the same time that LSR was working to influence a compromise position on the proposed Redwood National Park, he was actively pressing forward with a proposal to carve out of New York State's Adirondack Park and Preserve a major new national park. In 1967 he put forth concrete proposals that caught the residents of the Adirondack area by surprise. In a short, intense period of public debate, the proposal was defeated on its specifics, and there is no Adirondack national park today. However, some observers at the time and historians since have concluded that LSR may have produced almost exactly the result he had actually intended, for the effect of the release of his recommendations was to spur more effective laws and regulations with respect to the protection of the Adirondack region.

The Adirondack Park is the largest state preserve in the nation, so large and, relative to most state parks, so well protected that it is included in the *United Nation's List of National Parks and Equivalent Reserves.* For decades various conservation groups and the National Park Service have called the Adirondack Park the finest possible representative of the New England–Adirondack natural region, perhaps the most obvious gap in the National Park System. Only the Mount Katahdin area of Maine, much of which is protected within Baxter State Park, could approach Adirondack in adaptability to national park status. But even it pales by comparison. Equal in size to the state of Vermont, the Adirondack park protects over 220 species of birds and 50 species of mammals, including golden eagles, loons, black bears, and white-tailed deer. The Forest Preserve within the park is historically important, for it is not only the largest wilderness area east of the Mississippi River, it is one of the oldest, and is the only such preserve protected by a special provision in a state constitution. George Perkins Marsh had the Adirondacks in mind when, in 1864, he wrote of the values of watershed protection and soil conservation that accompanied forest preservation.

The Adirondack Park was established in 1892; it includes the Adirondack Forest Preserve, established in 1885. The forest preserve comprises 42 percent of the park, is public land, and is protected by an amendment to the New York State Constitution, passed in 1894, that declares the forest preserve should "be forever kept as wild forest lands." This provision became known as the "forever wild" clause of the state constitution. To change it requires an amendment to that constitution.

In 1967 the park consisted of nearly six million acres set off by "the blue line," a line that coincides roughly with the geographic region of the Adirondack Mountains. Over 60 percent of the land inside the park boundary was privately owned, mixed in a vaguely checkerboard pattern across the face of the publicly owned lands. The Forest Preserve comprises 2.3 million acres, and it was this, and only this, that was declared "forever wild." The economy of the Adirondacks depended on tourism, recreation, mining, and forest products. Inside the blue line were fifteen villages, and during the 1960s they grew by 16.5 percent, while towns partially in the park and on its margins grew by 24.2 percent. Administration of the park was exceptionally complex, as there was little coordination between the village and town governments, the twelve counties that had a slice of the park, the fire or school districts (which did not necessarily follow political boundaries), sewer, water, and park districts, or four regional planning districts.

Despite these complexities, and in part because the small communities in the heart of the park were depressed and experiencing little of the growth that was taking place at the margins, most visitors would not have been aware when they moved from the forest preserve to the park, from public to private land, except where they encountered logging roads, school buses, and advertisements at the outskirts of towns. Thus there was little reason, it seemed to local residents, to create local land use regulations, and less than 10 percent of the land within the park's boundaries was subject to such regulations.

This situation had been acceptable until the 1960s. Attempts to develop areas near the central park towns had been rebuffed in the past, though these attempts invariably returned, with proposals for second homes, condominiums, bobsled runs, and new roads. When construction began on a new interstate highway to link Albany with Montreal, a highway called the Adirondack Northway, which broached the park's boundaries, there was a sudden surge of fear for the future of the park, for the Northway would make it accessible at high speed to over fifty million Americans. There was a provision that permitted state highways to take up to 400 acres for essential needs without a referendum, but this did not apply to county and local roads, which sometimes were widened in a way that some viewed as unconstitutional. Further, the Northway had been put to referendum and had passed; what was to prevent further votes of this nature? The Adirondack Park (together with Catskill State Park, which also had forest preserve protected by the "forever wild" provision of the constitution) was administered by New York's Department of Conservation, while all other state parks were under the administration of the Council of Parks, of which, until 1966, Robert Moses was the chairman.

In 1966 Laurance Rockefeller succeeded Moses as chairman of the Council of Parks. LSR was worried about increasing demand for private campgrounds within the Adirondacks, the growing and aggressive constituency for offroad snowmobiles in the park, and the ever-increasing downstate clamor for more hydroelectric power. These concerns, as we will see in chapter IX, brought LSR into conflict with Moses and, in support of his brother Nelson, then governor of New York, had led him to support a power plant further down the Hudson River (which rose within the Adirondack Park), in part as a means of holding demands for more water and power away from the park itself. Further, LSR believed that a patchwork of local regulations, where they existed at all, would not provide for the "grand, unbroken domain" that park proponents had dreamed of when the Adirondack Park was created.

Laurance Rockefeller had first raised the question of an Adirondack National Park in 1961, when he wrote to Conrad Wirth, the director of the National Park Service, suggesting that a feasibility study should be made. Wirth had done nothing formal about this suggestion, but the idea had remained on their respective agendas. Wirth had seen a national park as a possible target for his ambitious Mission 66 program. But in 1963 Wirth was forcibly retired as director.

Now, as the new chairman of New York's Council of Parks, LSR ordered up a study. Prepared by Roger C. Thompson, research director of the State Senate Finance Committee, the study's conclusions were delivered orally to LSR and others in December 1966. Thompson reported that park and forest preserves were competing with each other, and he recommended reform of the administrative structure for both. Wilderness preservation and logging demands were in clear conflict. Boundaries of state-owned land were ambiguous, leading to many intrusions. Even a relatively small increase in the number of visitors, brought by the Northway, would swamp the park's administrators. There were few back country guides who could take nonhunters into the interior, there was virtually no tourist information, and the type of facilities visitors would expect were woefully inadequate. Something would have to be done and quickly.

At the same time Conrad Wirth was reminding Rockefeller of their earlier discussions. Wirth understood that the forever wild principle protected the forest preserve, but he believed that protection would be more secure—after all, an amendment to the constitution had created the forever wild clause and an amendment could at some future time undo it—if pressure were taken off the wilderness areas by more effective and more extensive recreational facilities in the park, somewhat along the lines of the management principles then in play at Yellowstone. LSR, always concerned with natural beauty and its enemies, feared that developments on the checkerboard of privately held lands within the park boundaries would destroy the integrity of the natural scenic views.

Early in 1967 Laurance Rockefeller, as an interested individual and not as chairman of the Council of Parks, commissioned a new study, to be prepared by Roger Thompson and Conrad Wirth (whose views he already knew), joined by Ben H. Thompson, former head of the Branch of Lands for the National Park Service. LSR undoubtedly anticipated the results of the report. Whether he actually expected the study—which recommended the creation of a new national park in the heart of the Adirondack Mountains, consisting of 1.7 million acres of land and water—to be acted upon is another question. At best Rockefeller would have provided the catalyst by which the East acquired a new national park; at worst, people would be alerted to the dangers to the state park and forest preserve and would, he hoped, be galvanized into corrective action.

The report, noting that a national park would bring great economic benefits to the region, concluded that only this measure would "assure the preservation of larger areas of wilderness than is now possible under the fragmented land ownership pattern" that prevailed throughout the park. To achieve a national park, the report recommended that 1.12 million acres be acquired from the state of New York, focusing on the already-held central mountain and lake core, with an additional 600,000 acres being acquired by purchase or donation from private owners over fifteen years. The report was sent to Governor Nelson Rockefeller for further study, without recommendation, and the governor appointed a commission to consider its implications.

At that time and since there have been astute observers who believed that LSR's initiative was meant to stimulate the state to action, to give his brother ammunition for establishing a new agency that would have regulatory teeth. These observers have suggested that there never could have been a national park since national parks are "solid land" (in this they were incorrect) and that the National Park Service would not have tolerated the patchwork nature that the state park presented. That is, they argued on the one hand that the Adirondack Park could not meet national park standards, and on the other hand these same critics argued that the forever wild provision in the state constitution gave the forest preserve better protection than any national park could provide, and that the state park was too precious to be surrendered to a federal agency. A few observers attribute special meaning to the fact that the first version of the report was released in a form that showed the seal of the state of New York on it, and that this version was recalled on the day of its release and replaced by one without the seal, for they take this to mean that the true target of the report was the state rather than the public. Others point out that when LSR rose to defend the park proposal at a public meeting sponsored by the Adirondack Mountain Club, he replied to virtually every objection to the park that some compromise position could undoubtedly be found. By being so agreeable, this school of thought suggests, LSR was revealing that he did not believe the park proposal would fly or he would have defended certain points more vigorously.

However, those who attended LSR's talk in Warrensburg on October 28, 1967, or who have read it since, would not agree that it was so mollifying. He was quite direct about the threat to the park, pointing out the risks the Northway posed, the virtual absence of zoning regulations, the problem of inholdings, and the development being carried out by the state in the Forest Preserve itself. This, he said, violated the letter of the state constitution: "It goes on because it is not challenged by lawsuit. But management by sufferance is no way to run a resource." Some present believed they heard a gentle warning that LSR might, as a friend of the park, himself institute lawsuits if necessary to prevent this unconstitutional development, and they heard his nostalgic reflection on how he and his wife had, after World War II, enjoyed the natural wonders and outdoor opportunities of Camp Canaras, on Upper Saranac Lake, where they had maintained a summer home for five years, as a gentle remonstrance about how those natural wonders were slipping away, especially in the Saranac Lake area. What he sought, LSR said, was to work in partnership with the federal government, much as was being done at that moment in the California redwoods.

The proposed national park would have been the thirteenth largest national park in the world, larger than anything in Argentina, Australia, or the Soviet Union, where large parks were expected. Its proposed size alone, when widely publicized, brought negative reaction, for people were so accustomed to thinking of Yellowstone as "vast" and "limitless" (when, in fact, it fell well short of protecting its ecosystem), they could not comprehend a park of such proportions in an eastern state. Privately Rockefeller was not happy with the extent of the proposal, and some years later he concluded that if he and his colleagues had begun incrementally by recommending a national park of, perhaps, 250,000 acres, a size that was more readily understood in an eastern context—Shenandoah National Park in Virginia was 196,000 acres—the proposal would have "sailed right through."

The person who has examined the history of Adirondack Park most closely, Frank Graham, Jr., attributes the failure to three major factors. The fact that the park was enshrined in the New York State Constitution complicated matters enormously. Some few opponents were convinced that Rockefeller wished to put a resort or other recreational development in the new national park, for this was the time when he was developing his Rockresorts. Others, though not cynical about Rockefeller's intent, noted that the very popularity of the designation "national park," and the National Park Service's strong tendency during Mission 66 to build roads and new interpretive centers and additional campgrounds, would fly in the face of their definitions of forever wild. After all, Bob Marshall, the person who had most vigorously promoted the official designation of Wilderness Areas, had developed his ethic as a young man in the Adirondacks, as had Howard Zahniser, founder of The Wilderness Society. The Wilderness Bill had been signed into law by President Johnson less than three years before, and conservationists were still on red alert against any infringement upon wilderness definitions. In his comprehensive speech at Warrensburg, Rockefeller anticipated this fear and correctly pointed out that the enabling legislation for an Adirondack National Park could incorporate the forever wild language and that the Wilderness Act could be embedded in that portion of the bill that would relate to the Forest Preserve. But as Graham remarks, the forever wild preservationists preferred to trust the people who lived in or near the park rather than the far-away federal government.[15]

The people, if by this one means those who lived among the Adirondacks, did not favor a national park either. Some were inward and shortsighted, concerned only that their own hunting and fishing privileges not be taken away. Others strongly believed that the federal government ought, on principle, to be kept out of local matters. Many others hoped to develop their land, to take part in the second-home boom that was seriously threatening the integrity of nearby Vermont. Each small town employed a number of administrators who might, it was argued, be out of a job if the park proposal went through. Those who favored the park contended that it would produce more jobs by bringing more visitors, but this was a two-edged sword: many people who were barely clinging to such work as they had in the remote, and relatively poor, mountain towns feared that any new jobs would go to more experienced outsiders, while those who most cherished no-growth values feared precisely an increase in jobs that would necessitate an increase in infrastructure.

Rockefeller tried to blunt the growing dislike nationwide for what was increasingly viewed as an obtrusive federal government, speaking of it as a "somewhat ideological" point of view, but there was a second level of concern about government to which he could scarcely respond. This was the belief that his brother, the governor, would act "imperiously," as one opponent put it. This was a time when the governor was doing precisely that, in connection with a controversy over Storm King (see chapter IX) on the Hudson, adding to the generalized suspicion. Further, the governor already was under attack for constructing what many regarded as an extravagant new state office complex in Albany, which was running well over budget, reinforcing fears that any economic predictions based on the proposed national park might prove equally erroneous; and he was engaged in a political battle with members of the State Senate, at least two of whom had special interests in the park. In short, Nelson Rockefeller politically could not afford to make the national park proposal his highest priority.

In hindsight, then, there are several reasons why the proposed national park was rejected. Local residents either did not believe the estimates of how much they would benefit from the park or they believed them entirely too much, fearing a predicted two million additional annual visitors. While some gateway towns would clearly benefit, their advantage might well be to the disadvantage of small businesses further into the park. There would be a loss of hunters and a gain in campers, and many locals already resented the presence of state park camping facilities, pointing out that campers did more harm, in creating unsightly mess, requiring facilities, even in vandalism, than hunters did. As one commentator has remarked, resentment of tourism and the "second-home culture" played a role: cleaning toilets for a minimum wage for motels filled with people who come and go breeds anger. There was a widespread misconception about how federal reimbursements for lands and lost tax revenues would work and what restrictions the government might apply. Clearly there would be a loss of lumbering income and employment. Misinformation was fed by real estate developers with their hopes to build vacation homes at stake. One scholar who subsequently examined public opinion on the park proposal concluded that despite clear evidence, which he accepted himself, that virtually any economic analysis favored the park, the people were convinced through their own shortsightedness, lack of experience, and trust in local interest groups that a national park would hurt them economically, and they related to the Adirondacks largely in economic terms. LSR's offer, in his defense of the proposal before the Adirondack Mountain Club, to work out a new plan for payments in lieu of taxes and to phase out lumbering gradually did not carry the day.[16]

LSR had concluded his appeal to the Adirondack Mountain Club with the admission that the national park concept was only one means of solution of the problems of the area: "If there is a better one, I shall enthusiastically endorse it." After a suitable delay, and with more time devoted to careful behind-the-scenes planning, Governor Rockefeller moved the issue back to a front burner. In September 1968, he established a Temporary Study Commission on the Future of the Adirondacks. Its chairman was Harold Hochschild, an Adirondack resident, creator of the first museum devoted to Adirondack culture, an opponent of the national park proposal, and chairman of Amax, a worldwide mining conglomerate. The author of the Conservation Department's critique of the proposed national park, former State Senator Harold Jerry, was made executive secretary of the commission. It was apparent at the outset that this commission would not report favorably on a national park option. It was equally apparent that it would recommend aggressive preservation-directed steps. LSR, as chairman of the Council of Parks, withdrew from the scene, his best case scenario perhaps defeated but apparently content with what was likely to follow.

In its eight-volume report, submitted in December 1970, the commission concluded that the Adirondack Park was at a crisis, thus effectively endorsing the Rockefeller-proposed analysis while rejecting its suggested solutions. State action was required broadly and immediately with respect to both public and private lands. The interaction between the owners could no longer be left to the personal relationships of the past. Large-scale subdivision was likely, as Americans grew more affluent and leisure-minded, as highways and automobiles improved, and as population growth in the northeast surged. Local governments in the Adirondacks could not meet the challenge. A planning agency was essential, but the Conservation Department was not the right agency. The state should create an independent agency. Nearly two hundred specific recommendations followed, the sum of which was to urge the creation of a regional regulatory authority that would acquire scenic easements, regulate outdoor advertising, regulate aircraft and motor boats, establish wild, scenic, and recreational rivers of the kind being established at the national level through the National Park Service, and control development along river corridors. Conservationists were ecstatic.[7]

Governor Rockefeller vigorously backed the report's recommendations. Additional information poured in. Potential developers and logging companies moved fast to achieve their goals before new regulations could block them. Upstate politicians battled against downstate. A dozen towns hurried land use controls into place, having exacted the promise that controls in place before July 1, 1971 would be exempt from any new agency's control. Draft legislation was delivered to the legislature late in the 1971 session and passed at the end of the year, creating an Adirondack Park Agency. Among the new commissioners were two former members of the temporary study commission. There were two *ex officio* members of the commission, Henry Diamond and Richard Wiebe, who were both close to the Rockefellers. Richard W. Lawrence, Jr., became the chairman of the agency and Diamond became Conservation Commissioner later. For the first time the Forest Preserve (as distinct from the Park) was to be viewed as an ecological system, not as land to be devoted to recreation. LSR had not won his national park but he surely had won his point.[18]

Thereafter the national park idea was allowed to wither quietly. Even the *New York Times* and the Wilderness Society had opposed it. Perhaps in another few decades, when the Park Service was less likely itself to infringe on the forever wild principle, and when the national park ethic had evolved to the point that there would have been less cause to fear new recreational infrastructure being built into a national park, the idea might have moved forward. If 1967 was not the right time, no later time became a better time. When the National Parks and Conservation Association, which loosely monitored land use in the state park thereafter, revived Laurance Rockefeller's idea in 1988 and recommended selective and phased transfer of portions of the park to the NPS "if the opportunity arose," it listed the Adirondack Park only 82nd in priority in a wish list of 99 new park proposals.

One must ask, has Adirondack Park proved to be better off in the hands of the state than it might have been with the National Park Service? The conventional wisdom says "yes," because of the forever wild clause in the state constitution that requires an amendment to the constitution, through referendum, to lessen protection. Yet there have been several studies of the park that suggest this is not so clear as one might expect. The question is, how well managed is the park? The cost of administration of the commission itself since 1971 has been $2 million annually. As one student of the park asks, might not that $50 million have been better spent on protection by an agency that already existed? One need only visit the park to realize that no one has been quite prepared to face down the more politically influential towns within its borders. Almost certainly there have been fewer visitors than if the area had become a national park, and many back roads undoubtedly have been left narrower than they would be under NPS management. But there also have been commercial developments that NPS would not have allowed. The question of being "better off" requires definitions, followed by the most careful investigation of alternative scenarios, and even then no one can really say whether by rising up to defeat the park proposal the people of the region saved it for themselves and posterity or whether a great opportunity to make a major contribution to the rise of the national park ethic was missed.

The Rockefellers did not let the matter rest. While the Adirondack initiative was just one of many that Nelson and Laurance undertook in the Adirondack and Catskill mountains and along the Hudson River, LSR kept the Adiron-

dack Park on his conservation horizon for the next two decades. He continued to attempt to spark the counties, the state of New York, foundations, and
other philanthropists into greater concern for the integrity of the park. In the
spring of 1989 Governor Mario Cuomo appointed a new commission, chaired
by Peter A.A. Berle, to report on the Adirondacks Park in the Twenty-First
Century, with funds from a variety of sources, including the American Conservation Association. Unhappily, despite early signs that he wished to take vigorous action, Cuomo did not prove to be a strong and decisive conservationist, and some of the impetus behind the commission's work was lost. The
massive report, released in April 1990, was viewed by many as heavy-handed,
and a recommendation that there be a moratorium on private development was
particularly poorly received both by land owners inside the park's boundaries
and by the state legislature.

Though the 1990 report is said to have been still-born, a reading of it today
suggests a different conclusion. The work of Berle and his thirteen other commissioners was not wasted, for they and a specialist staff produced a report that
confirms how, in the years after 1967, the park missed achieving greatness. As
an Open Space Task Force had reported in 1980, the character of the park was
not secure. The opportunity for "one grand, unbroken domain," as envisioned
by the park's supporters in the 1890s, had been lost irretrievably. Anyone reading the technical papers submitted to the commission in 1990 could not help
but conclude that the condition of the park was parlous and far more so than
in 1967. One paper asserted that the Adirondacks were of national park quality and argued that the creation of a park would bring national and international attention to it, with probable economic benefits; that a federal mandate
would preserve for all time the park's scenic beauty; that park-wide planning
would be enhanced and visitor services and interpretation improved in the
hands of the National Park Service. That the author of this technical report
then felt constrained to explain the various forms of protected area management in quite simple terms, comparing the Adirondack potential to such
national parks and monuments as Shenandoah, Voyageurs, Acadia, and Channel Islands, argued that the people of New York still did not know the real benefits in protection that a national park afforded. The report made it abundantly
clear that coordinated signage, sophisticated interpretation, and a strong sense
of environmental priorities still lay in the future for the Adirondack Park and
Preserve. That the report was ill-received simply underscores the persistence of
misunderstanding about the relationship of state and local responsibility to
national protection and recognition.

Still, the news at mid-decade is heartening, and it offers some evidence that rejection of the national park option has not proved fatal. The nature writer Bill McKibben has called the Adirondacks "the Yellowstone of rebirth, the Yosemite of revival, the second chance Alaska." There is hyperbole here, but recovery in the Adirondacks does look more likely. The state has slowly acquired land, and about 42 percent of the park is now held by the state. This is not enough to assure effective protection, but it does provide critical habitat and promise for the future.[19]

If on the surface LSR suffered a defeat in 1967 in his effort to promote a new national park for the eastern states, he was effective in other areas, especially during the Johnson administration, and in the less favorable administrations that followed as well, particularly with respect to historic preservation. Critics of the succession of Republican presidents, all from LSR's party but none from its liberal wing, often said that Republicans found looking to the past, and thus the creation of historic parks, more congenial than Democrats did. There may be some truth in this, though the better explanation for the decline in creation of new natural units of the National Park System in all except the Carter administration lies in the fact that historic parks are easier to create, since a resource is seldom being taken out of commercial use, and most national historical parks and national historic sites are, by their nature, relatively small units. Further, people who oppose the presence of the federal government may be appealed to through their local pride and patriotism, and offering to commemorate a historic event or figure already seen as significant within a region is an easier path to advancement of the national park mission than attempting to take vast areas of land out of mineral or timber or organized recreational production.

Laurance Rockefeller was interested in historical preservation, and perhaps alone among JDR, Jr.'s sons he took seriously the sometimes unproductive debate amongst the historical preservation fraternity about restoration, reconstruction, preservation, and interpretation. He was generally alert at a level of nuance not often encountered among nonprofessionals determined to achieve a merely preservationist goal, an awareness that perhaps began when he was a child visiting Bassett Hall. This awareness would be seen in his interest in the historic as well as the natural and scenic resources of the Hudson River Valley, in his work to protect, and make available to the public, the family home at Kykuit, in Pocantico, above the Hudson River, and in numerous other initiatives that focused on the great river that ran down much of the length of his home state. Most of these initiatives led to state and nongovernmental local protection, though LSR also wished to bring the federal government into play, and most often, as in his other initiatives, he worked with the National Park Service.

As a result of his efforts, numerous historic properties within the natural parks that bore his stamp—Grand Teton, Virgin Islands, and Haleakala—were protected. As we have seen, by restoring an ancient Hawaiian platform, he created Puukohola Heiau National Historic Site. Several properties were designated National Historic Landmarks as a result of submissions to the National Park Service that he supported: Kykuit itself, designated in 1976; the Williamsburg Historic District, named in 1960, in the year of his father's death and in part to honor his father's achievements in historic preservation; the Palisades Interstate Park, a long-standing Rockefeller philanthropy, which preserved the great rock cliffs along the New Jersey side of the Hudson River, singled out in 1965 as an early and highly successful symbol of cooperation between state conservation agencies; Founder's Hall, at the former Rockefeller Institute for Medical Research, now Rockefeller University, in New York City, which his father had established in 1901 and to which LSR contributed steadily and substantially, and at whose designation ceremony in 1974 he presided; and most obviously, Rockefeller Center, built by his father, of which LSR was chairman from 1953 to 1956 and again from 1958 to 1966. The product of the family's capitalist success, the center—designated a National Historic Landmark in 1987—was at the time perhaps the supreme expression of American financial and industrial strength in the midst of a city that had become within three generations the business capital of the world.

But LSR's most important direct contribution to historic preservation was his creation, in partnership with his wife, Mary, of the Marsh–Billings National Historical Park in Woodstock, Vermont. As the granddaughter of Frederick Billings, Mary had become the owner of the Victorian home known locally as the Marsh–Billings Mansion, and Laurance had acquired through the years the surrounding forest and farm land. As partners, they gave the mansion and 555 acres of land to the National Park Service to create the new park. At Marsh–Billings one can see LSR's ideas about historic preservation at work, including his desire to assure that a national park did not damage the local tax base by his providing payments in lieu of taxes and endowment to maintain crucially important aspects of operations. As this park proposal moved forward in LSR's usual deliberative way, he reflected on the changing nature of the historic preservation movement, even going so far as to offer to remove a handsome veranda that had not been part of the Marsh–Billings Mansion's original structure, an offer appropriately declined by the Park Service.

To people who did not understand how the national park ethic had evolved in the United States, the Marsh–Billings National Historical Park did not initially seem to meet their expectations of a unit of the National Park System. Indeed, even some park professionals were uncertain about its purpose, or how to fit it into the thematic studies the service had conducted over the years, and there were those who, to the annoyance of LSR, proposed turning the facility into a conference center that would complement the Horace M. Albright Training Center at Grand Canyon Village and the service's interpretive training and education center at Harper's Ferry.

The Marsh–Billings National Historical Park is unique within the Park System in both the theme it commemorates and illustrates and in the way in which it interprets the theme. The Committee on the Study of Educational Problems in National Parks, which was a predecessor to the present National Park System Advisory Board, recommended in 1929 that the NPS attempt a thematic classification of the nation's historic resources. A general outline was presented to and accepted by the Advisory Board on National Parks, Historic Sites, Buildings and Monuments in 1936, in keeping with the prevailing scientific principle that classification of resources was a necessary first step to both an inventory of needs and to creating a system of comparative analyses by which one could judge the relative significance nationally of various contending nominations for federal protection by inclusion in the National Park System. The themes were subdivided much as a high school or college textbook would segment various aspects of the American experience with, for example, European colonial exploration and settlement as a major theme, and Spanish exploration and settlement as one, and French, English, or other European national origins as second, third, and fourth sub-themes. These sub-themes were, in turn, further broken down into "facets" of exploration and settlement, as in the English settlement of New England. The scholarly community of historians was intimately involved in and approved of the themes and the process at the time.

Just as no generation, ethnic community, or group of scholars owns history, no one expected these themes to remain unchanged, and they did not. History is, after all, three things: what actually happened in the past, what people believe happened, and what scholars argue through their research and writing happened, and when people speak of history they generally do not differentiate between these types of history. Written history, and thus its themes, changes slowly but inexorably as the result of the discovery of new sources, new documents, diaries, letters, and journals of contemporary participants in events; from the opening of new archives; from new techniques for investigation, the interrogation of manuscripts, and asking better questions; and from changes in society, which make some themes appear outdated or less relevant than other, emerging themes. Thus in 1936 there were a large number of sub-themes on what were then the staples of the study of American history—European settlement, the westward movement, the rise of American business and technology, etc. By the 1990s these themes, though remaining, would be significantly supplemented by other themes relating to ethnic history, women's history, conflict as opposed to consensus in the shaping of America, even themes no group of scholars or Park Service analysts could have thought of in the 1930s, such as space exploration. Thus the guiding themes were changed and augmented, especially in 1982, 1987, and between 1993 and 1996. The number of themes grew as did the sub-themes and facets.

Clearly the National Park Service could not hope to acquire a unit to each of the sub-themes or facets, for by 1987 there were 72 sub-themes on indigenous American populations alone, with the sub-theme of the establishment of intercultural relations between native and settler peoples further sub-divided into eleven facets. The entire structure was complex, quite detailed, contentious, and open to the same criticisms that can be directed against any effort to categorize historical events to fit current interests. It was a process that also gave the National Park Service's program an intellectually elegant structure and provided a wish list for potential units. Since hundreds of facets were included under the many sub-themes, the NPS created a program by which it could examine potential sites and, if they were found to be nationally significant, illustrative of one of the facets, and still retaining substantial historical integrity in their physical setting, they could be designated National Historic Landmarks. NHLs, as they were called, would remain in the hands of their owner, would not become units of the National Park System unless they were threatened with severe degradation or loss, and unless it was clear that the best way to protect them was to bring them into the system. National Historic Landmarks were judged to be of national significance when they received the designation and the Park Service became a fallback protector—by restoration grant, by brokering a landmark into a state park system, or by possible inclusion in the National Park System.

The Marsh–Billings Mansion was designated a National Historic Landmark by this process in 1967. Thus when Rockefeller began to think about transferring the property by gift to the NPS, the question of national significance had already been settled. The question that remained was, if the unit were brought into the system, which of several themes most powerfully spoke to what it represented? Since the site qualified as an NHL under more than one theme, it also qualified to be designated a National Historical Park, a designation reserved for units with multiple resources of significance, rather than a National Historic Site.

The theme of stewardship was a natural one, for the concept is central to the combination of conservation and preservation represented by the earlier units of the Park System and also of the growing thrust toward environmentalism. Good stewardship over the land was important to both the conservation of natural resources and to the historic preservation movement. What set the Marsh–Billings site apart was that it exemplified a constant growth within nature as three different stewards applied the prevailing wisdom of their time to what was essentially an economic pursuit, farming. Thus the mansion had been designated an NHL under the sub-theme of the origin and development of the conservation idea before 1870, by virtue of its relationship to George Perkins Marsh; but it also spoke of late nineteenth century practices of reforestation (initiated by Billings in 1884, some six years before Gifford Pinchot launched his more ambitious plan at Biltmore, in North Carolina), of scenic preservation (especially at nearby Mount Tom), of the maturation of the conservation movement up to the Second World War, and of post-war environmental concerns.

Stewardship is a very real activity but it is also an abstraction that Americans often find difficult to understand. A Marsh–Billings National Historical Park, those who proposed it argued, would be an excellent site at which this abstraction could be made concrete, through the evidence of a growing conservation and ultimately environmental ethic at work. Since Marsh, Billings, and later the Rockefellers were responsible for this continuity of dedication to stewardship, the unit was to bear the names of the first two and, perhaps, ultimately of the third as well, but the national park was not created to celebrate these individuals. It was created to illustrate the principle of stewardship at work. This would prove a major challenge to the people who were asked to prepare the interpretive markers, the films, books, and other educational and information materials for the unit, since stewardship was more difficult to explain or visualize than a unit based, for example, on a Civil War battlefield.

The person who most effectively shaped the concept of stewardship to give meaning to places like the Marsh–Billings property was LSR's old friend and mentor, René Dubos, the French-born microbiologist from Rockefeller University. Based on St. Thomas Aquinas and on the teachings of St. Benedict of Nursia, "stewardship environmentalism" held that knowing abuse of nature was a form of sacrilege. Since the world belonged to God, the environment demanded respect; yet, Dubos argued, humankind had been placed by God in charge of the resources of this world and could manipulate nature to the interests of humanity provided this was done with reverence. This anthropocentric view, Dubos said, required an understanding of the symbiosis between earth and humankind.

Two types of landscapes were possible: undisturbed wilderness in which there had been no human intervention, and "humanized environments created to fit the physiological, aesthetic and emotional needs of modern, human life." Most people passed their days, at best, in an environment of "humanized nature," and this was desirable, for only in this way could humanity achieve the recreative "adaptive fitness" essential to reinventing itself in the face of each new environmental crisis. But there must also be genuine wilderness, both for the good of ecosystems and because there was a deep human need for a more primeval nature that would assert "a sense of community with the past and with the rest of creation." Dubos argued this position vigorously in scientific journals but also for the lay public in the *Audubon Magazine*, in public speeches, and in correspondence with conservationists and environmentalists, including Laurance Rockefeller. Caneel Bay did not contradict the wilder parts of St. John; Mount Tom complemented the Billings Farm; the ranchlands and hotels of Jackson Hole highlighted the majesty and wildness of the Grand Tetons. Conservation, stewardship, and the human heart—the title of one of Dubos's commentaries—were a self-reinforcing continuum.[20]

To begin an interpretive effort, the National Park Service, with the financial support of the Rockefellers, brought together fifty knowledgeable individuals for a conservation stewardship workshop in Woodstock in the fall of 1993. The participants included superintendents of national park units, the director of the National Park Service, the governor of Vermont, historians, folklorists, community planners, authors of biographies of Marsh and Billings, and LSR's long-term advisors on conservation matters, including Henry Diamond and Russell Train. LSR introduced the conference and Train spoke of his commitment to stewardship across a range of activities: "the protection of unique portions of America's natural heritage, . . . the building of citizen conservation organizations, . . . the development of ideas and the building of a conservation ethic, . . . environmentally sensitive investment, . . . dedicated public service, . . . the promotion of conservation action by government at all levels, and . . . private philanthropy . . . without parallel in history."[21]

In his introduction LSR related stewardship to the Judeo–Christian ethic, by which mankind had dominion over the natural world only in order to exercise a land ethic that would sustain life. He spoke of moral values being essential to survival, defining environmentalism as "an inter-personal relationship" that had evolved out of human experience. He pointed to Aldo Leopold's *A*

Sand County Almanac, originally published in 1949, and one of a handful of deeply influential classics in the environmental movement. Leopold had extended the study of ethics, which he (erroneously) believed to have been studied only by philosophers, to ecological evolution, concluding that ethics must rest upon the premise that an "individual is a member of a community of interdependent parts." The land ethic, he wrote, enlarged the boundaries of the community "to include soils, waters, plants, and animals, or collectively: the land." Once this was understood there would emerge an "ecological conscience." Mankind must learn "how to think like a mountain"—to understand the value of all life. Leopold's reasoning appealed deeply to the man who had written his Princeton thesis on values in relation to ethics.[22]

The Rockefellers concluded that when they transferred their summer home in Woodstock to the National Park Service, their name should not be part of the new unit's title. The mansion had been proclaimed a National Historic Landmark in commemoration of George Perkins Marsh. When Marsh had praised the utilitarian values of watershed protection and soil conservation, as well as the leisure pursuits that accompany forest preservation, he had the Adirondacks in mind; that, and the wide impact of *Man and Nature* stimulated LSR's interest in the man as well as the property. However, aside from some interior modernization, the property had retained its historical integrity largely because of its post-Marsh owner, Frederick Billings. Billings was less well known than Marsh, but he had been a highly successful lawyer in California from 1850 to the Civil War, a president of the Northern Pacific Railroad, and a person of some note in terms of philanthropy, reforestation, and concern for the environment. Thus the property was known locally as the Marsh–Billings Mansion, and LSR opposed the attachment of his name to the new unit of the National Park System.

Then a compromise was struck. Though the new national park would be officially designated the Marsh–Billings National Historical Park, the legislation that created it and the interpretation that would be carried out at the site would in due time, given its theme of stewardship over the land, include Mary and Laurance Rockefeller as an integral part of the story. "Stewardship" would be used in two contexts: to define conservation practices that emphasized the roles of "people, culture, nature, and community," and as "an expression of personal commitment and civic responsibility." That LSR had been a "good steward" land owner was clear, and though Woodstock was not his primary home, he came to accept that his many and extensive contributions to an evolving understanding of modern methods of land preservation, and his encouragement of other good steward owners, in Woodstock and elsewhere, could be commemorated at the new unit, which was an important culmination of his career in conservation as well as historical preservation.[23]

Still evolving in 1997, though opened to the public in 1983, the Billings Farm & Museum lay across from the Marsh–Billings Mansion, a half mile north of Woodstock from which the museum and farm could be reached by a simple roadside path across the historic Elm Street Bridge, itself the object of Billings and Rockefeller gifts. The museum, housed in four reconstructed barns, interpreted Vermont farm life in 1890, the year of Frederick Billings's death. There was a working dairy farm and a living history center, installed in a refurbished farm manager's house. The complex presented with a high degree of sophistication and clarity the use of farm tools, the nature of life in rural Vermont, and the Vermont virtues LSR admired, and it was the product of much careful professional advice with input from the best historical interpreters and preservationists in the country. LSR had moved the museum forward incrementally, each stage carefully pondered before action, with cautious efforts to bring the community and the state into consultation, so that it was not, in fact, a static museum so much as an interpretive center, a place based on research and directed to educational goals that would continue to evolve in order to remain relevant. Attractively sited, potentially fed by visitors staying at the nearby Woodstock Inn, and other amenities in the area, the Billings Farm & Museum was nicely representative of how LSR wanted to educate and entertain the public. He and the staff drew upon the precedents of the "model" farming practices established by Frederick Billings on the property and the traditions of the county fair that had long been held on the site, a fair for which the young Mary, her siblings, cousins, and friends had ridden their ponies with the color guard from village to farm. The new national historical park would, in its management plan, emphasize partnerships with other entities, cooperative planning to conserve and educate, in an evolving process that both reflected and illuminated the realities of conservation planning in the late nineteenth century, thus to illustrate the long history of association between the forest lands, the farm and the mansion complex, and the town of Woodstock itself. In 1993 Laurance and Mary jointly received the George McAneny Historic Preservation Medal from the National Park Foundation "for outstanding leadership in historic preservation," the first time the medal had been awarded to a husband–wife team, with the new National Historical Park as their joint achievement.[24]

Throughout his life LSR would provide similar catalytic gifts, often as his father had done, on a matching basis, to prime a pump, so that others would become part of the support system too. Through the foundations he established or aided, such as the American Conservation Association, the Woodstock Foundation, or the National Park Foundation (launched in 1968 with a gift of a million dollars in seed money); through the boards he chaired or held closely—Jackson Hole Preserve, Inc., Rockresorts, Rockefeller Center, the Rockefeller Brothers Fund, the Palisades Interstate Park Commission—he was able to supply the key gift to promote a needed study, report, or monograph on literally hundreds of projects. In doing so he was cautious, generally nondirective, happy with whatever might be learned, concerned that the delicate balance of human relations, scientific objectivity, historical accuracy, and financial prudence be kept intact. His acquisition of the David T. Vernon Collection of Native American artifacts by JHPI was a precise example of how he worked: acquisition, at a fair price, of a valuable collection, followed by consideration of what next should be done, resulting in a study group of artifacts going to the Museum of the American Indian in New York and a display collection of the 1,400 finest objects being loaned to the National Park Service for its Colter Bay Visitor Center at Grand Teton National Park, culminating in a formal transfer of ownership, with over half the artifacts on permanent display. LSR's gifts to the National Capital Parks, starting off with $75,000 in 1964, is a second example, and his support of the Lyndon Baines Johnson National Historic Site (later National Historical Park) is a third. Perhaps the most idiosyncratic and yet revealing example was his support for the maintenance of the Steamboat Hotel in Fredericksburg, Texas, which had become a museum to Admiral Chester W. Nimitz, the World War II naval commander in the Pacific theatre who had signed the instrument of surrender with the Japanese at the end of the war, with the thought that the museum should be included in the National Park System (which did not happen).

Like his father before him, Laurance Rockefeller focused on matching grants, on precipitating action, on being a catalyst; he seldom met the full cost of any undertaking, for he was convinced that a broad spectrum of support best assured success and continuity for a project. He knew that if he alone stood behind a major undertaking, he could easily be accused of throwing his weight around. He understood that a reputation for handing out packets of money to meet the total costs of an enterprise, however deserving it might be, would create a network of dependencies rather than a network of innovation and energy. The Marsh–Billings project was to some extent an exception to this, though he made it clear that the National Park Service was to contribute financially; more typical of his way of operating were his several purchases of land for the Virgin Islands National Park, his personal interventions in the proposed redwood park, and his galvanizing proposal for an Adirondack National Park.

Of course, also like his father, LSR would at times provide the discrete gift to meet the full cost of an activity that would have a multiplier effect. When a park superintendent somewhat casually mentioned how, if he only owned a school bus, he could turn his park into an outdoor classroom for nearby school children, the superintendent soon received a check, upon a promise of anonymity, for the cost of a bus. When the National Parks Association proposed to assist two young college students in their desire to launch a program to bring high school and college student volunteers to the parks during the summer to help park personnel with construction, maintenance, and research work, LSR made a grant to cover the full program in one park. He quietly met the tuition expenses of a college student from abroad, certain that the student would return to his home country to promote the park ethic. There were dozens, perhaps hundreds, of such relatively small, yet to the recipients giant, benefactions as these.

There were commentators who believed that LSR most probably would have done far more for the National Park Service had he been asked to do so. Park Service officials had worked closely with the Rockefellers. In 1928 both Stephen Mather, the director, and Arno B. Cammerer, the associate director, had been instrumental in convincing JDR, Jr., that he should give $5 million to help establish Great Smoky Mountains National Park. Albright, Wirth, and Hartzog worked for the Rockefellers after retirement, and Hartzog's papers show abundant contact throughout his directorship, though less so after retirement.

But the Park Service changed over the years, became more bureaucratic, less often in direct touch with the type of philanthropist that LSR represented. Some park officials felt uncomfortable with his continued, though substantially moderated, desire to see economic gain for a community from the creation of new units. Though Rockefeller was moving from conservationist to environmentalist, he still believed that a park had to be justified to people whose first instinct was to oppose it. As Ronald A. Foresta reported in an excellent examination of the problems faced by the National Park System, written for Resources for the Future in 1984, there were many in the service who believed that the third and fourth generation of Rockefellers could have been approached in the way Mather and Albright had worked with JDR, Jr., and with LSR in the days of Albright, Wirth, and Hartzog, but that somehow the agency was reluctant to do so, perhaps precisely because the Rockefellers held such potential for influence, as when LSR helped prevent Wirth's possible dismissal in 1953 and 1961 (though not in 1963), or when he rejected what he regarded as inappropriate proposed alternative uses in the Marsh–Billings unit. Nonetheless, when asked he responded.[25]

Indeed, Laurance Rockefeller had done far more than most people in or out of the National Park Service actually knew. Either by direct gift, or through

Jackson Hole Preserve, Inc., the Rockefellers had provided funds to purchase additional land in Big Bend, Glacier, Grand Canyon, Lassen Volcanic, Olympic, Rocky Mountain, and Yosemite national parks, at Antietam, Big Hole, and Fort Donelson national battlefields, and at Capulin Mountain National Monument; had helped to fund the Yavapai Museum at the Grand Canyon; had purchased land to buttress Ford's Theatre National Historic Site; had underwritten many of the costs of the National Parks Centennial Conference in 1972 and the Second World Conference on national parks; and had quietly provided George Hartzog with the money to fund research and publish several reports. LSR had intervened directly when his brother Winthrop was governor of Arkansas, asking him to reconsider his support for a dam on the Buffalo River, when it was to become a National Scenic River, and (often through the National Park Foundation) had assisted in a variety of other ways. When, in 1970, Director Hartzog proposed to place some kind of commemorative plaque at ten of the national parks to draw public attention to the Rockefeller contributions over the generations, LSR suggested that something more private might be done, and in the end the director sent him a series of photographic albums of each of the parks.[26]

In 1991 the National Park Service was seventy-five years old and appeared to have lost its way somewhat, to need a shot in the arm. What better way, then, to celebrate its seventy-fifth anniversary than to provide just such a stimulus with two or three conferences that would lead to recharged batteries and a clearer vision for the future? When Director James Ridenour raised the question, Rockefeller agreed to help.

Two conferences held between April and October 1991 thus bore LSR's stamp. The first, a Conference on Partnerships in Parks and Preservation, was held in Albany in September, co-sponsored by the New York State Office of Parks, Recreation and Historic Preservation, and the National Parks and Conservation Association. This was an opportunity to explore partnership proposals between private enterprise, the National Park Service, and state park authorities, and through several of LSR's representatives on the planning committee, the program, or simply in attendance, to encourage new linkages between the private and public sectors.

Far more important was an "international symposium" held in Vail, Colorado, which gave rise to what thereafter was known as "the Vail Agenda." Officially a conference on "Protecting Our National Parks: Challenges and Strategies for the 21st Century," this meeting was assisted by LSR both directly—he is listed as one of the two individuals who provided "generous support" for the symposium—and indirectly through two of the four co-sponsoring bodies,

The Conservation Foundation and the National Park Foundation. The symposium was organized by Henry Diamond as the general chair. Though LSR was in the background, and did not attend, all who were involved were aware of his interest and concern.

The Vail conference re-examined the Park Service from structure through policies, with a focus on four subjects, all close to LSR's heart: stewardship, environmental leadership, park use and enjoyment, and organizational renewal. Working groups produced reports and recommendations on each subject while fifty-two speakers and presenters had an opportunity to air their views.[27] In March 1992 the final report and recommendations were presented to Director Ridenour, and shortly thereafter he mandated a variety of internal study groups, a Strategic Planning Office, and a wide range of inquiries to evaluate and, where appropriate, take action on the Vail Agenda. The work of the co-organizers, Diamond and William J. Briggle, the chair of the Steering Committee, produced a range of common-sense and at times startlingly relevant recommendations that pointed the way to a rejuvenated National Park Service. An intervening election, the defeat of then-President George Bush by the governor of Arkansas, Bill Clinton, and the resulting change in secretaries of the interior and directors of the National Park Service early in 1993 clearly affected the pace of action, though the first two of the required reports on environmental leadership appeared on schedule in 1992 and 1994, respectively.[28]

Laurance Rockefeller was a park professional and he thought as the park professionals thought. Conservation leaders invariably and environmental leaders generally must think in terms of the politics of the possible. As long-time park observer Michael Frome has written, they would "rather build bridges than barricades."[29] The more militant environmental groups see it as their duty to go to the wall for the best, largest, most nearly pure park proposal, and they often leave to others the actual steps by which, through compromise, a new park or an expanded boundary is achieved. This is as it should be. Park "purists"—those who understand that the resource for which a park was created must always be put first when management decisions are made—are seen as in opposition to "the recreation crowd," to those who believe fully as deeply, and not alone from commercial judgments, that in the long run a park is better served by being known in all its seasons, and loved for the memories of good times enjoyed within the park. But these positions are simply points on a continuum. There is a tendency to forget that great national parks once were promoted as "the nation's playground" (Rocky Mountain), as tourist destination points for railroads (Yellowstone, the Grand Canyon), or because they had golf courses and ski runs (Yosemite). Horace Albright, much lionized today for what he did for the national parks, and with good reason, favored hotels in the parks, commercial development of the Yosemite Valley, and in 1968 was soliciting funds for the Shrine of the Ages Chapel on the rim of the Grand Canyon. The prevailing concept of what national parks are to be has changed dramatically in the last quarter century.

National Park Service professionals were generally for the middle ground, though as the national park ethic developed, they inched closer to protection and in some small measure away from use. Rockefeller was part of this gravitation, moving from multiple-use recreational arguments for parks more toward a centrist position, balancing protection and use as the park hierarchy itself had come to do. In this sense he was a mover, a shaper of the evolving ethic, and paradoxically he was also shaped and moved by it. On occasion LSR was referred to as "Mr. National Parks," and though he shunned this title, he more than almost anyone warranted it: he had shaped the parks through his many benefactions while also reflecting the changing ethic by which American national parks would come to comprise the best, most elegant park system in the world.

At the time LSR was involved simultaneously with the Redwood, Adirondack, and Virgin Islands projects, he was working closely with the White House on how to make Americans more conscious of the natural beauty around them. In 1965, in a message to Congress, President Lyndon Johnson spoke of the interrelatedness of these matters in words that might well have been LSR's: "Our conservation must be not just the classic conservation of protection and development, but a creative conservation of restoration and innovation. Its concern is not with nature alone, but with the total relation between man and the world around him."[30] LSR believed that man was responsible, as a steward, for all that happened to the environment, and that in this discovery humankind could renew itself. As René Dubos, the microbiologist he so admired, wrote, "Man shapes himself through decisions that shape his environment."

In his eighties, Laurance Rockefeller undoubtedly hoped to pass the torch, as it had been passed to him, to the next generation. His only son, Larry, born in 1944, had shown an early interest in conservation, and devoted himself in later years to environmental causes. LSR's daughters, Laura, Marion, and Lucy, born between 1936 and 1941, did not choose a career in conservation but each was also environmentally minded, as reflected in their life-styles and philanthropic interests. No one understood better than their father that everyone had to paint on their canvas in their own way; still, he had reason to believe that, through his children, he would see his work carried on. Larry was appointed to the Palisades Interstate Park Commission in 1979, succeeding his father, and ably defended New York's Minnewaska State Park from the threat of development. As staff attorney for the Natural Resources Defense Council, he worked long hours on behalf of a variety of projects. He took an interest in the nation's barrier islands and in Alaskan lands. He acted as go-between on behalf of the National Parks and Conservation Association and the Richard King Mellon Foundation when the Association needed money to complete its ambitious multi-volume study of the National Park Service's future requirements, leading to perhaps the fullest inventory ever of potential park units.[31] Larry wanted to develop his own ecologically sensitive resort project, Beaverkill, in the Catskill Mountains. He took part in the Earth Summit in Brazil in 1992. He was chair of the Public/Private Partnership to Save Sterling Forest, an endangered area in Orange County, New York, and Passaic County, New Jersey. For such initiatives, the National Park Foundation presented him with its 1988 Horace M. Albright Award for "sustained contributions to the enhancement of the nation's natural and scenic environment," and the Wilderness Society and NPCA likewise honored him in the 1990s.[32]

In 1994 Scenic Hudson, Inc. wanted to honor Laurance Rockefeller, and LSR's long-time advisor on national and state parks, Nash Castro, was asked to sound him out, since it was foreseen that on the whole Rockefeller did not care to be the object of this kind of function. Castro advised the sponsors that LSR would almost certainly decline and suggested that they broaden the honor, to four generations of the family. When this was put to him, LSR agreed, providing his son concurred and would serve as the "family spokesman and anchor." Larry did so, and at the dinner that June, a photographer from the *New York Times* caught a moment of transparent affection, as mother and son turned to each other, father framed between them, to accept the applause of the attending group.[33]

Stewardship, the theme of the Marsh–Billings National Historical Park, is an idea as old as Christianity—indeed older—a concept elaborated upon by St. Thomas Aquinas, and in more recent years a deeply held and particularly Protestant theology. Expressed in governmental terms, the "stewardship agencies"—the National Park Service, U.S. Forest Service, Fish and Wildlife Service, and Bureau of Land Management—have each evolved their own ethic, their own understanding of their responsibilities, from the legislation that created them. Each has taken the view that it was managing a substantial amount of real estate in perpetuity "in the name of the American people." The leading philosophers of environmentalism, as well as many of the most important leaders and actors—those who, as Aldous Huxley wrote, understand the answer to his question, "When a piece of work gets done in the world, who actually does it?" and accepted his reply, "Everything that gets done within a society is done by individuals"—have come from those who have followed a scriptural ideal of the good steward. JDR, Sr.'s Baptist faith, in which JDR, Jr., followed, and LSR's more ecumenical approach to religion and spirituality, meant that their contributions went beyond land and money. LSR more than any other Rockefeller held to a consistent vision—that conservation and use, even multiple use—were possible, *must* be possible, for the nation would not fail to grow and Americans would not fail to need both more places to live and more places to play. He worked to achieve what he viewed as a balanced end, a mid-position between those who felt that growth in itself was a social evil and those who felt that growth in itself was life's highest purpose. At a time when politics, social expectations, race relations, and the very fabric of life was increasingly polarized, he persisted in a search for a middle path, for compromise between commerce and conservation.

VII

Shaping a National Outdoor Recreation Policy

The idea of creating a federal commission to study the nation's current and future outdoor recreational needs apparently originated with Joseph W. Penfold, western representative and later conservation director of the Izaak Walton League, a national association for fishermen.[1] Penfold felt that the post-war surge of population was overwhelming America's capacity to provide outdoor recreational outlets, and that an inventory of needs with the then seemingly far-off year 2000 in mind was essential. He argued that there was little awareness of the relationship of recreation to conservation, especially at the state level, citing an instance when, at a water hearing in Colorado, the director of the Colorado Water Conservation Board testified, "Nothing stands in the way of a bright future for Colorado but a handful of conservationists—who don't need to have any attention paid to them."[2] This remark set Penfold on his evangelical path. He was no "tree hugger," no "purist": he wanted there to be land and water for hunting and fishing, for camping, for uses that included development lots; had the snowmobile been commonplace then, he would likely have favored it. In essence, though he had never met Laurance Rockefeller, he was a conservation and use man too. However, Penfold also realized, as he listened to spokesmen for the Army Corps of Engineers and the Bureau of Reclamation recite statistics about acre feet of water, timber yield, property values, and all the data that invariably were poured out to justify a dam, a reclamation project, or a realignment of a river, that conservationists had no reliable statistics with which to reply: they simply appealed to common sense and vague values of spirituality and beauty that were swept aside by number crunchers. What was needed to counter developmental arguments, Penfold reasoned, was a massive body of hard-edged answers backed by countervailing data.

From this realization would eventually come the Outdoor Recreation Resources Review Commission (ORRRC) and Laurance Rockefeller's public advent onto the national environmental scene. Penfold broached the subject of the need for a broader assessment and a commission to administer it with Senator Joseph C. O'Mahoney of Wyoming and Congressman Aspinall of Colorado. David Brower, head of the Sierra Club, was simultaneously speaking of the need for a Scenic Resources Review. In January 1957, a nonpartisan group of sponsors introduced a bill in the House that languished in the nether reaches of committee contemplation. Realizing that the project needed a little help from its friends, Nelson Rockefeller discussed the issues with the House Speaker Sam Rayburn, with the result that the legendary Texan whisked it through. Passed on June 28, 1958, the act created the proposed commission and the new body was assigned the task of finding answers to three basic questions: What were the recreation wants and needs of the American people (1960 would become the base line), and what would they be in 1976, the nation's bicentennial, and in the year 2000? What recreation resources were available to fill those needs? (This would call for an inventory of a kind never before attempted.) What policies and programs should be pursued to insure that those needs were "adequately and efficiently" met? The goal was "to preserve, develop and assure accessibility to all American people of present and future generations such quality and quantity of outdoor recreation resources as will be necessary and desirable for individual enjoyment, and to assure the spiritual, cultural and physical benefits that such outdoor recreation provides. . . ."

Even in the nineteenth century recreation as understood in the United States generally went beyond passive leisure activities to embrace a rudimentary conservation ethic that gave thought to "quality and quantity." Parks had begun as pleasure grounds, places of ornamentation and inspiration, where the growing nineteenth century middle class could stroll at leisure, enjoying themselves as they "transcended" the cities that were developing around them. Parks were filled with ornamental shrubs, accessed by landscaped drives, their designs often appealing to a taste for the picturesque; they were enhanced by "water features" where the play of light and water provided an opportunity for contemplation, with well-tended floral displays, rose gardens, and conservatories added to major parks. The ornamental park began to give way near the end of the nineteenth century to the "reform park," which would actively help society to improve, with playgrounds for children, especially of immigrant background, and opportunities for the discipline of organized play, drawing upon European and especially German emphasis on healthy bodies being essential to a healthy state. Athletic facilities, dance halls, public swimming pools, even vegetable patches for children, branch libraries, and dental clinics became part of the urban park, which was sited more and more in the neighborhoods.

Thus by the 1930s public parks were becoming recreational facilities, often with little beauty, targeting to the needs of leisure, intended to fill the hours for men and women, and their children, who were unemployed and unable to afford, as the Great Depression deepened, commercial entertainment. Parks became a service, even a universal right, not requiring justification, places where the people could have fun. The term *recreation* came into increased use from the early 1930s, perhaps because it did not imply, as *play* did, a facility limited to an age group, and city Playground Commissions became Recreation Commissions across the nation. This change at the city level led to a growing insistence that so-called wilderness parks should offer more recreational activities, in part to meet the needs of those living lives of enforced leisure and in part to give families under financial and social stress activities to do together outdoors, where the air was purer. The depression led to a reduction in park staffs, which produced a decrease in reform-minded group and educational activities and an increase in the development of open spaces where self-formed groups could recreate without supervision. To offset this trend, park professionals turned more and more to schools and colleges and to the federal government. More recreation facilities were blacktopped and fenced; trees were less important to the concept of the park.[3]

This trend was accentuated by World War II, during which many facilities were turned over to army training, swimming pools used as mock assault beaches, mountain slopes for ski patrols, and campgrounds for military rest and rehabilitation. After the war, recreation facility design was increasingly standardized, with mass-produced park benches and Cyclone wire fences, the first the universal symbol of park space and the second the urban demarcator of park lands. There was less intervention at playgrounds, requiring more signage. A consumer society produced more waste, requiring more waste containers. Parks grew uglier, more utilitarian, until the *New York Times* lashed out at what it called "Robert Moses's brick-and-tile lavatory style."

The study commission began its work at a moment of transition in outdoor recreation thought, and it crystallized that transition. More and more cities defined parks as open spaces, as lungs for rapidly growing and changing populations, as places to which the disadvantaged and underprivileged might escape on a hot summer's night. Parks were on the way to becoming pleasuring grounds in a new sense of the word, where rock concerts and jazz bands would be organized, where visitors did not seek solitude and quiet so much as community and action.

But in the countryside, outside the large cities of the east and west coasts, in rural and mountain areas, recreation continued to mean what it had meant since the day when mankind no longer had to hunt or fish for provender. Recreation meant more places to hunt and fish purely for pleasure, more places to hike, boat, or bicycle, more places to experiment with new activities such as downhill and cross-country skiing. ORRRC was constituted precisely in this moment of transition when recreation meant all things to all people, when it was a word suggesting unlimited activities requiring unlimited opportunities, when park creation and maintenance became an interest of philanthropists, a concern of businesses, and a demand by the general public.

Parks, whether municipal or national, no longer were to be reached by trolley car, railroad, or other public transportation. Access was to be by private motor car. This meant that seekers after recreation could roam much further afield—ORRRC used a five hundred mile perimeter for its study of need and use—and required more facilities, parking lots, gasoline stations, camp sites into which trailers could be wedged, showers, and modern toilets. In the past men had defined most recreational uses, including destinations, but by the late 1950s and early 1960s women were playing a far greater role in organizing family recreation. The nation was on the cusp of fundamental change, and the new commission had to measure that change and respond.

Sherman Adams, President Eisenhower's chief of staff, called all agency heads and Cabinet officers for their suggestions concerning an appropriate chairman for the commission. Penfold was considered, but he was a Democrat, and the chairmanship of so important a body should go to a Republican, or so Eisenhower's White House staff advised him. Samuel T. Dana, a brilliant environmentalist and professor of natural resources from the University of Michigan, who had a national reputation for his work on outdoor recreation, was urged by the Department of Agriculture, but he was seventy-five years old. Fred Seaton, the secretary of the interior, initially thought of Horace Albright, as well as Dana. While the chief of the Forest Service responded without any names, except to commend Dana and to oppose Albright, who would be too one-sided toward "national-park type" proposals, and to point out that the American Planning and Civic Association, of which Albright was chairman, and which had its offices in the Rockefeller building in New York, for he had apparently opposed the bill establishing the commission. The Izaak Walton League provided several names by category, including Laurance Rockefeller under "Development of National and State Parks." An industry-generated list included Dana, LSR (this time a bit improbably under Recreation, Mining, and Lumber), and his right-hand man on conservation, Fred Smith, then a senior vice president of the Prudential Insurance Company (under Grazing). All the lists were reviewed by Senator Clinton Anderson, New Mexico's powerful Democratic czar, a man of great integrity, who wanted to be sure that the person chosen was of the highest character as well as knowledge. Albright advised Anderson that Laurance Rockefeller was the best possible choice, for he was well informed on national parks but also understood the wide scope of the recreational issue and was unlikely to be opposed by the Department of Agriculture or the Forest Service. He had, however, been put into the wrong category: the next time a list was circulated, he appeared under "Recreation." Secretary Seaton, recalling the day just two years before when he had joined LSR in dedicating the new Virgin Islands National Park, also argued for Rockefeller. Thus the choice was made: President Eisenhower asked LSR to chair the proposed commission to study outdoor recreation. Rockefeller said that the idea of such a commission was "beautiful" and readily accepted what he would later conclude was "one of the most successful commissions in history in terms of legislative results."[4] This was not an over-statement.

Rockefeller was not able to exercise much control over the choice of Commissioners.[5] Four were appointed by the Senate: Senator Anderson, Senators Frank A. Barrett of Wyoming and Arthur V. Watkins of Utah, who were succeeded by Henry C. Dworshak of Idaho and Thomas E. Martin of Iowa, Republicans, and, until his death in March 1960, Richard Neuberger of Oregon, the only Senate Democrat listed simply as "Conservationist," who was succeeded by Henry M. Jackson of the state of Washington. The Speaker of the House appointed two Republicans, John P. Saylor of Pennsylvania and Harold R. Collier of Illinois, who was succeeded by Ralph J. Rivers of Alaska, and two Democrats, both also designated simply as "Conservationist," Gracie B. Pfost of Idaho and Al Ullman of Oregon, who would be succeeded by John H. Kyl of Iowa. The seven citizen-member positions to be filled by the president were open to Rockefeller's influence, however, and he was active in assuring good appointees. Fred Smith, as head of the Council of Conservationists, was chosen for his experience in multiple land use and because Rockefeller insisted. He was designated as from New Jersey and "Grazing." Dana (Michi-

gan) and Penfold (Virginia) were obvious choices. The other positions went to
Katherine Jackson Lee of New Hampshire, a director of the American Forestry
Association; Chester Wilson, a past director of the Minnesota Department of
Conservation, from that state; and Bernard Orell of Tacoma, Washington, the
one other person briefly considered for the chairmanship, who was a vice president of the Weyerhaeuser Timber Company. As soon as a vacancy opened,
Rockefeller saw to it that Marian Dryfoos Heiskell, from the *New York Times,*
who could assure that the commission's findings would not be ignored by the
press and who was widely influential in conservation and gardening circles, was
appointed. Henry Diamond was present as LSR's right hand and chief editor
for the proposed report.

In addition to the commission, there was to be an advisory council of twenty-
five members. Rockefeller knew the council would be important, for its membership would speak to the integrity of the process, and if the appointments
were largely political in nature, he would lose an opportunity to demonstrate the
standard he wished the report to set. Further, the right members of an advisory
council would provide significant outreach to a variety of overlapping interest
groups and could help take up the middle ground between opposing organizations. When he accepted the chairmanship of the commission, he made it clear
that he did not want to be bound by an act, passed in 1949, that limited the
choice of personnel. His first move, therefore, was to get an amendment to the
act passed, so that the commission was exempted from it, and thus he could get
the most qualified people.

He did have to contend with the White House, which had some political
debts to pay. There is no advisory commission, council, or board in government
that is not used in this way; the trick is to minimize the numbers and to be sure
that the people appointed to fulfill an obligation are nonetheless qualified. The
White House produced a list of individuals, at first four and then six, who
were "musts" for the advisory council. One was Francis Sargent, Commissioner
of the Massachusetts Department of Natural Resources and well grounded in
the hunting and fishing constituency, who Rockefeller thought would be an
excellent executive director for the commission. A second was Pat Griffin, who
Congressman Aspinall insisted upon, and both Clinton Anderson and Wayne
Aspinall must be allowed to fill one slot each if they wished to.

In the meantime, state nominations had been coming in, and the staff assistant to the commission, Carl O. Gustafson, working out of Rockefeller Plaza,
carefully reviewed everyone who was named and passed a compilation on to the
White House. There were 386 nominees, listed by twenty-one categories, from
State Game and Fish Departments to Municipal Governments, with Alaska and

"General" as noninstitutional listings. "General" included Horace Albright, Kenneth Chorley, still Rockefeller's man on Colonial Williamsburg, Robert Moses, and Colorado's Pat Griffin, from Fort Collins. Fourteen states were represented on the Commission, and the White House wanted advisory council members to come from unrepresented states. Rockefeller stood firm for quality, and his own list added only eleven more states to the tally, with —in the White House view—too many from the District of Columbia and from California. The White House countered with another "must" list, and as an anonymous White House staffer wryly remarked, "none of these will get anywhere." One person, Andrew J. Biemiller, the only nominee under Labor, who was the director of the Department of Legislation for the AFL-CIO, "could not be worst" (sic) in the view of the staffer. The list was massaged extensively, with individuals recategorized, and one or two who had two homes reassigned geographically. This was all fascinating, no doubt, but Rockefeller was not interested in the process: he wanted the right stuff, and his definition was not a politician's definition, even though he recognized clear political necessity when he saw it. The result, after many weeks of back and forth, was an advisory council that did not include the new "must" people. Albright and Chorley made it. (Andy Biemiller did receive a slot.) LSR had made his point: the council, like the commission, would be bipartisan and as independent of government as possible. When LSR released the names to the press in April 1959, he was very pleased with the result.[6]

Rockefeller had taken such pains over the membership of both Commission and Council because he realized that significant legislation could come out of the ORRRC process. Once the commission's report was submitted, Congress could bury its recommendations, but he thought this unlikely; indeed, he planned to frame the report in such a way as to make legislation easy and virtually certain, gaining the endorsement of the president, who would transmit it to Congress for action. While the advisory council was, as its name made clear, advisory only, he knew that the commission would take that advice most seriously provided the right people were on it. In short, the entire process was an instructive lesson in civics, though the members of the commission and council were all wise in the ways of government.

At once the wisdom in asking Laurance Rockefeller to chair the commission became evident. Congress took a year to appropriate funds for the commission's work; rather than wait, LSR drew upon his own funds and brokered effectively with foundations to put a staff into place. He established a liaison in the office of each state governor. He called for an immediate meeting and projected his sense of urgency. Knowing that many special interests would expect the commission to take stands for or against pending legislation, he insisted that the group must not arrive at conclusions before an objective study was complete: there would be no leaked recommendations before the report was due. By this announcement he gave the commission breathing room and protected its staff from being asked to anticipate the results. When the commission report was finished three and a half years after the bill creating it, LSR—by then well aware of how Congress could bury any document it did not care to grapple with—created an action group to follow up on the recommendations, using only foundation money to support it.

LSR had plenty of experience with chairing meetings, though none of this public prominence. He proved to be very good at it. He kept the commissioners firmly to the agenda, he asked searching questions, he outlined objectives from meeting to meeting, he showed patience at the infrequent outbursts of irrelevancies, and above all, he had a clear sense of priorities. A little exegesis on the legislation made it clear that there actually were six tasks to be performed, and he broke these down into manageable segments, then turned his notes over to Professor Dana, who drew up a sequential action paper. Nothing was left out, nothing was left to chance. No relevant state or federal agency was omitted from consideration.

Years later Fred Smith, still LSR's in-house consultant on conservation, would remark that no task was so well suited to Rockefeller's way of thinking. This was, after all, not only about patience; it required a team to apply extensive research and systematic thought; it spoke to questions of healing and of a community's sense of right and wrong; it would help the nation show thrift in use of its resources and in the creation of outlets for recreation. It was precisely the right assignment for the young man who had majored in philosophy at Princeton in order, he had told his father, to understand "conflicting desires and actions."[7]

LSR soon learned about those conflicting desires. Special-interest conservation groups volunteered to conduct some of the studies: they were fended off. Washington's "floating pool" of staffers, people willing to find data to support any side of any argument, were told they need not apply. Hundreds and hundreds of interested individuals, some hoping to see their properties turned into tourist attractions at government expense, wrote to the commission or directly to Rockefeller. Dozens of Congressmen broadly hinted at the special needs of their districts. Everyone received a courteous reply. Meetings were held on time, with full attendance, so (unlike many federal commissions) work was not delayed for lack of a quorum. The commission met in the field as well as in Washington. Throughout the period LSR would address various public groups, both to carry the commission's message abroad and to invoke responses that might have to be considered before the final report was issued. Always happy in an airplane, he personally visited sites throughout the country, taking a particular interest in the analysis of aerial photographs, seeing for himself the nation's inventory.

Outdoor Recreation for America was submitted to President John F. Kennedy on January 31, 1962, an election having intervened. It revealed that 90 percent of all Americans were involved in some form of outdoor recreation, that public demand for substantially increased recreational opportunities was rising rapidly and, in so far as measurement was possible, would triple by 2000. Quick and sweeping action was needed. Sixty recommendations, ranging from more national parks to more access facilities for pleasure boats, were summarized in a succinct program. The action summary emphasized the need for a Bureau of Outdoor Recreation to coordinate federal programs and provide assistance to the states and communities; the inauguration of a land classification system of almost classical elegance; quick action to protect beaches and national shorelines from environmental degradation; abatement of water pollution; far greater use of easements to provide public access to recreational resources; the establishment of more national wilderness areas; and the institution of a system of user fees by public agencies so that those who benefitted most from certain recreational facilities would contribute the most to maintain them. All were sound ideas; all would, in some form, come to pass. Every commissioner signed the report, unusual for Washington and even more unusual for so controversial a subject.

In addition to the summary report submitted to the president, there were twenty-seven different ORRRC study reports covering virtually every permutation of recreation. These reports, which ranged in length from a brief 42 pages on multiple-use criteria for land and water to a massive 568 pages on the future of outdoor recreation in metropolitan regions in the United States, were enormously influential. (Because two of the reports were issued in three and two volumes, respectively, and there was both a separate executive summary and a preliminary booklet, the entire ORRRC series actually came to thirty-two volumes.) The quality of each subject report varied, of course, in part because of the practice of farming much of the research and usually at least some of the writing out to carefully selected contract groups or individuals. The report on the role of hunting in the United States was the work of the School of Natural Resources at the University of Michigan, that on outdoor recreation potential in Alaska was prepared by The Conservation Foundation, and innovative recommendations on ways and means of acquiring open space in the more rapidly developing areas of the country was the work of the imaginative William H. Whyte.

This practice led to many benefits, among them speed and comprehensiveness, but also to some criticisms, especially by those who feared that the impact of the reports would affect their personal interests. Thus the fact that Whyte was associated with Laurance Rockefeller, or that Rockefeller had helped to establish The Conservation Foundation, inevitably led to loose and ill-informed talk of a cabal. In truth, as the voluminous ORRRC records show, LSR made little effort, either individually or as chairman of the commission, to influence the content of any of the reports toward any specific conclusions, even on subjects of immediate concern to him, such as resorts. To be sure, some of the reports were, as a result of the technique, better written or more thorough than others. If some commentators felt they detected bias here and there—as in the report on potential new sites for outdoor recreation in the Northeast, the product of the Economic Research Service of the U.S. Department of Agriculture, and thus not surprisingly skewed toward economic values—others felt they sensed insufficient grasp of economic realities, as in The Wildland Research Center's report on wilderness resources and problems. On balance, virtually all commentators who were not at one extreme or the other on conservation issues found the reports as a group deeply impressive—indeed, the finest survey of its kind ever undertaken, then and since, on behalf of the American people.

As one reads the 4,800 pages of ORRRC reports today, one is struck by a range of piquant oddities, as well as by the massiveness of the undertaking. In one volume is an essay by the distinguished anthropologist Margaret Mead, normally associated with the customs of Samoan islanders, writing on American cultural values. Another volume observes, almost as an aside, that water is the unifying element that will lead city and country people to make common cause. One report recommends changes in the relationship between the National Park Service and the concessionaires within the parks, changes still being fended off by interest groups in 1997. A virtual aside in the report on Alaska recommends the creation of an Alaskan regional office by the National Park Service, which the NPS eventually implemented successfully. Norman Williams, of Woodstock, Vermont (and Tucson, Arizona), provided a precise analysis of legal problems involved in land acquisition for outdoor recreation that served as the best summary of its kind for two decades and thirty years later impacted both his home communities. Rockefeller, quite early in the process, working with Francis Sargent and Henry Diamond, declared how long each of the individual reports was likely to be, committing estimates to print, and an estimate of 4,735 pages came out at 4,806, as near on target (and as far from a cost overrun) as any government commission is likely to get.

To be sure, there were deficiencies. The reports were at times too abstruse, especially those laced with mathematical formulae about cost factors, to be understood by most readers or those in a position to effect improvements. The population projections used—that the likely national population in 1976 would be 231 million and in 2000 it would be 351 million—were too high, the correct figure at the bicentennial being 216 million and the present projection for 2000 being 276 million. This would bring some of the attendant statistics into question, even though the projections for overall soaring recreational demand proved, in fact, to be quite accurate. Yet, what strikes one above the oddities and occasional miscalculations from the vantage point of 1997 is how prescient most of the reports were, and how unfortunate it is that all the recommendations in the executive summary were not acted upon with real vigor.

The ORRRC survey found that, among people over twelve years old, driving for pleasure and walking for pleasure ranked first and second, respectively, as forms of outdoor recreation in 1960, followed by playing outdoor games or participating in organized sports, and then in descending order, by sightseeing, bicycling, fishing, attending spectator sports, and taking nature walks. To these, in winter, were added hunting, ice skating, and sledding, though none of these activities involved nearly as many people as the lowest of nonwinter recreational pursuits. The study concluded that outdoor games and sports would grow most rapidly (except in winter, when ice skating would begin to overtake hunting nationwide). Since there had been no reliable immediate post-war studies, these projections could not be seen in a larger context, and the commissioners agreed that the figures represented at best good guesses to indicate the action that might reasonably be taken. Popular taste for outdoor activities was recognized as dynamic, open to substantial change as new technologies made new forms of recreation possible, water sports, winter camping, and snowmobiling being obvious examples. Still, the estimates were of value and not so far wrong in many regards: for example, national parks received 66 million visitors in 1960, with more than 300 million predicted for 1980 and from 500 million to 2 billion (a range so large as not to be very useful) by 2000. Though such visits combined categories of recreation—sightseeing, driving, and walking for pleasure, etc., and omitted others (hunting, for instance)—the actual number in 1991, a quarter century after the projections were made, was 356 million.

This lower figure can be attributed to a dramatic increase in recreational facilities provided by other federal and state agencies, especially by the Bureau of Land Management, created in 1946 and not in the 1960s yet given a recreational mandate, the Forest Service, and the Army Corps of Engineers. In short, the ORRRC projections, inflated as some proved to be with respect to national parks, would most likely have been fully accurate had the impact of the report not led to major increases in the creation of recreational outlets by alternative agencies. Thus, ORRRC's figures were not, in any larger sense, wrong at all and their release in 1962 helped to spur the expansion of responsibilities for recreation in other branches of government, taking pressure off the National Park System so that it could better perform its primary mission to the resources its units were created to protect. Stephen Mather had known that the National Parks required second- and third-tier defense lines—state and county parks, places where people who did not care about conservation and preservation could go to take part in organized play, to camp out, fish, hunt, or relax without concern for the integrity, scientific significance, or iconographic magnitude of the park in which they carried out their activity— and ORRRC helped quite substantially to promote those defenses.

In addition to the upfront conclusions of the reports, there were some perhaps unexpected side effects, which most observers today would see as highly beneficial. In an influential report on shoreline recreation resources, the Board of Conservation of the state of Florida was quietly and properly castigated for having no master plan. The report on wilderness would persuade many readers that nearby communities could benefit economically from such designations (the conventional figure was that any amenity that generated twenty-four visitors a day would offset any small business with an annual payroll of $100,000). A searching inquiry into the recreation needs for metropolitan regions would, by focusing on Atlanta, Chicago, and St. Louis, highlight the disparity in facilities for black Americans at a time when southern states still had segregated state parks, accompanied by unsparing conclusions on the so-called "colored state parks" of Georgia and the inadequacy of access provided to over one-third of the population of that state's largest and most progressive city. A section of "conclusions with respect to race" pointed out inequities of which most Americans, eight years after the Supreme Court had rendered its decision in *Brown v. Topeka School Board* on segregated school facilities, were probably quite unaware. The reports were dotted with such pointed commentaries on how American society was developing.

In some cases the ORRRC reports simply added more fuel to campfires already burning: the shoreline study, for example, came well after the National Park Service's own studies, conducted between 1955 and 1959, of the nation's vanishing shoreline, and six months after Congress had authorized the first National Seashore, on Cape Cod, as an addition to the National Park System.

The swearing in of LSR and fellow members of the Outdoor Recreation Resources Review Commission, created by President Dwight D. Eisenhower, 1958. *From left:* Chester S. Wilson, former Minnesota state commissioner of conservation; Bernard L. Orell, vice president, Weyerhaeuser Co.; Joe Penfold, conservation director, Izaak Walton League of America; Mrs. Katharine Jackson Lee, director, American Forestry Association; M. Frederik Smith, vice president, Prudential Insurance Company of America; Laurance S. Rockefeller; President Eisenhower; Frank Sanderson, administrative officer, The White House. (Official White House photo)

LSR and President John F. Kennedy, after the president signed the act establishing the Bureau of Outdoor Recreation, 1963. *From left:* Senator Hubert H. Humphrey; Stewart L. Udall, secretary of the interior; Senator Clinton Anderson, New Mexico; President Kennedy; Congressman John Kyl, Iowa; Congressman John Saylor, Pennsylvania; Laurance S. Rockefeller. (Official White House photo)

LSR with President Lyndon B. Johnson at the presentation of pens used in the signing of the bills that framed much of the environmental program of LBJ's "Great Society," 1968. *From left:* Henry Kimmelman, special assistant to Secretary Udall; unidentified; Tom Clark, attorney general of the United States; Laurance S. Rockefeller; President Johnson; Stewart L. Udall, secretary of the interior; Mrs. Nathaniel Owings, chairman, California Coastal Commission; George B. Hartzog, Jr., director, National Park Service; Harthon L. Bill, deputy director, National Park Service. (Jack Kightlinger/LBJ Library Collection)

LSR with President Richard M. Nixon, 1970. (Official White House photo)

LSR with President Gerald Ford at the Rockefeller home, Kykuit, on the occasion of it being declared a National Historic Landmark, 1976.

LSR with President Jimmy Carter at the memorial service for Nelson A. Rockefeller, Riverside Church, New York City, 1979. *From left:* Nelson A. Rockefeller, Jr.; Mark F. Rockefeller; Mrs. Nelson A. Rockefeller; President Carter, First Lady Rosalynn Carter; LSR; Mary Rockefeller; Mrs. John D. Rockefeller 3rd. (Rockefeller Archive Center)

LSR greets President Ronald W. Reagan on the grounds of Kykuit, 1986. *From left:* David Rockefeller (*taking picture*), President Reagan, Mrs. David Rockefeller, LSR, and Mary Rockefeller. (Official White House photo)

LSR with Vice President George Bush and Benno Schmidt at the ground-breaking ceremony of the Rockefeller Research Laboratories of Memorial Sloan-Kettering Cancer Center, New York City, June 24, 1986. (Christopher Little)

LSR and President Bill Clinton resting their hands on the statue titled, "Appeal to the Great Spirit," during the President's visit to LSR's JY Ranch, Jackson Hole, Wyoming, 1995. (White House photo)

LSR at the New York State Council of Parks meeting, Bear Mountain, New York, 1956. *From left:* Dwight G. Palmer, New Jersey Highway Commissioner; W. Averell Harriman, governor of New York; Robert Moses, chairman of the New York State Council of Parks; Rockefeller, commissioner of the Palisades Interstate Park Commission.

LSR's son, Larry, cuts the ribbon opening the final three miles of the Palisades Parkway, 1957. *From left:* Laurance; Governor W. Averell Harriman, New York; Larry; Governor William Meyner, New Jersey; George W. Perkins, president of the Palisades Interstate Park Commission. (Rockefeller Archive Center)

LSR's family at their home on Fishers Island, New York, circa 1952. *From left:* Lucy, Mary, Laura, Marion, and Larry. (Laurance S. Rockefeller)

Laurance and Mary Rockefeller at the Billings Farm, Woodstock, Vermont, mid-1980s.

Mary Rockefeller presenting the deed to her family home, which became the Marsh–Billings National Historic Park property, to Secretary of the Interior Manuel Lujan, 1993. LSR looks on. (Official White House photo)

LSR's Jackson Lake Lodge within Grand Teton National Park.

Caneel Bay and Virgin Islands National Park.

Aerial view of The Mansion, Woodstock, Vermont. (Skyway Photography)

View of the Billings Farm & Museum in Woodstock, Vermont. The farm is immediately adjacent to the Marsh–Billings National Historic Park. (Brian Vanden Brink)

At other points the reports lent authoritative weight to programs long if not necessarily well established, such as the Wilderness Areas, the first having been the Gila Wilderness in the mountains of southwestern New Mexico in 1924. Equally clearly, the ORRRC reports were instrumental to numerous new programs and individual achievements: for example, Thomas R. Cox, historian of the northwestern state park movement, credits ORRRC with helping to promote the first truly professional state parks department in Idaho.[8] The Wild and Scenic Rivers Act of 1968 was clearly anticipated by several of the individual ORRRC reports (as well as by a Senate recommendation and the NPS in 1960) as were the national lakeshores, the first of which, Pictured Rocks, in Michigan, was designated in 1966.

As it happened, ORRRC's projections, as they were applied to the Adirondacks, that area of Rockefeller concern in the late 1960s, were wrong. The war in Vietnam, the collapse of housing prices, increased mobility and disposable income, which led baby boomers to the expanding ski slopes of Vail and to the warm waters of the Caribbean rather than to camp sites and fishing streams, all meant that the Adirondack park was not subject to the onslaught of use ORRRC suggested or LSR's proposal of 1967 feared. The rise of public furor against mindless and sometimes clearly dishonest developers, as in 1972, when the Horizon Corporation, which built or planned thousands of houses in unzoned communities, was the target of the largest land sale fraud case in the history of the Federal Trade Commission and further undermined public confidence. By 1980 use of Adirondack and Catskill campgrounds had fallen by 46 percent from a mid-1970s peak. ORRRC's hopeful suggestion that urbanized ethnic communities could be drawn into distant rural pursuits proved quite unrealistic in the face of declining public transportation, persistent racism, the breakdown of the family, and the nation's growing loss of identity. LSR had known that lovers of the outdoors tended to be urban and middle class; he had believed, based on ORRRC's research, that the base of supporters for federal and state cooperative planning could be broadened to achieve recreational goals. In this he was wrong: by the 1980s only 1 percent more of inner city residents expressed any interest in the subject.

Looking back, historians would single out six major accomplishments of ORRRC, many of which still have profound impact on national recreation policy today. From ORRRC came the Bureau of Outdoor Recreation, placed in the Department of the Interior, which drew together the activities of twenty uncoordinated government agencies, creating for the first time a federal recreation policy. Second, the weight of the reports on urban centers began a shift from great natural parks and major historical sites toward finding units for the

NPS closer to major cities. This was accomplished both by creating new national recreation areas and by searching out small, urban-focused historic properties. The concept, later to be known as the "national urban park movement" or "bringing parks to the people," would be taken up by the Johnson and Nixon administrations with controversial results. Third, the reports generalized the U.S. Forest Service's concept of "multiple use" to other types of resources, arguing that various activities could occur on lands essentially recreational in purpose, including grazing, lumbering, and mining, without materially damaging the recreational values of the land, and conversely, lands theretofore seen largely in commercial contexts could have noncommercial recreational amenities added to them. (The enlarged concept of multiple use, already under attack by the Sierra Club, would soon prove controversial.) Fourth, the report urged that a fund be established for federal purchases of land and from which grants would be made to state and local governments for buying and developing open spaces for limited-use recreational purposes, and this, after modification, would become the Land and Water Conservation Fund. Fifth, the reports were used by President Kennedy's successor, Lyndon B. Johnson, in part because of Laurance Rockefeller's influence, to become the basis for much of the environmental program of his Great Society. Finally, the reports plotted a sensible course for federal and state cooperation at a time of dramatic change in the nature of American federalism.[9]

ORRRC's significance was, therefore, far greater than the sum of its parts. For the first time a federally appointed commission had studied the needs of the entire New York–New Jersey–Philadelphia megalopolis, for instance, seeing issues at several levels of responsibility simultaneously: federal, state, county, municipal, even individual. For the first time a commission had sought to project forward beyond the customary American conception of "long-term planning" (which usually, and at best, embraced ten years) to attempt to predict needs over a forty-year span, or nearly two generations. For the first time the outdoors was examined as a whole, with recreation deemed both a public good and a public right. A calm, balanced assessment of the consequences of delay was attempted, with sensible statements on the cost of guessing too high with respect to recreational needs set off against the cost of guessing too low. A federal commission had sought to assess the impact of absence—of the lack of recreation opportunities in everyday life—rather than the impact of presence, and it had done so for the entire American landscape. Taking a comprehensive aesthetic and environmental view, ORRRC was nothing less than the first national inventory of how Americans related, and would relate barring substantial changes in trends, to their land. To some environmentalists the achievements of the ORRRC might not seem so monumental. Seen in the context of the time, however, profound changes in attitude cannot be denied. The reports marked the beginning of a new mood in America in which it was no longer manly to ignore the question of beauty, no longer patriotic to insist on unfettered exploitation of natural resources, no longer politically acceptable to ride roughshod over the fears and needs of those who opposed pollution, over-population, and over-consumption.[10]

Laurance Rockefeller's leadership was pivotal to all this. He never missed a meeting. He communicated, as the voluminous files in the Rockefeller Archive Center and the Eisenhower presidential library attest, with every fellow commissioner with courtesy, skill, and an eye to the special concerns of each. Possibly he contributed a bit more to the portion of the report on the Catskill Forest Reserve, the Hudson River Valley, or the question of public access through public transportation and automobile corridors (for these were special interests of his) than he necessarily contributed to the discussion of the future of Alaskan lands, though this was an interest too. But his stamp was on every report, both directly and through his special assistant, Carl O. Gustafson, and the chief editor for the final reports, Henry Diamond, or hand-picked advisors and specialists such as Whyte or George Lamb of Jackson Hole Preserve, Inc. Many years later LSR would remark that the ORRRC business had been great fun and perhaps one of the two or three most important things he had ever done in the field of conservation. As chair, diplomatist, and catalyst for outdoor recreation he was at his best.

ORRRC was a watershed, for Rockefeller, for conservation, and for the nation. The end result of the commission's deliberations, as orchestrated by LSR, may not have been precisely what Penfold and others had in mind when they began, for though they did not wish to lock up the land, they were initially focused on the traditional issues of wilderness, of public land policy, and of water resources. It was Rockefeller's leadership that catalyzed the commissioners toward a people-oriented approach to resource management, as he persistently argued that conservation meant relating parks and outdoor recreational resources more directly to the needs of the people. Outdoor recreation, LSR concluded, had "evolved from a luxury of the few to a necessity of the many." As Henry Diamond was to note years later of ORRRC, and of subsequent efforts, "Laurance brought people into the environmental equation, where before they had been excluded both physically and from a policy-making point of view." The key, LSR said time and again, was not "how many acres" but how effective were the acres for people. To be sure, not everyone was happy with this perspective. Sierra Club leadership, for example, complained that LSR had been captured by Penfold and the Walton League, who as conservationists lacked an environmental ethic—that is, they conserved in the interest of man rather than protecting species for their own sake. The very idea of a water "resource," David Brower, the Club's president, said, was directed to man's needs and uses. Rockefeller agreed that this was true, and he argued that it must be so if the nation's future needs were to be met. Thus LSR became a major figure, again in the words of Henry Diamond, "in the transition from the old conservation to the new people-oriented ecology."[11]

LSR's projected action group was put in place early in 1963. Known as the Citizens Committee for the Outdoor Recreation Resources Review Commission, or CORRRC, it could, as the government could not, receive charitable donations. Amid jokes about how ORRRC and CORRRC sounded like a vaudeville team, a law firm, or a pair of large birds mating, the members went to work with $190,000 brokered by Laurance Rockefeller. He was again in the chair, with Dana, Heiskell, Orell, Penfold, and Smith carrying over, and with two members of the advisory council added, together with the Pennsylvania Commissioner of Natural Resources and LSR's staff assistant from ORRRC, Carl Gustafson. The Citizens Committee went to the people, publicizing the commission's report, and issuing a modest brochure that called for immediate action.[12]

President Kennedy sent a special message to Congress on conservation, touching on all parts of the ORRRC report and other matters as well, recommending the creation of a special Land Conservation Fund of up to $500 million, financed by user fees, diversions from the Highway Trust Fund of taxes paid on gasoline for motor boats, new sums assessed on recreational boats, and receipts from the sale of surplus federal nonmilitary lands. He also asked that Congress move quickly on nine new national park units, that state and local governments be assisted in acquiring federal surplus properties for their own more local needs, and that open-space land programs within the cities be jump-started. Kennedy called for the passage of a National Wilderness Preservation System Act along lines already introduced by Senator Anderson. In time, with the exception of one of the recommended national parks, all were achieved.

LSR lobbied hard for these goals. He urged the establishment of a Bureau of Outdoor Recreation (BOR) in the Department of the Interior. He worked on behalf of the proposed Land Fund—later, the Land and Water Conservation Fund—by which both the state and federal governments would be able to purchase areas for recreational purposes. He spoke out on behalf of primitive areas and referred often to the dignity of intelligent use of leisure time. The BOR act passed triumphantly, the product of ORRRC, and the Wilderness Act followed in 1964.

The Bureau of Outdoor Recreation, created on April 2, 1962, was less than triumphantly successful. The first federal agency created for recreational purposes, and the first to have the word *recreation* in its title, the BOR managed the Land and Water Conservation Fund, by far its most important task. It also conducted surveys of recreational resources and needs, sponsored research, encouraged interstate and regional cooperation, and coordinated federal recreation programs. These somewhat amorphous tasks were not helped by the fact that the National Park Service was initially hostile to the new agency. The BOR never found a clear identity among the many federal bodies charged with promoting recreational facilities in one form or another. It was unfortunate that the National Park Service did not embrace the BOR and, indeed, transfer to it most of the Park System's National Recreation Areas, for these recreational units compromised the Park Service's primary responsibility to designate and manage resources of clearly national and even world significance. They also served to confuse the public, who reasonably enough could not understand why NPS policy was to oppose organized recreational activities in most NPS units while actively appearing elsewhere to promote such activities by virtue of the very title of an entire series of units. In 1978, Cecil Andrus, secretary of the interior for President Jimmy Carter, abolished the BOR and replaced it with a Heritage Conservation and Recreation Service (HCRS), which proved ineffective and short-lived, being terminated by President Reagan shortly after he took office. Most of the programs of the HCRS were transferred to the National Park Service, often with deleterious effects, since some of the programs were potentially at odds with national park ethics.

However, the Land and Water Conservation Fund was, for years, enormously successful. Normally 60 percent of the fund was to be made available to the states on a matching basis, provided development or acquisition projects were in accord with a comprehensive statewide outdoor recreation plan prepared at the state level and approved by the secretary of the interior. The state could then transfer grants to countries and municipalities in accord with the overall plan. In this way this key ORRRC recommendation promoted more comprehensive and integrated recreational planning than ever before. From 1965 until 1981 all fifty states participated. (When federal subsidies were greatly reduced in the first year of the Reagan administration, many states cut deeply back on their planning. The fund was scheduled to expire in 1989; reauthorized until 2015, it once again supplied substantial grants, though the total fund is no longer being used as Congress originally mandated.) By 1995 the fund had provided over $3 billion, matched by state, local, and private sector money, and had added three million acres to the public domain for recreational purposes. Its matching format was precisely modeled to the manner in which JDR, Jr., and

LSR had provided grants to create national and other parks in the years before, the vast sums more catalytic than anything a person of even great wealth could hope to provide, but in the same manner.

If imitation is the highest form of flattery, ORRRC was much flattered. A succession of federal reports on outdoor recreation followed in subsequent presidencies. BOR released its own Survey of Outdoor Recreation Activities in 1965. In 1974 the Environmental Policy Division of the Library of Congress prepared a 1,200-page "Nationwide Outdoor Recreation Plan" for the Senate Committee on Interior and Insular Affairs, chaired by Senator Henry M. Jackson, who had served on the original recreation commission under LSR's chairmanship. In 1979 the Heritage Conservation and Recreation Service would revisit the ORRRC report, even in format, with a multi-volume set of recommendations, *The Third Nationwide Outdoor Recreation Plan*, while in 1983 the Reagan administration would issue a new *Nationwide Recreation Survey*, which, breaking from tradition and format, was issued solely (and unfortunately) by the National Park Service. By the 1980s the original impetus of the ORRRC report had been lost, but the Land and Water Conservation Fund, even when its original intent was stymied, remained a significant legacy.

The impact of the Land and Water Conservation Fund alone would have entitled LSR to the gratitude of his country. In thirty years it would provide over $7 billion to fund 37,000 state and local projects. The fund became the most important backup for federal acquisition of land for national parks, wildlife preserves, national forests, and Bureau of Land Management properties; it was used as the chief federal vehicle for improving the quality of outdoor recreation broadly, of parks, and of open space. In 1994 LSR would again show his commitment to ORRRC's achievements, assisting in a review of uses of the fund. As the year 2000 approached, seemingly so distant when the Outdoor Recreation Resources Review Commission was established, the influence of its report was everywhere.

Perhaps ORRRC's success can be measured, if ironically, by the successor study conducted by the Heritage Conservation and Recreation Service in the Carter administration. When asked what most limited them in their enjoyment of the nation's vast infrastructure of outdoor recreation opportunities, most Americans responded with the single word, *time.* In the 1920s, surely, they would have said *health*, in the 1930s they would have said *money*, in the 1940s *transportation*, and in the 1950s they might have invoked *crowding.* But by the 1970s facilities were so abundant (if still insufficient), well known, and accessible, the inhibiting factor was *leisure time.*

Rockefeller was intellectually engaged by the ORRRC exercise, which he felt

was potentially the most important contribution he might ever make to conservation in America. Outdoor recreation combined all of his interests: preservation of cultural landmarks, landscape design, multiple use that had the
potential to link commerce and conservation, stewardship of the land for the
health of the people. His extensive travels as chairman of the commission gave
him a far wider sense of the variety and beauty of landscape in America, and
the potential for recreation, than he had ever had before. His subsequent positions on the Adirondack Park and Forest Preserve and on the Hudson River
Valley Commission were shaped by the convictions he came to while chairing
ORRRC.

To be sure, the concept of multiple use would produce problems. The language was enshrined in the Multiple Use Act of June 12, 1960, and it applied
solely to the U.S. Forest Service, embracing the idea that land could be used for
many purposes—grazing, forage, timber, water resources, recreation, etc.—that
under some circumstances were incompatible and under others wholly consistent. The act ended with a disclaimer, however, to the effect that multiple use
was not to be taken as meaning the achievement of a "combination of uses that
will give the greatest dollar return or the greatest unit output." Though advocates of new national parks or recreation areas frequently argue that a dollar
figure can be given to the value a nearby community will receive should the unit
be created, such figures are guesswork at best. When uses incompatible with the
resource are ruled out, there may be no direct economic gain at all. Park professionals know this, and LSR knew it (though he was not above invoking economic gain to offset the equally ambiguous argument of economic loss used
against park proposals), but the public did not always understand it. Thus the
idea of multiple use came, especially in the minds of committed environmentalists, to suggest a willingness to compromise environmental values for economic gain. The Bureau of Outdoor Recreation was committed to enlarging
the concept of multiple use to embrace an outdoor recreation component, and
to many environmentalists this placed the bureau in the camp of the measur-
ers of economic benefits, handicapping the BOR in its efforts to promote new
park opportunities and conflating recreation with economic development. Certainly some new Park System units emerged from the BOR process, most
notably North Cascades National Park and Assateague National Seashore, but
without the Land and Water Conservation Fund, the BOR would have proved
a disappointment. Still, it, like ORRRC, also prepared the way for special commissions and councils in the Johnson and Nixon administrations on environmental quality, recreation, and natural beauty, and while the subjects were different, LSR was as concerned for the last as he was for the first.

VIII
In Quest of Natural Beauty

Following President Kennedy's assassination on November 22, 1963, Vice President Lyndon B. Johnson succeeded him. On May 22, 1964, before a massive crowd of students and parents in the football stadium of the University of Michigan in Ann Arbor, President Johnson declared that the protection of natural beauty was to be one of the three pillars of his "Great Society." His vision was large, and it demanded large responses; his conclusion was almost Biblical: "Once man can no longer walk with beauty or wonder at nature, his spirit will wither and his sustenance be wasted." The next morning LSR was observed reading the speech, then the editorial crafted by John Oakes, senior editor of the *New York Times'* editorial page. "I can't believe it!" Laurance was heard saying, "Imagine!" He had not expected such language from Johnson, and he was at once deeply engaged.

In August 1964, Laurance Rockefeller received a letter from Lady Bird Johnson, the president's wife. She had accompanied Secretary Udall to Grand Teton National Park, where she and others enjoyed a float trip down the Snake River. Afterward she had stayed at LSR's JY Ranch. She wrote to "Mr. Rockefeller" to tell him how much his vision and taste meant to her, and he responded warmly. Though they had met before, they soon found that they shared enthusiasms, a common definition of natural beauty, and an intense desire to make America "the beautiful" once again. LSR's invitation to become a citizen advisor to the president followed Johnson's triumphant election to his office in his own right in November. In December Johnson announced his intention to appoint a commission to review public land policy as mandated by the Public Land Law Review Act, and he did so in February 1965. This commission was to undertake the complex task of reviewing law and land policy with respect to the use of public lands in the United States, a subject that was always of great, and generally contentious, issue in the western states in particular. The Fish and Wildlife Service, the Forest Service, and the National Park Service held lands throughout the nation—the Bureau of Land Management's holdings were all west of the Mississippi River—and they interpreted the three thousand relevant laws somewhat differently and managed their responsibilities to quite different goals.[1]

Rockefeller was an obvious person to appoint to the Public Land Law Review Commission, since each of these land-holding agencies had presented reports to the Outdoor Recreation Resources Review Commission. The other commissioners, largely trained in law, were Robert Emmet Clark of New Mexico, Maurice K. Goddard of Pennsylvania, Philip H. Hoff of Vermont, Mrs. John Glessner Lee of Connecticut, and H. Byron Mock of Utah, all well-placed and largely from the east, which was unusual for such bodies. The commission's charge was a more narrow one than LSR anticipated, however, for Congress directed it to focus first on federal policy with respect to mineral rights and extraction. Service on this commission did not prove to be the same happy experience that ORRRC had been, for the subject was highly technical, the group was fractious and slow moving, and as LSR was not the chair, he could not bring his customary sense of urgency and orderliness to the proceedings. He also felt the commission often bowed to local interests, especially in the Rocky Mountain West. The commission's final report, *One Third of a Nation's Land,* which appeared in 1970, was the first comprehensive assessment of public land laws in the twentieth century. The report received little attention and had little impact at the time, though it would undergird several future reports and provide a useful base for a potentially more influential study (to which LSR wrote a foreword) by Henry Diamond and Patrick Noonan on *Land Use in America* that was released in 1996. When Rockefeller looked back on his service with the commission years later, he dismissed it as "an experience I'm sort of numb about."[2]

But President Johnson had other things in mind for Laurance Rockefeller. In January 1965, partially at his wife's insistence, LBJ decided to call a White House Conference on Natural Beauty, to be convened in May. Johnson wrote to Rockefeller to ask him to serve as "coordinator and chairman." This was something LSR could sink his teeth into, for it grew logically from the trend of his thought toward the end of the ORRRC report. The conference was asked to produce "new ideas and approaches for enhancing the beauty of America." It was to look to private action as well as to government, and at all levels. The president remarked upon the need to unravel the conundrum, that people moved from the city to get closer to nature, "only to find that nature has moved farther from them." He also reminded those who thought this a new interest on his part that he had spoken of the need to protect natural beauty even when he was a young congressman in the 1930s.[3]

The White House Conference was a resounding success. There were fifteen panels divided into two groups, one focusing on problems of the city, the countryside, and highways, and the second on action programs. There were nearly a thousand participants. LSR's experienced team, Henry Diamond and William Whyte, were co-managers of the conference, which was largely underwritten by the American Conservation Association. Except for opening remarks by the chairman and the First Lady, there were no speeches, everyone getting down immediately to working sessions, shortened by a rolling thunderstorm that forced people into the East Room of the White House, reminded of the force of nature by the smell of wet coats. Practical discussions ranged across highway design, the underground installation of utilities, what to do with automobile junk yards, the future of the California redwoods (then under discussion with Governor Reagan), the preservation of farm landscapes, and much more. The panels produced 190 often highly specific recommendations (two of the panels did not provide recommendations, one—that on highway design—clearly unable to reach consensus), ranging from the desirability of there being a National Council on Natural Beauty and Recreation to the need for the president to instruct all agencies of government to review their activities with respect to the environment, through cleaning up the headwaters and length of the Potomac River, to requiring the U.S. Weather Bureau to report smoke as "smoke" rather than "haze" in order to alert citizens to air pollution. In his closing remarks, Rockefeller said that the conference had recognized that natural beauty would be determined by the ways the American people used their air and water, their land and their countryside, and that education lay at the center of the problem.

President Johnson moved quickly to embrace the report and implement most of its recommendations. He instructed all agencies of government to review their activities with respect to the environment and to report forthwith. He proposed new national recreational areas, new forms of inter-governmental cooperation, a new look at the design criteria of the federal interstate highway program, and a review of resource management practices. Governors' Conferences were convened in thirty states, leading to the creation of new state environmental protection agencies. Within the year Congress sent to the White House thirty conservation bills. In May 1966, one year after the conference, Johnson established a Citizens' Advisory Committee on Recreation and Natural Beauty with twelve members. No one, least of all Laurance Rockefeller, could have been surprised to learn that he was to be its chairman, and he called it to meet hours after the president signed the order that created it. He would serve this and successor committees for ten years through three presidents.

President Johnson read his overwhelming victory in 1964 as a virtually unlimited mandate for change. He was determined to expand educational opportunities, attack sex and race discrimination, wage war on poverty, address the deepening problems of the environment, achieve victory with honor in Southeast Asia, prevail in space over the Russians, promote public financing of broadcasting and the performing arts, provide expanded medical care to the defenseless, in order to make America the most powerful, most compassionate, most competitive nation on earth. To aim so high was, perhaps, to invite failure on one or more fronts, but he was determined to try. He was filled, he said, with the "excitement of great expectations."

How to begin? LBJ turned to the idea of the task force, a group of people assigned a discrete task, working in semi-anonymity, outside the glare of the media, to prepare confidential, off-the-record studies and recommendations. He quickly established task forces on national resources, education, transportation, foreign economic policy, and a dozen other subjects. One of these was on the preservation of natural beauty. By 1967 he had up to sixty groups working in this way each year.

Laurance Rockefeller headed up the task force on natural beauty, and he took his writ as being large, not limiting his group to either preservation or to "natural" beauty alone. Told that membership on a task force, and the force's report, would be kept confidential, LSR set about exploring what best could be suggested to the president for his legislative agenda in 1965. He drew heavily on ORRRC's recommendations since they were still fresh and largely valid, and his task force was one of the first to report. This was fortunate, for the president read all the early reports personally, together with the Bureau of Budget analyses of them, while he did not follow later reports so closely.

LSR was too prominent a public figure for his chairmanship to remain confidential for long. People of a conspiratorial cast of mind worried that Johnson was creating a secret government through his task forces and that "the Rockefellers" were exercising too much power, especially since David was highly influential in Latin American affairs at the time. The result was neither secret government nor a transformation of society, but many sound ideas were, through this method, put before the president and his cabinet.

The president and Mrs. Johnson shared an interest in the so-called *new conservation*, which was an early term for what would soon be called *environmentalism*. Together they moved the federal government's concern for "the national estate" to new ground. Though LBJ liked to suggest that the call for national beautification was "Lady Bird's business" (and some thought this was a dismissive view), he was there, as Mrs. Johnson's press secretary Liz Carpenter wrote later, "every step of the way." Scholars who have subsequently mined the rich treasure trove of the Johnson administration's papers agree. The beautification initiatives also spoke to Laurance Rockefeller's soul, to his childhood, to his desire to influence the man at the top, to be a catalyst from behind the scenes, to contribute significantly to a public good. The program was not, as a few critics at the time implied, simply a social line into the White House, for any Rockefeller had a line on which to draw at any moment. The president liked to joke that when he tried to get a little nap in the afternoon, he would "more likely" hear Lady Bird and LSR "planting daffodils in the next room." This was not dismissal, it was affection, and no doubt relaxation from thinking about the unpredictable war far away across the Pacific. LBJ was, as one historian has written, "a water-respecting and horizon-loving southwesterner," and in LSR he quickly realized that he had a person with an eye for the picturesque, for the Olmstedian, improved landscape.[4]

A major challenge was immediately at hand: Washington itself, which was a blighted and shameful national capital. Lady Bird Johnson was just the person to improve her backyard. As India Edwards, a member of the Democratic National Committee, remarked of her, Mrs. Johnson would prove to be "one of the great women" of the time as she worked to "pull back the curtain on a beautiful America that everyone could see."[5]

Mrs. Johnson worked outward from the center, beginning with the White House, moving on to the city of Washington, and then to the nation. Worried that the restoration of the White House, begun by Mrs. Kennedy, would be put on the shelf, Mrs. Johnson persuaded the president to issue an executive order to create the post of curator of the White House and to establish a Committee for the Preservation of the White House. The First Lady chaired the committee, and it included the director of the National Gallery of Art, the chairman of the Fine Arts Commission, the secretary of the Smithsonian Institution, and others, with Nash Castro from the National Park Service as executive secretary. President Johnson appointed public members, including the distinguished historian Bruce Catton, and the committee began its work in May 1964. As the White House was a unit of the National Park System, the committee would report to the president and also advise the director of the National Park Service on matters of preservation and interpretation.[6]

No one could recall precisely who first thought of the beautification program—probably Mary Lasker, widow of the philanthropist Albert D. Lasker, whose deepest interest was family planning and medical research, though she also promoted many beautification projects in New York City—but Lady Bird Johnson so quickly and fully made it her own, her claim surely was paramount.[7] When she was a girl, going out onto Caddo Lake from her hometown of Karnack, Texas, she had expressed a particular interest in nature's beauty. Traveling with her husband during the presidential campaign of 1964, she later remarked, she saw so much that was ugly during the "early sunups and cold pancakes" of campaigning that she became even more sensitive to the uglification of America. Unshielded junk yards and billboards were her *bête noire*. It seemed that all over America abandoned cars littered the streets, sat in backyards, and crouched like beasts on the roadsides. Secretary of the Interior Stewart Udall was working on a book, *The Quiet Crisis*, throughout 1963, for publication the next year, and after Udall accompanied Mrs. Johnson to the dedication of the Flaming Gorge Dam in Wyoming, he began to draft some of her speeches. At the same time Mrs. James H. Rowe, chair of the Capital Planning Commission, saw an opportunity to expand Jacqueline Kennedy's work to the city itself, especially after a depressing visit to Glen Echo Park, along the Potomac, which impressed on her how polluted the river had become. Udall urged the president to include natural beauty in his 1965 State of the Union message to Congress, and he and Liz Carpenter talked about the message and decided to help Mrs. Johnson create a committee of thirty or so people to focus on cleaning up the Potomac River and on beautification of the city, with Udall providing staff support from the Department of the Interior.

No one was ever really satisfied with the word *beautification*, and at the first meeting of the ad hoc committee, beneath the portrait of Mrs. Theodore Roosevelt in the Queen's Room of the White House, everyone went around the circle of those attending and no one could come up with a better term. Later Mrs. Johnson advised against too much use of the word, which she felt could be trivialized, and the official title for the group became The First Lady's Committee for a More Beautiful Capital. In time, "First Lady" was dropped from the committee's letterhead.

The Committee for a More Beautiful Capital met twenty-three times between February 11, 1965, and December 17, 1967, and LSR was in attendance, sometimes with his wife, Mary, nearly every time. On the first occasion he was present as "an observer," for the membership of the committee had not been firmed up, and afterward Mrs. Johnson wrote to him to say that she could not imagine he had ever been only an observer at anything, and asked him to accept formal membership on the committee. His name had been placed on the initial list of invitees by Mary Lasker; her initial memorandum, which at the time spoke of a National Landscape Committee, listed fourteen possible members, all but three from outside the District of Columbia. The list was reviewed by Elizabeth Rowe, who added more names from Washington, with everyone agreeing that if he would serve, LSR was an obvious choice. He accepted at once.

Laurance Rockefeller and Mary Lasker were among the largest financial contributors to the committee's work, though Mrs. Vincent (Brooke) Astor, Mrs. Paul Mellon, and until his death Stephen Currier, were very generous as well. Walter Washington, head of National Capital Housing and later mayor of Washington, had much input, urging beautification projects around the city's predominantly African-American public housing projects. Through the Department of the Interior, LSR gave the committee its first gift of $75,000— soon some of the members created a Society for a More Beautiful Capital, to receive gifts directly—and two-thirds of it was used at Watts Branch Park, then a derelict area from which five truck loads of refrigerators and abandoned truck tires were removed and into which, after landscaping, playground equipment was put. The other third was applied to a plan to clean green oxides off the city's eighty-five sculptured memorials, choosing one statue as an experiment. The National Park Service—which was responsible for nearly all of the city's small monuments, memorials, and statues—wanted to clean General William Tecumseh Sherman first; he looked out on the city from Sherman Square, between Pennsylvania Avenue and the White House, and he was in very bad shape, suffering from dirty air and the moldering carcasses of birds. However, southern tempers were running high over school desegregation, and the more conservative members of the committee thought the symbolism would be misinterpreted. Unsuccessful efforts were made to find another appropriate statue for the experiment, and when Interior concluded that the starlings were about to do to Sherman what the Confederate army could not do, they went ahead with Sherman's bath and made no public announcement. This pilot project proved very expensive, and LSR came up with another $25,000 (which went to Jeanne d'Arc and an armillary sphere in Meridian Hill Park) to keep the momentum up and to attract donations from other members of the committee.

Rockefeller also gave $50,000 to launch a practical work–education–recreation summer program for inner city youth. This was Project Trailblazers, which brought educational and recreational programs to the Anacostia area where local teenagers were paid to turn an old theater into a neighborhood African-American heritage museum. LSR made a further gift of $25,000 to make possible better directional signage at each end of Theodore Roosevelt Memorial Bridge when the highway department put up giant signs that blocked the view to the Lincoln Memorial. As with all his endeavors, he made it clear that if these programs proved a success, he expected the District of Columbia to take them up: "ever a catalyst, never a patsy," was the remark of Sharon Francis, the feisty assistant sent over by Stewart Udall to help the committee with its rising tide of mail. Most of the programs did prove successful and in time various agencies of government, federal and local, took them over.

Following a presentation to the committee by Nathaniel Owings, landscape architect from Skidmore, Owings, and Merrill, whose quite extensive plans for Pennsylvania Avenue and The Mall would take a decade and more to complete, the group visited two park areas picked out by Nash Castro, the National Park Service's assistant regional director for administration, who attended all meetings and began the work that would lead to the planting of a million daffodils, thousands of dogwoods and azaleas, many hundreds of cherry trees, pink magnolias along Pennsylvania Avenue, crepe myrtle along New York Avenue, and other injections of color and charm into the capital city, beginning with the first plantings of decorative shrubs and trees on March 9. Over the next months, Castro produced a list of other needful parks in parts of the city, and LSR and Mrs. Johnson spoke often about this list.

There were, of course, disagreements on the committee. Rockefeller wanted to emphasize landscaping at public schools, the creation of more new parks, especially in the African-American section of the city, perhaps the construction of mini-skating rinks, and modest planting of trees and flowers. Mary Lasker wanted only flowers, trees, and shrubs in the central part of the city and around the airport and its approaches. "Plant masses of flowers where masses pass," she said, and wrote a check for $30,000. Brooke Astor underwrote school and community playgrounds, as did the Washington Post Company. Mrs. Paul Mellon provided the money to relandscape Lafayette Park, directly in front of the White House, and the Rose Garden and Jacqueline Kennedy Garden (now called the First Lady's Garden) at the White House. Lawrence Halprin, landscape architect of San Francisco's pioneering Ghirardelli Square, was brought in to plan some amenities, and he recommended parks along the Anacostia, a giant ferris wheel hanging out from the bluff south of Bolling Air Field, and an elaboration of the Kenilworth Aquatic Gardens, then in rather poor shape

IN QUEST OF NATURAL BEAUTY

and situated between two declining residential neighborhoods. LSR preferred Nathaniel Owings's presentation, knowing his work first hand from his Mauna Kea complex, and helped to promote the creation of a Pennsylvania Avenue National Historic Site under the partial jurisdiction of the National Park Service.

By 1966 Mrs. Johnson had a strong sense of urgency about the committee's work, for she felt that there were only two years left to her, suspecting and perhaps hoping that her husband would not run again in 1968. A person of enormous discipline, great strength, and intelligence, she was very skillful at blending the diverse interests of her committee to produce the most good for the city, for she was determined that she would be a First Lady who was known not for her words but for her deeds. She liked to tell the story of the French nobleman, Marshal Lyautey, who once instructed his gardener to plant trees along his drive. Why plant them, the gardener said, these trees would not grow for a hundred years. In that case, Lyautey replied, plant them today. For herself, Lady Bird wanted a very simple epitaph: "She planted three trees." Two more years would not be enough time.

The prospect of delay often was resolved by either LSR, who frequently stepped into the breach, speaking last at the committee's meetings and weaving a compromise position by which action could be taken immediately rather than waiting for yet another meeting, or by Nash Castro, who the White House social secretary, Bess Abell, called "the Miracle Worker." Energetic and able, Castro was also the administrative officer of the White House Historical Association, and he knew how to get the answer to a problem quickly. So many of the projects were to be carried out on National Park Service lands that he went far beyond presenting lists of desirable projects to become a "mediator and expediter par excellence." Where entire park design was involved, he generally wanted NPS staff to do it, for he was much too aware of how an outside architect or landscape designer could come in, create something quite glorious, and then go away, leaving the city or the federal government with an ever-mounting maintenance problem. Where the NPS was responsible for maintenance, the work was generally well done, but if schools or roads were involved, the work generally was done badly. Working with Walter Washington and LSR, Castro produced commitments from those who would benefit from the projects to look after them once they had been installed, and for the most part this worked well. LSR was impressed by him and in due course Castro would leave the National Park Service to work more closely with him.

Moving on a separate track, the Highway Beautification Bill was before Congress. Time and again the bill appeared on the verge of defeat, usually over some estimate of cost. The undersecretary for transportation, Alan Boyd, drew upon members of the beautification committee for help, and they all lobbied furiously to see to it that their Congressional delegations voted the right way. Lowell K. Bridwell, the head of the Bureau of Public Roads, met with the Committee for a More Beautiful Capital and the Citizens' Advisory Committee on Recreation and Natural Beauty often, and LSR saw to it that staff from the Bureau of Public Roads accompanied the committee members when they toured in Virginia so that they could hear the discussions of scenic easements and aesthetically enhanced waysides.

The Citizens' Advisory Committee was to the fore on this issue, recommending that federal highway aid to the states be contingent on route selection procedures that would give "full consideration to resource, recreation and aesthetic values." The Committee also urged that a special Scenic Roads Fund provide matching grants to states, that on lesser roads there be a moratorium on implementing a federal 30-foot highway safety rule as it related to the removal of trees, and that an outdoor advertising program instituted by the state of Vermont, perhaps in combination with programs used in Michigan, California, or Hawaii, be extended nationwide. All but the last were achieved by the end of the Johnson administration.

The billboard lobby was especially tenacious. It argued that it had a right to advertise along the nation's roads, that travelers needed information on how to find hotels and restaurants and which cigarette to smoke, and that restrictions on advertising were anti-capitalist. Signed on October 22, 1965, the Highway Beautification Act, commonly called the billboard law, passed by a single vote; no legislation that session presented so much difficulty or took such effort to bring senators into line. The president lobbied ruthlessly for it—some of his aides felt that he considered his and his wife's personal honor were at stake—and even after the act was passed, those in favor of beautification had to remain constantly vigilant. In 1966 Gerald Ford, congressman from Michigan and minority leader in the House, said that he wanted to abolish the beautification program and only the intervention of Laurance Rockefeller, on behalf of the Citizens' Advisory Committee, brought his fellow Republican around. Ford's view on highway construction, in particular, was purely utilitarian—he wanted the fastest, safest, least expensive highways possible, without regard to aesthetics or damage to historical or natural resources—and LSR found that he frequently had to speak or write to Ford lest the beautification program suffer a major reduction in funding. When the Highway Beautification Act was passed, both Mrs. Johnson's Committee and the Citizens' Advisory Committee were credited with crucial support at the needed moment.

The Committee for a More Beautiful Capital extended its work well outside Washington. There were several bus trips into the Virginia and Maryland countryside, again with Nash Castro as the coordinator, to plant trees, dedicate new highway waysides, and to scout out future projects. When the group wished to go further afield, especially to Charlottesville and to Abingdon, in the southwest corner of Virginia, Laurance Rockefeller often loaned his personal airplane. He insisted on flying with the First Lady, for as he remarked, how would he feel if anything happened and he was not aboard? Liz Carpenter organized even more far-flung journeys into the deep south, the midwest, and the Rocky Mountains, selling space to the press on the plane that took the First Lady to her destination, and using those sales to pay for the plane, so that there could be no charge of "jaunts" on the taxpayer's dollar.

While President Johnson's interest in issues of White House, capital, and national beautification was real, and he liked to talk with LSR about conservation broadly, he was a creature of politics. He was happily persuaded by Rockefeller to address the National Recreation and Park Association. In 1967 he asked LSR to chair a new Advisory Committee on Environmental Quality; he felt there was an obvious affinity between liberal Republicans and southern Democrats. Obviously there was a political side to the relationship between the two men. Johnson was working with David Rockefeller's Business Group for Latin America, hoping it could resuscitate a moribund Alliance for Progress. LBJ also was aware that he might well be running against LSR's brother for the presidency in 1968, for the governor of New York was the obvious leader of the Republican Party's liberal wing, and the crushing defeat of its conservative candidate, Barry Goldwater, in the election of 1964 might lead the Republicans to nominate the governor. Johnson may even have hoped for a public defection from the party by Laurance Rockefeller, though if he did harbor such hopes, he did not know his man, for loyalty to Nelson was one of Laurance's most deeply held traits. Secretary Udall might consider recommending LSR for the cabinet, and one or two of LSR's highly placed lieutenants might suggest to him that they were thinking of publicly joining the Democratic Party, but LSR would not, for all the respect he had for the President, the admiration he entertained for the First Lady, and the pleasure he took from his role as a citizen advisor to both, have deserted a lifetime commitment to liberal Republican values.

By the election of 1968, the question was moot. Johnson had taken himself out of the running. Nelson Rockefeller hoped to receive the Republican nomination but by June it was clear that the race was between Nixon and Reagan. LSR had no reason to support breakaway Democrats, such as Eugene McCarthy or George Wallace, and the latter was repugnant to him because of his history of racism. When on March 31, 1968, in a television address devoted to the war in Vietnam, Johnson abruptly announced that he would not run for another term as president, the question of whether Johnson's interest in LSR's advice and skilled brokerage on conservation matters was in some measure politically motivated became irrelevant.

Lyndon Johnson's presidency lasted for five years and three months. Notable for the raw energy he brought to all that he attempted, Johnson had wanted to rewrite the American political and social landscape. His contributions to civil rights, to providing medical care for the aged and poor, and to conservation and the environment would win him praise from most historians; his policy in Vietnam would earn condemnation. These years were intensely divisive, fraught with problems that deepened as time went on. When Johnson left the White House in January 1969, the nation was in turmoil, filled with hate, indecision, and cynicism; yet he had entertained the highest vision of what the American people might achieve. He had sought consensus and produced conflict.

In this context Johnson's concern for natural beauty, his White House conference, the committees that LSR chaired, and the work of Mrs. Johnson to achieve a more beautiful capital struck some members of the media then, some scholars since, as ironic at best. The week in which LBJ appointed LSR to the chairmanship of the White House conference, the Vietcong began furious attacks against American installations, and two weeks later Operation Rolling Thunder, by which the United States responded with the sustained bombing of North Vietnam, began. A decade and a half later a new National Park Service responsibility, a somber Vietnam Memorial, would grow out of The Mall, with 57,939 names inscribed on it, enumerating Americans killed or missing in the war.

But there is no cause and effect here. Fewer American lives would not have been lost had there been no interest on Johnson's part in a campaign to promote natural beauty. Johnson's New Conservation—indeed, all of the domestic programs of the Great Society—suffered deeply from the effects of the war, from its cost, its divisiveness, its creation of new problems, new wounds, and new failures. Still, the achievements of the Johnson administration, especially in conservation, were not trivial. No one can possibly say how those achievements and failures will be judged in fifty years' time. But surely the quest for beauty, contradicted as it was by the ugliness of war, was not a negligible matter. Perhaps the quest was naive, but it was no less sincere, or desirable, for that. LSR did much to keep that quest on track, and though it may be argued that by the 1970s there had been, in the face of undoubted victories for environmental advocates and an increased sense of the role of beauty in daily life, a countervailing increase in moral despair, how much greater might that sense of despair have been had there been no effort to strive for the beautiful.

What was LSR's contribution? Until the White House conference the pursuit of "beauty" had tended to be viewed as "woman's work," even as the concept of just what "woman's work" might be was beginning to change. Texas politicians and multi-millionaire businessmen did not concern themselves with the ephemeral, undefinable, even metaphysical world of beauty. Some Washington regulars, the inside-the-beltway crowd, had dismissed Mrs. Johnson's initiative as simply a First Lady finding something productive to do with her time. When the president endorsed the pursuit of beauty, some suggested that he was doing so to please his wife and to keep her occupied, while others more darkly hinted that LBJ was seeking escape from the growing dismay over the war in Vietnam. But LSR had considered this call for a rededication to natural beauty to be at the heart of one of the president's most important domestic initiatives. If some pundits doubted that *re*dedication was involved, not being able to find any previous time when Americans had paid much attention to beauty as a matter of national interest, they were simply making LSR's point. His association with the projects, to beautify the nation's capital and to extend concern to what was beautiful to towns and cities across America, gave it weight, validation, the backing of the "practical men of business": that he and not, say, the chairwoman of the Federated Garden Clubs of America led the new committee suddenly meant that it was acceptably masculine to care about such matters. Rockefeller's simultaneous efforts to find a compromise by which a Redwood National Park might be created were seen as a man's activity, even a businessmen's activity, for it involved high-level negotiations, getting down to the nitty-gritty with tough timber merchants. Concern for the ethereal concept of beauty was an entirely different matter, and because Rockefeller was unrelenting and unembarrassed in his effort to define it, find it, protect it, and promote it, he legitimized it as a corporate and male concern.

Laurance Rockefeller was well aware of the international implications of the New Conservation. He had traveled abroad often enough to recognize how environmental issues spilled across national borders. There was the time when he and Charles Lindbergh were traveling together, to Hawaii, to Tonga—where they persuaded the monarch of that small independent kingdom in the south Pacific to set aside several prime beaches as national parks—and elsewhere. Lindbergh was a member, by LSR's invitation, of the 1965 task force. LSR knew from Nelson's interests in South America, and from David's worldwide financial activities, how each problem was linked to every other problem. He was fully alert, in part because of the work of JDR 3rd, to the impact an ever-rising population had on resources, amenities, and the general quality of life. He understood that there was an environmental basis to political stability. He deeply distrusted the policy of defoliation in Vietnam, but LSR expressed his interest in international affairs most directly through his work on behalf of the worldwide Wildlife Conservation Society (see chapter IX), and in his conversations with and high regard for such individuals as Maurice Strong from the United Nations and René Dubos of Rockefeller University. However, LSR felt that his personal contribution was best made closer to home, through his role as a bipartisan citizen advisor to presidents, foundation directors, secretaries of the interior, and others.

For his work with the Johnson administration, Laurance Rockefeller received the Medal of Freedom. He remained close to the Johnsons, and after LBJ's death in January 1973, with Mrs. Johnson. He helped to promote the Lyndon B. Johnson National Historic Site at the Johnson Ranch in Johnson City, Texas, in 1972, and in 1973 the creation of the LBJ Memorial Grove on the Potomac. The idea for this memorial in Washington came up almost spontaneously as the Rockefellers, Brooke Astor, and other family members were flying to the president's memorial service, and when looking down, he realized that there must be something simple to memorialize LBJ, Brooke Astor said it should be a grove of trees. LSR and Lady Bird set out to raise $2 million; Nash Castro (who had been aboard the plane) accepted chairmanship of the working committee, which soon numbered seventy members; and on April 6, 1976, in time for the nation's bicentennial, the memorial was dedicated by President Gerald R. Ford and his Vice President Nelson Rockefeller: a massive block of Texas granite within a 17-acre stand of 980 white pines in Lady Bird Johnson Park on Columbia Island, close to the Virginia side of the Potomac. The result was a "simple, rudimentary, totally unpretentious" memorial, precisely as LBJ would have wished.[8]

In 1969 a Republican said to be hostile to environmental issues became the president: Richard M. Nixon. When Nixon launched his campaign, there was no reference to the environment in his various position papers. The suggestion was made from the Rockefeller corporate headquarters at Room 5600 that he should take an interest in the matter. Shortly, a Conservationists-for-Nixon Committee was proposed by one of the candidate's advisors. From 5600 came the opinion that this was not a good idea, and that if Nixon won the election there should be a transition team devoted to conservation with a bipartisan approach. Such was created and Russell E. Train from the American Conservation Association (the man LSR always thought of as "Mr. Conservation," resisting the title when it was applied to himself) became the chairman of the task force.

To the surprise of many, candidate Nixon took a genuine interest in conservation matters. Just over two weeks before the election, he delivered a radio address on the subject, using material generated at 5600. When elected, he proved to be a generally good conservation president. Nixon created a new fifteen-member Citizens' Advisory Committee on Environmental Quality and asked LSR to be chairman. Rockefeller would serve as chair until February 1973 and remain on as a member until 1977, into the presidency of Gerald Ford. The Citizens' Advisory Committee initially reported to a cabinet-level Environmental Quality Council, initially chaired by the president himself, and it submitted its first report in August 1969. Four months later Nixon signed a National Environmental Policy Act that established a three-member Council on Environmental Quality, to be chaired by Russell Train, to which the Citizens' Advisory Committee on Environmental Quality reported thereafter. In this way LSR kept his environmental concerns to the fore. Rockefeller and Lindbergh worked together on Nixon's 1970 environmental message to Congress and persuaded him to use the full resources of the Land and Water Conservation Fund to create new public recreation facilities near disadvantaged communities. Rockefeller also urged Nixon to convene a White House Conference on the Environment, to focus on the two vital building blocks, clean air and water, and he and Lindbergh proposed a possible "Rand Corporation for the Environment."[9]

The new advisory committee met every three months, usually in Washington. It included Arthur Godfrey, a widely popular television star, Pete Wilson, then the mayor of San Diego, Henry Diamond, and several others with established credentials on conservation issues. The committee's major report, *Community Action for Environmental Quality*, delivered in 1970,[10] was the product of close thought and careful writing, though it was neither as systematic nor as extensive as the earlier ORRRC effort. What it lacked in breadth, however, the slim report made up for in pungency. As typical with LSR-generated documents, it focused on recommendations for action, this time in four areas: open space and recreation (with much common-sense discussion of zoning), townscape and landscape, clean air and clean water, and the training of young people for careers in environmental affairs. The audience was the general public, for a concluding section on "follow-through" was addressed, as the title to the report made clear, to voluntary community action groups. Again, there were interesting side effects: a passing observation that few lawyers were interested in the environment was taken up by commentators and soon a new field was springing up in the nation's law schools, not because of the report though clearly pricked by it; comments on how to capitalize on bad breaks, how to stage public meetings for maximum impact, how to use the media, were all surprisingly direct for a government-initiated document. The prose bore the acknowledged imprint of William H. Whyte once again. Broadly distributed to the media, the National Conference of Mayors, universities, and environmental groups, the report resulted in a three-part television series, "Mission: Possible" (the title a take-off on a widely followed spy thriller program), sponsored by the Xerox Corporation, which, after prime-time airing on the American Broadcasting Corporation, was shown on two hundred public television network stations in 1971.

That year, with the scientist René J. Dubos of Rockefeller University and Tom McCall, the liberal and environmentally minded Republican governor of Oregon, who lobbied hard for the position, as new members, the advisory committee focused on how to stretch the environmental dollar. Steadily the committee's emphasis moved toward public purpose–private partner relationships, toward innovative ways of getting the dynamic motor of capitalism to help achieve environmental goals. With the creation of an Environmental Protection Agency in 1970, the road from ORRRC had merged with dozens of roads from other distant points, with the committee at last reporting to a sub-cabinet independent agency of the kind LSR always had envisaged.

LSR continued his practice of brokering funds for environmental reports through one or another of his philanthropic organizations. In 1972 he persuaded the Rockefeller Brothers Fund to underwrite a new task force to study land utilization and urban growth. This fund was the vehicle for collective as well as many individual philanthropies of each of the brothers. From its creation in 1940, it was involved in numerous activities. Once the fund came into "big money"—JDR, Jr.'s gift of $58 million in 1952—it supported New York's Museum of Modern Art, the Population Council, and programs for equal rights, environmental integrity, and civic values. The brothers met at 5600 or Pocantico as equals and talked out their priorities with respect to funding. For the most part they remained markedly consistent, some would say stubborn, and this meant that at times there was friction between them.

Here too, as always, LSR tended to be the conciliator, drawing his brothers toward compromise positions, though with a leaning toward Nelson's positions in general, while never losing sight of his own goals for conservation and the Memorial Sloan-Kettering Cancer Center. There was, as one would expect, disagreement on how prudent it was to make capital grants of one sum or another, with Laurance and David pressing for larger grants, arguing in favor of expending half the fund's endowment. LSR for twenty-two years led RBF as either president or chairman.

The new task force included LSR as chairman, Henry Diamond (at the time Commissioner for the New York State Department of Environmental Con-

servation), Pete Wilson, still mayor of San Diego (later senator from and subsequently governor of California), Paul Ylvisaker, dean of the Graduate School
of Education at Harvard University, Vernon Jordan, executive director of the
National Urban League, and other figures prominent in the civic and business
communities. Published in 1973, the task force report, *The Use of Land: A Citizens'
Policy Guide to Urban Growth*,[11] was edited by William K. Reilly, then director of
The Conservation Foundation and future head of the Environmental Protection Agency in the Bush administration. It was a major document, unlike the
public relations gestures that so often issue forth from committees appointed
to assure some constituency that something is being done about a perceived
problem. The report concluded that the time was past when governmental programs could hope to remedy the defects of urban growth. It spoke eloquently
of the failure of many suburban communities to provide adequate housing for
low income people, of the dehumanization of once prosperous downtown
areas that were empty of charm by day and empty of people by night. Still, the
conclusion was hopeful in tone, for the task force recognized how quickly an
aroused citizenry could bring change in a democracy. The sense of resignation
one often detected in reports of the late 1960s and early 1970s was replaced
with a quick-step admonition to act immediately, indeed in time for the
nation's bicentennial, by then only three years in the future.

LSR, as a citizen advisor, felt this report was a model for future citizen participation. It was far-ranging, invoking comparisons with other nations, and it
drew upon case studies in New York, Florida, Colorado, and California. It was
realistic, for it recognized that the nation would continue to grow. It supported
his lifelong contention that protection and use could cohabit, that with appropriate regulations on development, sufficient public involvement, and a greater
sense of responsibility toward the land that nurtured society, the nation could
protect "the beauty of our countryside, coastal lands and mountains; and the
delicate rhythms of nature" without shutting out any segment of the population. The report outlined what the individual citizen could do to help shape the
environment. Hailed as ground-breaking, as the best summary of the dilemmas
of development available, and even as unusually readable, the report stepped
well back from the recommendations of most of its predecessors in its recognition that Americans had grown skeptical about the efficacy of centralized
governmental regulation.[12]

By the time *The Use of Land* appeared, Laurance Rockefeller no longer was
chairman of the advisory committee, having been succeeded by Henry Diamond. Various members had urged that he be reappointed to the chair, as the
"guiding light, leader and inspiration," for so many years, but he did not want

this though he accepted reappointment to the committee as an ordinary member. LSR felt that the many reports, good as the last one was, were becoming somewhat repetitive. Almost from the moment of Nixon's easy re-election in 1972, the president was beleaguered by the growing Watergate investigation, and Rockefeller found him increasingly inaccessible.[13] Then, in August 1974, when Nixon resigned the presidency and was replaced by his vice president, Gerald Ford, the man who had spoken bitterly against Johnson's beautification efforts, especially of highways, Rockefeller sensed that the president's heart was not in the work of the Citizens' Advisory Committee. McCall, having made strongly anti-Nixon remarks in public, left the committee, and in 1975 became a member of the board of The Conservation Foundation. The federal environmental agenda was receding, problems in New York State were calling, and when President Ford appointed Laurance's brother Nelson to the vice presidency, LSR concluded that prudence and integrity dictated withdrawal from the Washington political scene.

LSR had experienced a remarkable period of public exposure and influence for a person as reticent as he. He had served five presidents in succession, and that was enough. He would remain ever hopeful and nationally active through the conservation doldrums that followed the Carter administration, most particularly under President Ronald Reagan. A 1988 report of the president's special Task Force on Outdoor Recreation Resources and Opportunities, a group from which LSR was notably absent, marked a stark contrast. Badly written, the product of scissors and paste, the report began with an egregious typographical error (the misspelling of the word *President*) symbolic of the apparent indifference that lay behind it. The task force was made up of mid-level and lower figures from within the government, and it included not one person from the Department of the Interior. It contained fifty-nine references set against an entire volume of bibliography that had accompanied the ORRRC reports. It made no recommendations. Frustratingly, Reagan's secretary of the interior, James Watt, was refusing to use the Land and Water Conservation Fund as intended. Understandably, matters closer to home came to dominate LSR's agenda into the 1990s. Still, when he looked back on the many reports that emerged from his chairmanships, LSR saw each stage as the unfolding of a map, as the nation "evolved ... into renewal." He had been, he felt, "on a moving train." That map and train now led to New York once again.

The battle for natural beauty had not been won—indeed, it could never be definitively won—any more than battles against ignorance, racism, drugs, or apathy could be definitively won. Rockefeller thought of these years as a citizen advisor to presidents with great affection, as a time when he and often

Mary were involved in matters that reflected his renewed search for the spiritual dimension in life. He also thought of them as years when he had formed some of his most lasting friendships. He never failed to respond to any call from Lady Bird Johnson for assistance with beautification projects elsewhere, and when she founded the National Wildflower Research Center, near Austin, Texas, in 1982, he was on the first board and, in 1995, present at the dedication of the new center that bears her name. He seldom failed to respond to calls for help from the National Park Service, as when he helped to underwrite the Vail Agenda. He never stopped supporting new studies and new reports that would promote more rational, socially beneficial land use in America. Even so, in 1980 he was seventy years old, and he wanted to be more consistently attentive to matters in New York State and along the river—the Hudson—that ran through his life as it had run through his father's, for it had many intellectual tributaries.

IX

A River Runs Through It

Laurance Rockefeller is a New Yorker by birth. However much the air age and high finance made him an international figure, he would always return home, and home was New York. Home was an apartment in Manhattan, an estate in the Pocantico Hills north of Tarrytown, a distinct landscape with real weather and real seasons, where one could sense changes in America rather than buffer oneself against them. He cared deeply about many things, but a river ran through nearly all of those things: the Hudson River, the "Rhine of America," great, cold, glacially entrenched, rising deep in the Adirondacks, on the slopes of Mount Marcy, the highest point in New York State. As the mountains melt into spring, the Hudson flows down from the narrow confines of a flattened gorge, past the heights of Saratoga, where the nation staked out its independence, bringing frozen reminders of winter through the industrial corridor where Mohawk and Hudson merge, along past rising factory walls that, as much as any place in the land, gave birth to the American industrial revolution. The river deepens, broadens, moves inexorably between rising, slab-sided cliffs, past the homes of presidents, past old Dutch homesteads, past the mansions of the rich, sliding under the great brooding dome of Storm King and cutting through the Hudson Highlands, past Bear Mountain and High Tor, widening for Haverstraw Bay and the Tappan Zee, slipping by the hills of Pocantico and along the high palisades of the New Jersey shore, to flow almost imperceptibly into New York Bay to meet the sea. No river, not the James, not the Mississippi, not even the wide Missouri, has had any greater claim to being America's river of history. This was the river and the land that the Rockefellers saw as home. Here Laurance Rockefeller's interests in historical preservation, in conservation, in maintaining beauty in the landscape, came into personal focus in a way that was intense, deeply felt, and almost baronial.

In New York State LSR had four overriding conservation interests. Close to home he devoted growing attention to the protection of the great estuarine Hudson River Valley and its highlands, of which Pocantico was a part. Across the Hudson he received a torch from his father, to continue the growth and protection of the Palisades Interstate Park in New Jersey and New York, a torch he held high for forty years before passing it on to his son. In the city he focused in particular on the New York Zoological Society: its aquarium, the Bronx Zoo, and its satellite in Central Park. Upstate he sought to be the catalyst for converting the great Adirondack Park and Forest Preserve, decreed to be Forever Wild and so clearly threatened, into a national park and, as we have seen, failing that, into a more coherently managed and fully protected reserve. These were all in his backyard, part of the land for which, as a New Yorker born and bred, he felt personal responsibility. Each radiated out from the hills of home to a land he saw as spiritually his own.

The most long-standing of LSR's direct Hudson River interests was the Palisades Interstate Park. He became a member of its commission in 1939 and he served until 1978. It bound him to both his father and his grandfather.[1]

To fully understand the significance of this park, one must think back to the time when Progress was the dominant signifier in American society. To pay large sums of money to enhance a view was not the nation's ethic. For those who did have such a concern, often men of great wealth with large estates, substantial staffs, and knowledge—sometimes sophisticated, often not—of European notions of the groomed park (French), the "natural" wood and meadow that was in fact closely observed, trees placed just so, that they might appear casual while framing a view (English), or rustic rock shelters and hiking trail guard rails above splashing waterfalls and fern-green gorges (Swiss), the goal was to "enhance" nature. This was a human concept, of course, and it did not always include the fauna among the flora, for the one sometimes destroyed the other.[2]

The search for the scenic has been a nineteenth and twentieth century middle-class phenomena in the Western world, most especially in the United States. Roadmaps would denote "scenic routes," parents would take their children on Sunday "scenic rides" by carriage and, later, "scenic drives" by automobile. Americans would set off on the European Grand Tour, or more likely See America First, choosing "scenic areas" to visit in preference to art galleries, museums, and libraries. This love of the Great Outdoors often included shaping it to a more cunning eye.

Certainly Laurance had learned this from his father, whose carriage roads at Acadia were engineered, maintained, and curried to assure the finest views from the winding drives and the cut-stone bridges toward the sea. JDR, Jr., disliked the sight of dead trees, hence his quick willingness to volunteer funds to Horace Albright to clean up the roadsides in Yellowstone.[3] Indeed, at Acadia he ordered the destruction of the beaver because their pond-building destroyed trees, and not until the 1950s was the National Park Service able to convince him that beaver were essential to the ecology of the park. Acadia became a built landscape to a large degree, and while it was less wild, few would say that it was less beautiful. Thus the shaped landscape, the protection of natural "wonders," and the framing of a scene as though for the camera was analogous to a great art gallery or museum, and this sensibility would mark eastern parks until the late 1930s.

The Palisades Interstate Park in New York and New Jersey is of this style. It is "the most notable example in the United States of interstate cooperation for the conservation of outstanding scenic features and the promotion of outdoor recreation."[4] Created and extended with public and private money, it represented a triumph over the encroaching forces of suburbanization. The palisades had gazed for centuries across the Hudson toward New York, increasingly a silent rebuke to those who would with graffiti put their name, school, or loved one ahead of the unmarred face of nature. As early as the 1860s it was clear that something would have to be done to protect the palisades. Even so, heavy quarrying continued in the trap rock on the west side of the Tappan Zee until near the end of the century.

In 1894 both states enacted laws that ceded the face and water frontage of the palisades from Fort Lee, New Jersey, to Piermont, New York, to the U.S. government for a military reservation. This would keep the area intact and one day the whole might be open for recreational purposes. The leaders of the movement to protect the land running back from the top of the cliff were Andrew H. Green, the founder of the American Scenic and Historic Preservation Society, and Governor Theodore Roosevelt, who appointed a commission empowered to acquire land in 1900. Major gifts from Mrs. Edward H. Harriman, J. Pierpont Morgan, Sr., John D. Rockefeller, Sr., and many others made it possible to develop a park northward, and in 1910, 1917, and 1924 bond issues approved by public vote provided the funds for extensive additional purchases.

In 1917, The Rockefeller Foundation also donated $1 million and in the following years the foundation, the Laura Spelman Rockefeller Memorial, and individual members of the family would provide millions more to acquire land, set up summer camps, construct park buildings, and build trails.

Palisades Interstate Park was especially important in the evolution of landscape design. Given its location, it was the focus of much attention, and more than any other park in New York or New Jersey, it represented the Rockefellers' concept of how to combine conservation and use within a park. The Bear Mountain unit—an area that had been intended as the site of a state prison—would be extensively developed and its inn and other buildings would be the prototype for the "rustic style" throughout the East. The Storm King Highway, carved out above the Hudson in the 1920s, would (together with Acadia) set the early standard for attractive and functional highway guard rails; and the majestic great cliffs that one could see from New York's Hudson River shoreline, running from Fort Lee, on the Jersey side, north to the state line, were made accessible, yet protected, by the building of a parkway that was for its time a model of efficiency and beauty.

JDR, Jr., made $11 million in land available so that the scenic area between the federal highway that snaked along the western cliffs to the New Jersey–New York line and the edge of the palisades also could be protected. Night clubs and other inappropriate structures were removed, lookout points, wayside automobile parking areas, and center island gasoline stations were constructed, and the whole of the land along the New Jersey cliffs was bound up by the beautifully designed and landscaped length of the new parkway. Constructed between 1947 and 1958, forty-two miles long, running between the George Washington and the Bear Mountain bridges, this was the most attractive of the several new parkways that would send their tentacles out from New York City toward the north.

In the 1940s the very notion that a highway should be regarded as beautiful seemed anachronistic to some. But when the parkway system was built from New York City into Westchester County, when the Merritt Parkway was constructed from the state line deep into Connecticut, and when the Palisades Parkway was designed for the west escarpment of the Hudson River, aestheticians, highway engineers, and conservationists, too, called them beautiful. By any comparative standard, this judgment was and is correct. Those responsible for the design of the Westchester and Palisades parkways were also the principal advisors on the construction of the Skyline Drive in Shenandoah National Park in Virginia.[5]

Laurance Rockefeller was appointed a member of the Palisades Interstate Park Commission by Governor Herbert H. Lehman on September 12, 1939, when he was twenty-nine years old. He was chairman of the commission's finance committee, then secretary of the commission from 1941 to 1960, vice president until 1970, and president until 1977, resigning from the commission the next year in order to clear the way for Governor Hugh L. Carey to appoint LSR's son Laurance to the commission early in 1979. "Larry," as he often was called to distinguish him from his father, would serve as vice president from 1986 to 1991 and, from 1991 to 1995, as president of the commission. LSR had been on the commission for forty years; father and son thus served for well over half a century.[6]

The Rockefeller stamp was clear on this land even before LSR joined the commission, through the family's many gifts, which included the steamboats *Clermont* and *Onteora*, which from 1920 brought thousands of city dwellers to Bear Mountain State Park. LSR's own first gift, in 1942, was for the acquisition of land for Tallman Mountain State Park. The Rockefeller Brothers Fund and Jackson Hole Preserve, Inc., over the years made additional large gifts. In 1960, when LSR became vice chairman of the New York State Council of Parks, under Robert Moses, he insisted that more had to be done in the Hudson River Valley and in 1965 he led the way in acquiring Iona Island, with its historic marsh. Few places along the Hudson are more symbolic of the way in which, despite repeated human adaptations of the environment, a site might be brought back into harmony with nature and made part of a significant park. Over twenty acres of this three hundred acre island had been devoted to vineyards in the mid-nineteenth century, and more than three thousand pear trees had borne fruit for years. The West Shore Railroad had cut across the island via a causeway at one end and a trestle at the other, and there had even been a railroad station. The island had also been the location of a spectacular train wreck. In the 1870s Iona was the site of a summer resort reached by steamers from New York City. The island also was a U.S. Naval Arsenal from 1900 until the end of World War II, was used by the government to store rubber, and sported an iron shot tower. In short, Iona Island was scarcely an untouched nature preserve, though the fact that two-thirds of it was a marshy meadow had helped protect it somewhat. If this island could recover, surely many points along the Hudson Valley could be saved.

Incorporated into Bear Mountain State Park, Iona did recover. Designated a National Natural Landmark in 1974 for the many rare plants found there, and a National Estuarine Research Reserve in 1983 for its outstanding ecological value, Iona so extensively revived that it was proposed as one of four suggested segments recommended by the National Parks and Conservation Association in 1988 for a potential Hudson River Valley unit of the National Park System. Where multiple use had once been applied, single-purpose management had brought the land and its brackish marsh back to life, proving that it was possible to use the land in different ways and then, at the appropriate moment, to restore it.

During LSR's tenure as president of the Palisades Interstate Park Commission, the system of parks grew from 64,000 to 81,000 acres (and the number of park units from 12 to 23). The largest single acquisition, Minnewaska State Park, was inveigled by LSR through the federal Land and Water Conservation Fund and matching state grants, when in 1971 Rockefeller traveled to Washington to meet with President Richard Nixon's secretary of the interior, Walter Hickel, and persuaded him to allocate $2.5 million to fund a master plan and to purchase 6,995 acres of land (the park now approaches 12,000 acres). LSR also helped with the acquisition and development of Rockland Lake State Park, and under his leadership the commission developed Fort Lee Historic Park and reconstructed the historic Bear Mountain Inn originally built in 1915. During LSR's term snowmobiles, power boats, and "artificially induced form[s] of recreation" requiring infrastructure were banned in natural areas, and park visitors increased from 1.5 million to 6.2 million. Where formal recreational parks were concerned, LSR and the commission measured achievement in such statistics, for as he had remarked in connection with the ORRRC report, he believed that the number of people using recreational facilities was an important indicator of the nation's health.

There were contrary views, of course. A hostile report on LSR's view of conservation had been offered by David E. Pesonen of the Sierra Club in 1962. Pesonen was a research assistant on the wilderness portion of the ORRRC report. He denounced the document as a compromise, a set of volumes that would "look at home on a shelf crowded with dusty plans for The Orderly Development . . . and The Wise Management of . . ." America's future. He feared that the report's emphasis on recreation would militate against the preservation of wilderness areas, and that LSR's advocacy of multiple use to meet the nation's contending needs in a balanced way would produce a succession of compromises rather than victories for the nation's "irreplaceable scenic and recreational sites." Pesonen was particularly fearful of a proposed nuclear power plant that the Pacific Gas and Electric Company planned to build on Bodega Bay, just north of Point Reyes in California.[7] However, his fear might more directly have been addressed had he been thinking of another power company in another irreplaceable scenic site: the Consolidated Edison Company of New York and Storm King Mountain on the Hudson. Here the advocacy of compromise in the interests of both recreation and power would be tested against a position of no compromise on the part of the growing environmentalist movement.

On September 23, 1962, the Nature Conservancy, a national nonprofit group that was buying natural areas to "bank" them for long-term protection, established a committee to consider whether Beacon Mountain should be purchased. This mountain, on the east side of the Hudson, dominated the Highlands as Storm King did the west side. The committee did not consider Storm King, for they thought it was safely protected by the Palisades park authority. Four days later the chairman of Consolidated Edison, the prime supplier of electrical power to New York City and downstate areas generally, announced its intention to create the largest privately owned pumped storage hydroelectric plant in the world. Initially identified as simply being "near Cornwall, New York," the announcement did not mention that a tunnel for the massive hydroelectric pumping station would obtrude directly on the face of Storm King and would be, if permission were given, inside state park boundaries.[8]

The resulting controversy is worthy of a fresh new book unto itself. It was the most dramatic clash over industry versus conservation of the decade. The ensuing legal battle lasted for seventeen years and, to many historians, marked the definitive shift from conservation to environmentalism as a public concern. It pitted Nelson and Laurance Rockefeller against a wide range of conservation agencies and organizations, including the Department of the Interior, and led to the charge that Nelson, in particular, was a "cosmetic" conservationist. It gave rise to a significant new local force, Scenic Hudson, Inc. The controversy seriously damaged the credibility of the utilities industry, as Consolidated Edison proceeded in a high-handed way against those who opposed the project. When Con Ed studies were shown to be biased, incomplete, and incompetent, it drove public opinion against the giant power producer.

The pumping station was intended to provide reserve power for peak capacity needs in New York City, and with the Cold War at its height, there was a sense that America's largest city was vulnerable without such reserves. New York and its suburbs were growing and new sources of power seemed inevitably needed. Yet Consolidated Edison handled its assault on Storm King so badly, when New Yorkers were confronted with the most serious power blackout in American history, on December 29, 1965, leaving thousands of people without heat or light and hundreds stranded high above ground in the city's tall buildings, the public and the media did not conclude that more power was needed but that Con Ed was so guilty of mismanagement, the company could not be trusted to be honest or efficient about the massive Storm King project.

Between 1962 and 1965 Governor Rockefeller remained resolutely behind the project, despite mounting adverse publicity, proposed legislation to block it, and even clear defeats in the courts. In 1965 he sought to meet the mounting opposition as political figures often do, by appointing a temporary study commission to consider how best to protect the many resources of the Hudson River Valley scenic and historic corridor which, in effect, might link the Adirondack and Catskill state parks. Laurance Rockefeller's foundation, the American Conservation Association, provided half the funds for the study.

As part of the exercise Arthur D. Little, Inc., prepared a substantial report on the prospective development of industry along the Hudson River and identified many sites for, in particular, the building materials industry, quarries, pulp and paper factories, bulk petroleum storage, and the generation and transmission of electric power. The report also noted that the Hudson was, in fact, an estuary as much as it was a river, and that the estuary extended virtually the entire way from New York City to the state's capital in Albany. There was very little gradient below its juncture with the Mohawk River and therefore no gravity flow of significance. For this reason the river had not built up a flood plain and for much of its distance was bordered by high, irregular valley slopes, steep bluffs and, south of Storm King Mountain, rugged embankments that gave way on its western side to the sharply pronounced and dramatic escarpment of the Palisades. For industry to develop, adequate rail and highway transport was needed along the river route, and for much of the distance between Albany and New York, any railroad had to hug the waterfront in search of escape from the slopes or strike off at an angle some distance from the river, as the New York Central had done for its west shore division. There were, the Little report concluded, few sites on firm ground for industrial development for over 150 miles up the river.[9]

The temporary Hudson River Valley Commission, chaired by Laurance Rockefeller, reported that an arbitrary strip definition to protect areas in the valley would not suffice, since a good bit of the land immediately along the river was protected already, while, given the topography, much that was a mile or more away and that fundamentally influenced the view to or from the river was not. The commission therefore recommended a visual corridor to follow the river, a concept then little known in the United States though well understood in Europe. When the commission submitted its formal recommendations, which included the creation of a permanent commission, the governor approved and the state assembly established the Hudson River Valley Commission.

The commission monitored development in the valley, identified land for new parks and recreational areas, and worked with towns along the river to promote scenic easements and to enhance the area's attractions and resource protection. However, it also almost immediately became ensnared in a second controversy, a proposal to build a Hudson River Expressway down the east side of

the river. Even before Little had completed its report, or the temporary commission had delivered its recommendations, a bill was introduced to provide for
constructing a new highway from near Beacon some thirty miles south to
Ossining, there to link up with the network of older Westchester parkways,
several of which had been promoted by New York City's czar for highways and
parks, Robert Moses. Two assemblymen and the mayors of seven of the towns
that would be bypassed by the new road opposed the bill, as did the U.S. congressman from the district, Richard L. Ottinger, while the Westchester County
planning commissioner, other assemblymen, and the mayors of towns below
Hastings-on-Hudson favored it, maintaining that a new highway would provide a scenic drive that would bring New Yorkers north along the river and, not
incidentally, would clean up unsightly sections of riverfront.

The Hudson River Valley Commission concluded that the proposed
expressway would provide motorists with better visual access to the river and
suggested that 95 percent of the traffic on the new highway would be passenger cars. Further, said the HRVC, new recreational facilities could be placed
between the highway and the river's edge. Tarrytown's newspaper strongly
favored the expressway, and many of the residents of the congested community,
which was clogged with traffic and noise when the General Motors assembly
plant (located on a point of land on the river) changed shifts, hoped for a
scenic bypass. However, under pressure from Representative Ottinger and many
local residents, and in the face of claims that the expressway would benefit the
Rockefellers financially—and the fact that the state highway department's studies of alternative routes clearly had been hasty and insufficient—Governor
Rockefeller organized the repeal of that part of the highway act that would
carry the expressway south of Tarrytown. Thus only seven miles, between
Ossining and Tarrytown, remained in contention. There, critics said, the state
was confusing beautiful highways with highways through beautiful areas and
was attempting inappropriately to ride on the coattails of President Johnson's
interest in national beautification.[10]

Governor Rockefeller had created the Hudson River Valley Commission in
order to take some of the sting out of the fact that the Federal Power Commission had given the green light for construction of the Storm King facility
in March of 1965. But this decision, and the existence of the commission, simply fed the fires of opposition, especially by the Scenic Hudson Preservation
Conference (which in time became Scenic Hudson, Inc.), which included some
younger members of the Rockefeller family, and notably LSR's son Larry. The
secretary of the interior, Stewart Udall, waded into the fray, opposing both the
Hudson River Expressway and the Storm King power project; the superinten-

dent of the U.S. Military Academy at West Point opposed the latter; and even when Consolidated Edison offered compromise proposals—to bury the power transmission lines under the river, rather than stringing them across the face of the mountain, to hide the plant more effectively, to reduce its size, to mitigate this or that impact, to create a fund for further study of the fisheries, and especially of the striped bass, and to move the facility just beyond the state park boundary—opposition grew rather than diminished. In 1966, with LSR in the chair, the Hudson River Valley Commission proposed even further lines of retreat for the power company, and clearly by that point LSR had realized that his personal support for the Storm King project was inappropriate and unwise.

There were charges at the time that the Rockefellers would benefit financially from the project, but this charge had little merit. Some opponents declared, without evidence, that LSR had used his position on the Interstate Park Commission to persuade the commissioners to support the pumping station. A search of the minutes of every meeting of the commission provides no support for this charge. The commissioners were prepared to see the necessary excavations for the pumping station take place immediately outside the Storm King boundary, but when Con Ed later proposed an alternative site inside the boundary, and the city of New York initially supported the proposal, the commissioners declined to accept it. LSR found the boundary distinction important and at first did not believe that he was supporting anything that might "desecrate" the state park. Opponents, determined to stop the project in its tracks, felt the difference between land inside and land outside the park boundary was not significant.

Read today the arrogance of Consolidated Edison is difficult to comprehend. When attorneys from Scenic Hudson warned that the rocky bowl Con Ed would construct might, as a similar pumped-storage project near St. Louis did, leak millions of gallons of polluted water a day, Con Ed replied that there might be "a little" seepage. When advocates of unspoiled countryside protested against the initial proposal to run overhead wires on towers as high as ten-story buildings, with a right-of-way cut 125 feet wide and ten miles long, a treeless line marching over the mountains, Con Ed simply said that high transmission lines were "a fact of life." When people spoke up for White Oak Swamp and its bird and wildflower life, Con Ed struck out at "misinformed birdwatchers, nature fakers, . . . and militant adversaries of progress." When early studies suggested that fish might be sucked up into the plant, Con Ed produced a tame scientist who opined that the maximum effect of the entire project on striped bass egg life would be that of a single active sports fisherman. When a Sierra Club witness complained that polluted water would flood a valley, a Con Ed witness responded that everyone knew that a large lake was handsomer than a small lake. When historians contended that the Hudson Highlands were important to an understanding of the American Revolution, Con Ed declared that "nothing of historical significance ever took place on Storm King Mountain, in Black Rock Forest, or in Cornwall." Such ineptitude is staggering, and it brought its own reward.[11]

In the end there was no Storm King pump storage project. Escalating costs, alternative and cheaper sources of reserve power, a recalculation of peak loads, the opposition of the growing alliance of conservation groups, the conclusion that the power project would damage habitat for Hudson River fish, the editorial voice of the *New York Times,* and a mounting apprehension by LSR that compatible development was not possible or desirable at Storm King, all contributed to killing the project. Ultimately, the Palisades Interstate Park Commission was the beneficiary of the failed effort by Con Ed, which donated the several hundred acres it acquired for the project to enlargement of Storm King State Park.[12]

LSR knew that a growing metropolis required power, and he had believed Storm King could be an exemplary instance of combining conservation and use as he often had advocated. He was not one to hide behind a NIMBY defense, the recently coined satirical acronym for those who would say "Not In My Back Yard" to any new power plant or highway without offering up an alternative solution. The nation did need power, a crowded metropolis did need motor access, and the question was not whether to provide it, but how. He had thought Storm King was the right place; in the end he agreed with those who insisted that it was not. Looking back, most historians of the conservation movement have concluded that LSR was wrong, too slow to change his position, and too committed to growth and to his brother.

It was, in a way, too bad that LSR and Scenic Hudson had come to loggerheads. He had done a good job with the Hudson River Valley Commission, gathering information and commissioning studies—unhappily the collection he built was dispersed some time later—and he had tempered his brother's rather headstrong insistence on full speed ahead. At the first public hearing on Storm King, when asked to stand up and be counted, LSR backed away on the technically correct grounds that, as chair of a purely ad hoc commission, he could not take a public position. This led most people to conclude that he was backing the governor, though in fact he was urging caution and more study. When he realized how incomplete and faulty the studies Consolidated Edison had submitted truly were, he was dismayed, for he had trusted the utility's science and was surprised to find it flawed and, quite possibly, distorted to serve its purposes. As the facts emerged, he made a graceful retreat, absenting himself from the conflict, for at the time he felt that any public break with his brother, indeed any confirmation that Nelson had proceeded needlessly, was to be avoided at all costs.

In time LSR and Scenic Hudson made common cause. There were subsequent joint ventures, and as LSR broadened his focus to the length of the Hudson, there was a gradual healing process, helped by the fact that his son Larry had sided with Scenic Hudson and gone to work for the Natural Resources Defense Council. When the Hudson River Conservation Society, which had been less militant against Storm King, was merged with Scenic Hudson, LSR helped persuade *The Reader's Digest* fund to provide support, and with Nash Castro as an effective conciliator, he became a player on the Hudson once again. On Storm King, even more on the Hudson River Expressway, LSR was behind the parade, not leading it. Many people were inclined to attribute the imbroglio largely to "Rocky times," a not very veiled reference to the governor, and they expressed appreciation for the way in which LSR showed no bitterness when the arguments put forward by Scenic Hudson prevailed in the public arena. In the end, Russell E. Train, the president of the World Wildlife Fund-U.S., mediated the river disputes, bringing to an end in 1980 a seventeen-year series of legal battles.

How did Laurance Rockefeller come to be on what history so clearly will show to have been the wrong side in the Storm King controversy at all? The question has many answers, but like so many questions, it has one big answer: dedicated loyalty to his brother Nelson, the persistent candidate for the U.S. presidency. No doubt LSR's conviction that it would be possible to have one's cake and eat it too—that multiple use could be made to work—was important to his slowness to back away. He had held to this view for a long time and in many settings, and he was unlikely to abandon it easily. No doubt his awareness, through his brother JDR 3rd, whose interest in population control he shared, of how the need for power was likely to grow as the population of metropolitan New York grew, and that to supply power would require compromises, was instrumental. Certainly his penchant for seeking the middle way, for compromise, as shown over the Redwood and Adirondack national park proposals, by which he not only felt that half a loaf was better than none but that in getting the half loaf one often assured getting a good bit more, was significant. Trusting his friends played a role, and so did his famed tenacity and persistence. Possibly economic interest was involved, but not critically, surely, for he had voted against his pocketbook on other occasions, and even his severest critics did not think LSR orchestrated matters over Storm King for personal gain. In the end, the desire not to let his brother down, not to back away unless the governor blinked, not to contribute to anything that would weaken Nelson Rockefeller in his administration (and thus in his long-running effort to capture the presidency, not to be abandoned yet) appears to have been the dominant factor at work.

In the end, Laurance Rockefeller did change his mind. Some observers thought that he simply backed away when he realized that he and the governor were going to lose, or that they considered the furor not worth the candle. No doubt such calculations were part of the decision process. Yet, there is good evidence that LSR truly had a change of heart, that when he saw that people he greatly respected, people who had been long-time advisors, like the former director of the National Park Service, Conrad Wirth, or Rockefeller University's noted microbiologist, René Dubos, opposed the plans for Storm King, he concluded that he had been wrong.

One of the most telling letters of protest came from LSR's long-time mentor and friend, Horace Albright, who served loyally on the Palisades Interstate Park Commission for sixteen years. Albright was a little disingenuous, for he certainly knew that Rockefeller was, at least initially, supporting the Storm King project; however, he wrote to LSR as though he were unaware of the facts, suggesting that he was informed only through "a friend": "Isn't it a pity that almost every very fine bit of scenic grandeur in the country presents strong potentialities for some kind of defacing commercial development or for some kind of military installation?" In the same breath Albright thanked LSR for sending him a copy of a book, *Country Beautiful.* The irony was not lost on his old friend.[13]

The significance of the Storm King controversy to the work of Laurance Rockefeller as a conservationist lies in the fact that he changed his mind, and in doing so, moved from being a conservationist to being an environmentalist. The essence of the latter, as suggested earlier, is in seeing the connectedness of all decisions and in taking into account hard scientific, factual, and statistical evidence. Conservationists tended to argue from aesthetics, or from guesswork—well-reasoned guesswork, to be sure, but intelligent guesses nonetheless—while environmentalists had more often hitched their stars to the scientific community. LSR backed away from Storm King not because he had no stomach for battle, for he had fought several, and not because he resigned himself to losing, but because all those studies of the impact of the Storm King project on the river that ran through his life convinced him that the trade-offs were not sound. The environmentalists had won the fundamental battle and he had aligned himself with them.

In fact, while Nelson still was governor, he and LSR worked together on a variety of successful environmental projects. Though political commentators at the time and some historians since have not given Governor Rockefeller high marks on the environment, in part because of his love for large-scale building projects, his environmental initiatives often were quite effective on a number of fronts, and during his administration New York was often ahead of the federal government in seeking reform. His Pure Waters Program, for instance, was supported by a billion dollar bond issue in 1965–66, a strategy promoted by LSR in 1962, when the federal government's expenditure on remediating water pollution was a quarter of this. New York banned DDT and other deadly pesticides before the federal government did and established a Department of Environmental Conservation in 1970, some months before the federal Environmental Protection Agency was created. Further, after Nelson appointed LSR chairman of the State Council of Parks in 1963, he and Laurance succeeded in centralizing operations, and in decreasing the power of some of the regional park systems, notably the Long Island State Park Commission, which Robert Moses had used as a power base. Under LSR's leadership, state parks were brought down the Hudson, into New York City, which had no state parks at all, beginning with Roberto Clemente State Park along the Harlem River. He was the moving force behind the Hudson Highlands State Park, and he and Jackson Hole Preserve, Inc., paid half the cost of those lands, which were left undeveloped. LSR led the Council in a quiet and effective effort to keep the Georgia-Pacific Lumber Company from building a wallboard plant in the Hudson Highlands, successfully persuading the company to abandon its plans for the factory and making it possible shortly after to add a vital piece of land to create the state park, while letting the governor take the political credit. Dedicated in 1970 and encompassing the highest land in the state south of the Adirondacks, Hudson Highlands became a wild gem of the Hudson Valley's parks.[14]

A reality of New York State politics was persistent upstate–downstate conflict. Upstate was generally Republican, conservative, rather inward-looking, and decidedly suspicious of New York City, its politicians, and its people. Downstate (which embraced the city, Westchester County, and Long Island) had the population and was the engine of commerce and believed that what it needed it should get. It tended to be Democratic, though with complex divisions. Populous upstate cities, despite their size, tended to identify with upstate views. Nelson Rockefeller was from downstate, but he was a Republican, and he was adept at getting the two states of New York to speak to each other.

Downstate wanted electric power, it wanted breathing spaces, it wanted to consume that which others produced from the land. It wanted upstate to provide that electric power, to protect numerous parks and pleasuring grounds even if their lands were taken off the tax rolls. But both upstate and down-state grew in population and, across the years of Rockefeller's governorship, changed substantially. Upstate saw New York City, in particular, as the source of problems.

Nelson Rockefeller was the most dynamic governor of the state of New York since World War II. From the time he first thought about running, in 1958, until he resigned in 1973 and, in 1974, became vice president of the United States under Gerald L. Ford, he was the dominant political force in the state. Friends and enemies alike would agree that he left a legacy of strong executive leadership, widely expanded the state's physical facilities (and left behind a large state debt), increased the number of statewide public authorities, promoted significant environmentally directed bond issues, and greatly improved guber-natorial–legislative cooperation. Friends called him "full of confidence" while enemies called him "arrogant," perhaps nearly the same thing; he was, as students of his governorship have written, the embodiment of pragmatic liberal-ism in American politics. He hoped his pragmatic policies would carry him to the White House, and he sought his party's nomination in 1960, 1964, and 1968, only to be denied it each time.

Nelson Rockefeller had charm, drive, and charisma. He was able to motivate people to work for him and his policies to a degree unusual in even the most dedicated politicians. He used his personality, his money, and his power to get things done for the people of New York and for himself. He evoked personal loyalty and relied on receiving it. He delegated authority well, counting on this loyalty to his policies, which were seldom ambiguous, and he broadened the practical authority of heads of various operating agencies, in particular the Public Service Commission, the Urban Development Corporation, the Met-ropolitan Transportation Authority, and the Commissioner of Environmental Conservation. He kept his staff on a tight rein but he also listened to those who held strong opinions that ran against his, though in the end he was not loath to issue a direct order. He counted on his brother Laurance's support and advice on conservation issues.[15]

Governor Rockefeller was one of the architects of the New Federalism, a term he made his own. People were growing restive under what they viewed as too many federal regulations. The Great Depression, mobilizing and manag-ing the nation's economy in war time, and the civil rights movement had led to a significant shift in power between the individual states and the central gov-ernment. Increasingly, emphasis on the flexibility of the American federal sys-tem, spread across a continental-sized nation, led to state initiatives in activities that, while they also required interstate cooperation, might be better handled at something less than the national level. Education, land use, laws governing the consumption of alcohol, for example, had always been more state than national. The Kennedy and Johnson administrations had returned to federal formulas to meet what many regarded as state problems. Rockefeller declared that state government had to be revitalized.

What this meant in practice for conservation was that the governor tended to believe that issues such as pollution abatement, water quality, and zoning regulations belonged to the state; further, he preferred to use state rather than federal authority to meet the recreational needs of the people. Time and again Nelson Rockefeller would resist what he viewed as federal incursions over issues that had environmental implications. He insisted that the Storm King project, the Hudson River expressway, and ultimately the Adirondack National Park proposal were state matters.[16]

LSR was more likely to look to the federal government to deal with conservation matters. This was his experience and that of his father before him. His chairmanship of ORRRC, his close connections with the National Park Service, his belief that highway beautification could be achieved best at the federal level, made him more likely to look to Washington than Albany for help. Unless, of course, his brother was in the state house, when LSR would propose a $100 million state land-acquisition program and nudge the governor to provide $400 million for park and recreation development. Between the 1970s and the 1990s, the recreational needs of the nation would become more state than federal. Even the National Park Service, which strongly advocated outright ownership of all land within the designated boundaries of a unit, and which believed that it had a special expertise in park management, began to work with local authorities. "Friends" groups—nongovernmental organizations dedicated to raising funds for and influencing programs in specific units of the National Park System—were formed across the nation, and locally such associations sought to help restore historic homes, rehabilitate abandoned landscapes, or clean up polluted lakes. From these friends groups grew the idea of partnerships for the environment, by which advocates and amateurs would work with professionals to achieve commonly defined goals.

However, partnerships and alliances of this kind also represented a slippery slope to the ethic of the National Park System. Local interest groups might persuade their member of Congress to pressure the NPS into accepting a worthy but less-than-nationally significant historic building into the system regardless of a standard that emphasized uniqueness and the superlative. Friends and partners sometimes tried to call the tune on management policies. Virtually unmanageable checkerboard patterns of ownership and responsibility would emerge in parks. Though LSR held out longer than most for the older national park ethic of integrity of site, quality of resource, and rigor of protection, his proposal to create an Adirondack National Park was his last major effort of this kind in the state of New York. Thereafter he too followed the path of the New Federalism, seeking partners in management. When, by 1995, there was a resurgence of interest in the Adirondack Park, for example, the interest was in a coordinated strategy for public and private sectors, in environmental quality as an asset to building a tourism economy, and in working out "partnership parks." This strategy was more likely in the 1990s to create new recreational areas; it was less likely to assure the total protection of a resource, or that the resource would be of national significance. Indeed, the question of national significance was tending to become less important, and as a result, much as LSR had feared, the National Park System was more vulnerable to new forms of "park barrelling." The solution for the Hudson River Valley, for example, became just such a partnership.

In 1970 the governor created a Department of Environmental Conservation. The Division of Parks and Recreation, which had been in the Conservation Department, was transferred to the Executive Department. The regional commissions remained the centers of power, however, until further reorganization in 1972, when operating authority was taken from the State Council of Parks and the regional commissions and passed to a commissioner of parks. That year the governor's cousin, Alexander Aldrich, became parks commissioner, and early in 1973 LSR stepped down from this chairmanship as well.

After Nelson Rockefeller left the governor's mansion, the Hudson River Valley Commission fell victim to budget cuts and lack of interest on the part of subsequent state administrations. LSR persisted in his advocacy of some type of Hudson River heritage corridor. In 1982, when the liberal Democrat Mario Cuomo became governor of New York, the situation improved. A 4,200-acre Hudson River National Estuarine Research Reserve was established in 1984, comprising four outstanding wetland complexes within the area of oceanic tidal influence, at Stockport Flats, Tivoli Bay, Piermont Marsh, and Iona Island. A vigorous program by the State Historical Preservation Officer and historical societies within the communities along the Hudson meant that by 1988 at least the most important of the historical sites identified earlier by the Rockefeller-financed study, including no less than forty-two National Historic Landmarks, were preserved.

In August 1988, Governor Cuomo signed into law legislation to create a Hudson River Valley Greenway Council. Its twenty members included the commissioner of the New York State Office of Parks, Recreation, and Historic

Preservation, the chairman of Historic Hudson Valley, Inc., the commissioner for transportation, and three state senators. An initial report that year was followed by a more elaborate one in 1987, prepared not by the council itself but by "a group of citizens concerned with the future of the Hudson River Valley." This group was chaired by LSR's long-time assistant on conservation matters, Henry Diamond, former commissioner of the New York State Department of Environmental Conservation, and included Nash Castro, then the executive director of Palisades Interstate Park Commission, Dana S. Creel, former president of Sleepy Hollow Restorations, Inc., and George R. Lamb, the executive vice president of Jackson Hole Preserve, Inc., all LSR enterprises, together with Patrick Noonan, president of The Conservation Fund, and the executive directors of Scenic Hudson, Inc., and the Hudson River Valley Association. Thus virtually all of the proactive Hudson Valley organizations, as well as LSR's principal conservation groups, had input to the report.

The document was quite without frills.[17] It led with a succinct statement of the greenway concept, which was in good measure Laurance's own idea for the valley, and one that he was contemplating in an altered form for his lands around Woodstock, Vermont. Several other people had also thought of the greenway proposal, of course, for most good ideas have more than one point of origin; certainly the idea could be traced back to New Deal Greenbelts or even to Frederick Law Olmsted's necklace of green parks around Boston. But the combination of natural lands, recreational opportunities and historical heritage sites implied by the Hudson River proposal bore LSR's mark. The report presented a clear case for improving the quality of life of all who lived along the Hudson, from Battery Park north to the juncture of the river with the Mohawk just north of Albany. The argument was unintimidating, unlikely to be viewed as threatening to private land owners, and did not directly invoke the specter of the federal government or the National Park Service. The report also reminded readers of how many sites along the greenway already were in the public domain. It argued for stabilizing "the Valley experience" and placed emphasis on "sense of place and community." A call for public participation led to six meetings at which testimony was taken by the council from two hundred speakers, nearly all of whom were positive.

This was a proposal for what soon would be called "cultural tourism." Readers learned that families often spent three days or a week at Williamsburg, Cape Cod, or in the California wine country: why not on the Hudson? They learned that the Smithsonian had concluded that Troy and its neighboring communities were the "birthplace of the American Industrial Revolution" and that a thus far not well advanced RiverSpark Urban Cultural Park could become "labor's Williamsburg"—and labor union officials testified to this effect. The report noted that already there were 82,000 workers who depended on tourism, earning $732 million, in the Valley. Without concerted action the valley would become less attractive and tourism would decline. Through the greenway, the report suggested, income would at the least double. Then-assemblyman George Pataki, who in 1995 would become the governor, and in 1996 successfully launched a $1.7 billion environmental bond issue of his own, was a strong supporter at the time.

For the report Laurance Rockefeller wrote a short introduction about the opportunity the greenway concept presented. He emphasized how the valley was an educational laboratory, how it was of international as well as national significance, how it had inspired America's first "great burst of artistic expression," the Hudson River School of Artists, and how a greenway could make the conciliation between the Valley's sometimes competitive interests possible. He concluded by quoting his brother when, as governor, Nelson said that Americans do not wait for government to solve their problems but like to tackle the problems themselves.[18]

Within the body of the report, the Cuyahoga Valley National Recreational Area in Ohio and the Big Thicket National Preserve in Texas were cited as examples of what might be done; both were units of the National Park System. Further, the Greenway was generically referred to as a national heritage area, a program supported by NPS, though without making reference to the Park Service. In short, without suggesting that the Hudson River Valley Greenway might be affiliated with the National Park System, LSR nonetheless opened the door to this resolution, to designate "a federal heritage area focusing a national spotlight on the region's role in American history."[19]

In 1986, the Rockefellers transferred land north of Pocantico to the state to create Rockefeller State Park Preserve: the first park in New York to bear the family name. At the dedication LSR spoke of the ecologically sensitive areas along the whole of the lower Hudson and of the more than a hundred significant historic sites in the valley. The Hudson River Valley could become a model for the restoration and preservation of historic and scenic landscapes throughout the country, he said. The river might yet become an American Rhine rather than an American Ruhr. It was still possible, he concluded, to use the valley to demonstrate how to combine the "economically productive, culturally rewarding and environmentally sound" in compatible ways, still possible for it to be protected in such a way that it would remain forever, like the school of artists that bears its name, an indelible part of the American memory.

The state legislature ultimately created a Heritage Task Force for the Hudson River Valley, and in 1991 the legislature passed a bipartisan Greenway Act designed to encourage communities to use federal, state, and private monies to create a regional planning compact for the Hudson River Valley, with the goal of increasing tourism by making the entire valley a destination rather than a series of disconnected and unrelated historic and scenic spots. The act gave two existing groups, the Hudson River Valley Greenway Council and the Heritage Task Force, a new mandate, restructuring the council to work with local governments while instructing the newly created Greenway Conservancy for the Hudson River Valley, which replaced the task force, to help communities and organizations implement the projects that emerged from the council's work. There were three goals in particular: to establish a coherent Hudson River Trail system on both sides of the river, to promote and protect agriculture both for its economic benefits and for the scenic enhancement it represented, and to resolve the entire valley into "a single tourism destination area."

The work began in 1992 with an inventory. By 1996 it had achieved much, though there was still a long way to go before "coherence" could be claimed. Still, by the omnibus national parks bill of that year, the Hudson River Valley Greenway was named one of six new National Heritage Areas that, in cooperation with the National Park Service, would become a new type of NPS unit, based on partnership rather than federal ownership. In this way the national park LSR had hoped for began to take some rough shape. American Heritage Areas were not, yet, precisely national parks, but they represented—to the pleasure of many and the concern of some—a significant step in that direction.

The Greenway Communities Council was founded in 1992 on the basis of a gift of $100,000 from Jackson Hole Preserve, Inc., together with five other much smaller grants. In each of the following years JHPI remained the largest source of funds, with the SURDNA Foundation also contributing handsomely. The council was chaired by Barnabas McHenry, who had worked closely with LSR on a variety of charitable projects based on the Lila and DeWitt Wallace/Reader's Digest Fund, while the long-time executive director at Bear Mountain State Park, Robert O. Binnewies, was an officer of the council.

At the point where the Hudson and Mohawk rivers joined, there had been established for some time the urban cultural park rather catchily called RiverSpark, inside the area of the greenway. This park celebrated work in American life, the dignity of labor, and the extensive development of industry in the area of Troy, Watervliet, Cohoes, Albany, and Rensselaer. Here, by late 1996, it was apparent that the National Park Service might create a new unit to commemorate those activities, and thus the greenway would be anchored by nationally significant sites at the top and bottom, and within its precincts (if one could as yet use such a term for so incomplete a process) the traveler would find four, and perhaps soon, five units of the National Park System. This greenway national heritage corridor is the product of many hands, LSR being only one, but it nonetheless realizes some portion of a dream he has entertained as long as anyone.

LSR's enthusiasms were contagious, and he could be most persuasive in getting other foundations, personal friends, and even presidents to support a favored enterprise. Since neither he nor any other person, however wealthy, could carry major activities such as Palisades Interstate Park or the protection of the much-abused Hudson River alone, and since his approach always had been to match the money of others and to act as a broker between donors and destinations, he continued to work to get the help of others in supporting his key projects in New York. In 1986 he gave $36 million to the Memorial Sloan-Kettering Cancer Center for research, but any medical research facility can swallow up money endlessly. Rehabilitation of damaged lands, great libraries, world-class art galleries, these are bottomless pits, as any member of their boards well knows.

Rockefeller was active in suggesting ways in which his friends and Hudson River neighbors, DeWitt and Lila Wallace, the founders of *The Reader's Digest*, one of the most influential publications in America, could use their vast wealth to help these goals. In 1967, LSR had invited the Wallaces to vacation at the JY ranch in Wyoming, and from that time they became increasingly close. They were happy to see the *Digest* be a conduit for making the nation's national parks better known, especially since the parks were, in their eyes, expressions of patriotism, and DeWitt Wallace in particular was an unabashed patriot. Wallace apparently was unhappy with the quality of leadership at his company, and a close friend who was also his banker asked Wallace whether there was anyone who could succeed him, and upon hearing that there was not, suggested that he select some well-versed friends and make them voting trustees of his stock. Wallace had an almost religious-like belief that *The Reader's Digest* had an obligation to its millions of essentially middle-class readers to inform and educate them and hold them to the paths of patriotism, and that money counted for less than these goals. Worried that after his death the top executives at the *Digest* might carry the enterprise in directions he did not approve, or would attempt to make the operation into a purely money-earning empire, Wallace decided to appoint two outside directors who presumably would stand above money, having no need for more themselves. Laurance Rockefeller was one of these. The other was Harold Helm, Wallace's personal banker and chairman of Chemical Bank. Wallace did so by a change in his will in 1973.

LSR saw *The Reader's Digest* as he saw *The National Geographic*, as the best possible publications through which a broad but not academic reading public could be induced to consider conservation goals as important in their own lives. He wrote for both and no doubt helped to arrange for articles to be placed in them. He shared the Wallaces' values in the *Digest*, against the advertising of alcohol, in favor of informative articles and a clearly expressed but not strident sense of patriotism, especially where matters of the nation's scenic, artistic, and historical heritage were concerned. For this reason some top level executives at Reader's Digest no doubt feared that he and other outside trustees might persuade Wallace to move in directions other than the ones they favored.

To some extent this proved to be the case. In 1978 DeWitt Wallace suffered a mild stroke; a week later his wife Lila sustained a far more severe one. It soon became apparent that by his will Wallace intended that his very considerable fortune was to be used largely for charitable purposes. There were many at the *Digest* who hoped to see this reversed, so that the Wallace fortune could be plowed back into the commercial business, and when the "outside trustees," LSR among them, appeared to be intent on major donations to charities, there was a good bit of bad feeling expressed.

The Wallace fortune went, in significant measure, to Macalester College in Minnesota, DeWitt Wallace's alma mater, to New York City's Lincoln Center, to the Memorial Sloan-Kettering Cancer Center, the Metropolitan Museum of Art, the Bronx Zoo, and the Fund for the Hudson Highlands. Those who wanted the money for other purposes were bitter[20]; yet there was plenty of evidence that both Wallaces would have approved of this use of their money, and it seems difficult to understand the suggestion that the outside trustees, of whom LSR was only one, had used the Wallaces' generosity badly in supporting cancer research or the Metropolitan Museum or the preservation of the Hudson Highlands, into which the Wallaces' home (and their interest in Boscobel, a Robert Adam–designed house built on the Hudson River opposite Storm King in 1804, and once called the "most beautiful home in America") readily fitted. Some commentators suggested these were gifts the Wallaces would not have approved, others said they were precisely what they would have done had they been able. One cannot really know. But one cannot reasonably fault the choice of such charitable recipients.

After the governorship of Nelson Rockefeller, during which three successful bond issues provided much of the financing for major assaults on pollution and major initiatives on behalf of the environment, environmental money became more difficult to find. Despite his wealth, no Rockefeller could do everything, and some problems were so intractable and the proposed solutions so expensive, only careful planning and cooperation between government and the

private sector could hope to produce lasting achievements. While LSR continued to fund some projects directly, he turned more and more to brokering
grants through the foundations he, his brothers, his grandfather, and father had
set up as avenues for giving at arms-length, or through sitting on boards of
foundations and conservation-oriented organizations. His longest standing
commitment of this kind was to the New York Zoological Society.

The New York Zoological Society—that is, the Bronx Zoo and its ap-
pendages—received enormous attention and devotion from Laurance Rockefeller. To some extent this was a matter of family honor. His grandfather was
among the founders of the society in 1895, and beginning in 1909 his father
included the zoo among his benefactions. LSR was elected to the board of the
society in 1935, when he was only twenty-four years old; it was his first major
board membership and his longest. He was made chairman of the executive
committee after his first meeting, the same year in which Fairfield Osborn
became the society's secretary, and he served on the board for sixty years,
including a term as chairman, three years as president, and (since 1977) as a life
trustee. LSR grew with the zoo, learning its important lessons, organizing a
safari to East Africa to bring back new specimens for it, and helping to bring
in a giant panda from western China for the zoo's exhibit at the 1939 World's
Fair. As William Conway, general director of the zoo from 1966, remarked
shortly before the society celebrated its centennial in 1995, there may have been
larger donors to the zoo "but no board member has been such a catalyst, so
imaginative and persistent in his interest, and so ready to go the extra mile."[21]

When the zoo opened its gates in 1899, administrators had emphasized rar-
ity and quantity. At the time zoos were virtual freak shows displaying exotic
wild animals for entertainment, even for shock value. By 1910 the Bronx Zoo
had 5,163 specimens of 1,160 species. Fairfield Osborn began to change the zoo
when he became president in 1940, abolishing cages, putting the animals into
open land that was constructed so as to resemble their natural habitats in
miniature. He recognized that the animals needed company, even affection, and
once told the keepers to act as though they were in an election campaign and,
if the animals were given a chance to vote whether they wished to return to the
wilds or not, work so that they would elect to stay in the Bronx. He (and other
revolutionary zoo directors elsewhere in the world) changed zoos from static
displays, sad incarcerations of cowed animals that often depressed the more
empathetic visitor, into sanctuaries, gene pools, and research and educational
centers. From cage to habitat, the zoo became a wildlife conservation park,
striving to forestall species extinction. In 1993 the Bronx Zoo's census was down
to 4,355 animals and 633 species, with well over a thousand births and hatch-

ings reflecting the new emphasis on captive breeding; it was still the nation's largest urban zoo. That year the Zoological Society changed its name to the Wildlife Conservation Society to reflect these trends.

This changed title is entirely appropriate. The society played a major role in saving the prairie bison from extinction in 1915; today there is an exhibit of such bison, opened in 1971. The zoo was instrumental to the saving of the Roosevelt elk, the Alaskan tundra wolf, and Kodiak and polar bears, all on view in areas developed between 1959 and 1966. The World of Birds exhibit—a spectacular indoor display of a hundred species opened in 1972—and the World of Darkness, opened three years earlier, bring visitors up close to life not to be seen on any urban street or in any suburban park. Since 1972, the zoo has been breeding gorillas, and since 1973 it has maintained a rare animals range, where three species not to be found in nature any longer may be seen: the Mongolian wild horse, European bison, and Père David deer. The zoo's snow leopards are one of the largest breeding groups in captivity. In 1977, Wild Asia was added to the zoo's attractions, so that between May and October visitors may ride a monorail high above elephants, gaur, Siberian tigers, and sika deer. In 1984, Jungle World was added just inside the zoo's south entrance.

LSR enjoyed the achievements of the zoo he served, recognized that for animals as for mankind, the quality of life was fundamental to an understanding of the environment, and he pondered the problem of species protection and diversity. How long, he asked, does society preserve animals whose natural habitat was gone? "How long do you play Noah?" LSR's portrait, painted in 1956 by Albert Murray, looks down from a corridor of the zoo's administration building, perhaps thinking of the annual occasion when he would invite the members of the New York Board of Estimates—the people responsible for the New York City budget—to his estate at Pocantico to play golf, using the moment to tell them of the zoo's accomplishments, supplying golf balls no matter how many his guests put into the rough, while talking of species preservation, of national parks around the world, but above all, of the very real needs of his beloved Bronx Zoo. LSR was a very good salesman when he wanted to be and for the zoo he was at his most charming.

The New York Zoological Society came to be responsible for much more than 262 acres in the Bronx. There was also the Central Park Wildlife Center, opened in 1988, the Queens Zoo, opened in 1992, the Prospect Park Zoo in Brooklyn, opened in 1993, and a Wildlife Survival Center on St. Catherines Island off the coast of Georgia, established in 1974. The society (often with the support of The Conservation Foundation) helped to create over a hundred wildlife parks and reserves around the world and to run 130 conservation programs in 50 countries. As William Conway reported in 1995, it "worked to inspire, to guide, or support . . . 89,253,816 acres in eleven nations" in the 1990s alone. In 1994 LSR wrote that the zoological collections were paramount to "conserving the world's important and varied species of wildlife" as an essential step to habitat preservation.[22]

There is another unit of the society whose history is not quite so bright. The New York Aquarium is the oldest public institution of its kind in the United States. It began in Castle Clinton, in Battery Park, at the tip of Manhattan Island. Since 1896, Castle Clinton was home to fish tanks, at first stocked with purely local fish, and after 1902, when the Zoological Society took over management of the aquarium, with more exotic inhabitants. The aquarium served New York well, and at its height received some seven thousand visitors a day. By 1939 the aquarium was the city's most popular attraction. Then in 1941 Robert Moses, bent upon building a vehicular tunnel between Brooklyn and the Battery, decided that the fish were in the way.

LSR was chairman of the Zoological Society's executive committee during the struggle over relocation of the aquarium, and his admiration for Moses was tinged with frustration over the older man's incapacity to listen. Many New Yorkers opposed Moses's initial plan for a Brooklyn–Battery Bridge, preferring a tunnel, because a bridge would destroy Battery Park, the aquarium, and perhaps the most stunning views of the lower Manhattan skyline; others opposed the bridge for its proposed cost. Moses was out-maneuvered on the bridge versus tunnel decision, and he was angry, for he was convinced that the cost savings of a bridge were worth the devastation of the Battery. When he reluctantly settled upon a tunnel in 1941, he promised Rockefeller that he would pay $10 million to move the aquarium to the Bronx. He never did so. Moses may have wanted to mollify this or that group when, despite careful cultivation and many friendly letters from LSR, and with no advance warning, he decided that the new aquarium would go to Coney Island, not to the Bronx. Research then and since has made it clear that, in fact, the aquarium could have been kept at its familiar and easily accessible Battery Park location, and Moses's biographer concludes that the irascible and imperial city planner simply wanted to exact revenge on those who had forced him to accept a tunnel instead of a bridge, for the advocates of the tunnel were also supporters of the aquarium's move to the Bronx Zoo.[23] Laurance was never prepared to believe quite so ill of a man whom he admired, however irritating he found him, and he was inclined to think Coney Island was chosen because it was somewhat more accessible to public transport at the time. In the end, Rockefeller took some comfort from the site, since its beach and ocean background provided an appropriate habitat setting for the fish. However, because admission was no longer free and because the new site was not accessible to weekday crowds as it had been in Manhattan, attendance dropped to about a quarter of what it had been.

In tearing down the old aquarium, allegedly because it would be undermined during the construction of the tunnel, Moses was defeated by a coalition of groups, including the American Scenic and Historic Preservation Society, in which Laurance was deeply involved. For Moses had set his sights on Castle Clinton itself, not just the aquarium. Never actually used as the fort Castle Clinton was intended to be when built in 1808–1811, it had been, in turns, a concert hall (in which the city had honored General the Marquis de Lafayette on the occasion of his triumphant return to the United States to whose independence he had contributed so much), the site of the first demonstration by Samuel F.B. Morse of the telegraph, and an immigrant landing depot before the construction of Ellis Island. Moses called Castle Clinton a "large red wart" on the face of New York, the city he was reconstructing, and because of his virtually unlimited power over decisions regarding city parks, he was able to condemn the aquarium and force its removal and then board up Castle Clinton and leave it to decay.

Building the tunnel did not destroy Castle Clinton, however. Those who had wished to save this bit of New York and the nation's history, with George McAneny as their leader and with Laurance Rockefeller among them, were able to have the building stabilized and, in 1950, taken over by the National Park Service as a national monument. It would reopen, a handsome space brilliantly refurbished, in 1975, and is now an exhibit area and the ticket offices for visitors to the Statue of Liberty and its adjunct, the new Ellis Island museum, both run by the Park Service as well, an ensemble of three unique properties that anchor the city at the final edge of the Hudson and protect its most vital visual approaches. Still, Moses had won on the location of the aquarium, and in the end the city had to spend $11 million on a cold new structure that did not open for fourteen years.

Rockefeller had seen from the outset that it was a mistake, whatever public transport might provide, not to put the aquarium next to the Bronx Zoo permanently, where visitors could take in two attractions on the same outing, rather than placing the two most public aspects of the work of the Zoological Society at opposite ends of the city. New Yorkers never gave the aquarium the centrality of affection they had when it was at Battery Park, and despite strenuous efforts, it did not become the pacesetter it could have been. Nonetheless, it too moved to breeding—its official title is the Aquarium for Wildlife Conservation—and it scored some notable triumphs, being the first to successfully breed beluga whales in captivity and conducting pioneer research on fish diseases.

As William Conway has observed, however, LSR did not often allow himself to be disappointed, and he could always be counted on at the crucial moment, whether for the Bronx Zoo, the Coney Island Aquarium, or the Central Park Wildlife Center, the last so much more accessible than any other facility of the society. With a staff of over four hundred the Society was like a small university, and Rockefeller was very proud of it. With Osborn (and a timely assist from Rachel Carson), he campaigned to raise $7 million for the zoo at a time when this was an enormous sum of money, beginning in 1946 and, with great patience, continuing to 1961. In 1957 the society and The Conservation Foundation sent a biogeographer, George Treichel, to Africa to study the destruction of wildlife, beginning the society's impact on the improvement of standards of protection in African national parks, and in 1968 Osborn and Charles Lindbergh worked together to draw attention to the plight of the Amboseli park in Kenya. Rockefeller returned to the battle in 1970, when the zoo set out to build its $10 million tropical South Asian exhibit (now Wild Asia). He and Mary were numbered among the society's twenty-five "Best Friends," not only for their contributions but for more practical matters as well, as when Laurance's skillful diplomacy with the city—which provides an important part of the funding for the zoos and aquarium—led to a free admission day at the zoo once a week, so that the inner-city population that lived near it might better come to appreciate and understand the long-range values of wildlife. LSR kept his eye to the educational mission of the society: the zoo should be a focus of "curiosity and wonder," he thought, part of the geography of childhood, a teacher of diversity in the fullest sense of the word, helping "man place himself in perspective."[24]

From afar, in the Adirondacks, to the river that ran through his life, and across its widening swath to the Palisades, LSR had worked more or less simultaneously to apply his conservation principles. His tightest focus was on the Zoological Society. But his closest was on his home at the Rockefeller estate at Pocantico, just outside North Tarrytown, New York. The Brothers were not always in agreement about the estate: Nelson was primarily interested in preserving "the Park," the site of Kykuit (Dutch for "lookout") and other historic buildings. The Park was also the location of the Japanese House that Nelson had built for Happy and their two sons. He considered the "Open Space"—the 3,600 or so acres outside the Park—an investment. John D. 3rd had no interest in preserving the Park, which he considered ostentatious and not what the family should be remembered for. However, he strongly wanted to preserve all

of the Open Space and believed that he and his brothers held this property as
stewards for the public. David believed the entire estate had great public value
and favored preserving the Park as a historic area and the Open Space as a natural preserve. Laurance was torn by differing views. He was never in favor of
preserving Rockefeller family homes, often pointing out that they had all been
torn down. Rockwood Hall, he would say with a smile, had been pushed into
the Hudson. Thus he was not interested in preserving Kykuit or the other
structures with the Park and he believed Westchester County had ample open
space parks. His primary interest, a dream not realized, was to see Rockwood
Hall developed as an extensive recreation facility that urban citizens could reach
by river and rail. Each brother thought of the estate's future in terms of what
he knew best.

Substantial in size—at its largest, four times the acreage of Central Park—
the Rockefeller family estate consisted of rolling hills, meadows, and stark out-
crops of rock interspersed with rich woodlands, representative of the Hudson
River landscape. It was close in proximity to other Rockefeller historical benefactions, the five properties managed by Sleepy Hollow Restorations, Inc.'s successor, Historic Hudson Valley. These were Washington Irving's home at Sunnyside; two properties dating from colonial times, Van Cortland and
Philipsburg Manors, the first perhaps the most authentic surviving eighteenth
century Dutch–English manor house in the Hudson River Valley, the other a
large stone manor house dating from circa 1683, both declared National Historic Landmarks by the National Park Service in 1961 (as was Sunnyside a year
later); the Union Church of Pocantico Hills; and at Annandale-on-Hudson,
Montgomery Place, built in 1805 in the Federal style and subsequently transformed to Classical Revival style and acquired in 1986. Since National Historic
Landmarks must pass tests of significance and integrity that, in effect, make
the case for inclusion in the National Park System itself, these enclaves might
be the basis for a new national historical park, especially if much of the Pocantico property were included, thus to illustrate four centuries of human occupation of the Hudson highlands. Further, since there were Native American
archaeological sites associated with Pocantico and elsewhere in the valley, such
a park might commemorate a thousand years of humanity.

The senior John D. Rockefeller had begun purchasing property in the area
late in the nineteenth century, beginning with Rockwood Hall. In 1909 he built
Kykuit as a country home in modified Georgian style. In time an orangery, pat-
terned after the one at Versailles (itself restored with a gift from JDR, Sr.), a
coach barn, and a playhouse in French Norman style were added. Around these
structures grew the well-tended core known as the Park, about three hundred

acres in all, which contrasted with the outlying remainder of the estate, kept
in natural condition except for the addition of riding trails. Though in no sense
a public park, much of the land, held in common by the Brothers, was kept
open to the public for hiking and horseback riding. In 1976 Kykuit also was
designated a National Historic Landmark. There were then six NHLs in close
proximity, owned or managed by Rockefeller interests, and from the perspective of the National Park Service's historians, the idea of a potential national
historical park was increasingly attractive.[25]

In 1951, John D. Rockefeller, Jr., had turned the estate at Pocantico over to
the Hills Realty Company, which he had created, and the following year he sold
the Hills stock in Pocantico to his five sons, each of whom paid for a precise
one-fifth share. Each brother agreed to sell his shares only to another brother
to hold the entire estate intact. JDR, Jr., continued to pay for the operation and
maintenance of the estate, added a playhouse and indoor swimming pool, and
effectively continued to manage Pocantico. In 1954, four of the brothers,
Winthrop having moved to Arkansas, bought the Park from Hills Realty, and
this was divided into various allocations, with the second largest being purchased by LSR.

The balance of the Pocantico estate remained in Hills Realty until after the
death of JDR, Jr., in 1960. In the ensuing years the Hills Realty holdings, which
included the Eyrie at Seal Harbor and the great Parke-Bernet auction house in
New York City, were liquidated and the assets were distributed to the Brothers.
David took the property in Maine, Nelson received cash, Winthrop was bought
out, and Laurance took most of Pocantico to facilitate the liquidation. David
and JDR 3rd owned homes in Pocantico, Nelson owned the camp, Laurance
owned Rockwood Hall, on which there no longer was a structure, and the Park
with Kykuit was owned by the four New York brothers jointly.

For some years thereafter the Brothers struggled with the question of what
to do with the property. After all, 3,600 acres of land in mid-Westchester
County could be used in many ways. The Rouse corporation was invited to
submit a plan, which included multiple-use, housing, an upscale shopping mall,
etc.; however, this plan was rejected. The children of the Brothers, led by
Steven, David, Jr., and Larry and supported by David's wife, Peggy, wanted to
see the property protected. JDR 3rd held Fieldwood Farm on the northern
edge of the estate; David lived in Hudson Pines, which was adjacent to the
Park; Laurance lived in Kent House, which was located within the Park; and
Nelson owned the hunting lodge or camp property and stayed in the Hawes
House within the Park when at Pocantico until JDR, Jr.'s widow, Martha, built
Hillcrest, after which Nelson moved into Kykuit. (Hillcrest was never lived in

and became the Rockefeller archives building.) Some of the Cousins had bought property at Pocantico, under the Aldrich plan, which followed the rejection of the Rouse proposals, but most of this generation wanted to live in real communities. They too, however, loved the property, wanted to see the family keep it together, and urged that there be further studies.

In 1972 the planner Hideo Sasaki came up with precisely the right idea. Donal C. O'Brien, who was chief counsel to the Rockefeller family, later recalled the moment as virtually revelatory. Planners had come and gone with their complex designs, charts and elevations, and black and white displays. Sasaki gave his presentation in the board room at Room 5600 using maps and other displays that were green—all green, or nearly so—and even as he began to speak, everyone in attendance could see the simplicity and the rightness of the plan: Pocantico should remain green. This was, as O'Brien said, a dramatic moment in its directness and clarity.

This did not mean that the historic structures on the property were safe. Nelson spoke for the Park; JDR 3rd for the Open Space; David, like Nelson, felt an almost dynastic sense of the historical importance of the Park. He, more than all the Brothers, had bought into Sasaki's view that the real challenge to the Brothers was to retain the entire estate in its present condition. Laurance was not interested in preserving the structures, for he thought that Kykuit in particular was ostentatious, and he was prepared to see it dismantled stone by stone and returned to green space. Neither he nor JDR 3rd had any interest in having Kykuit, the most imposing of the Pocantico homes, preserved as a monument to the family.

The Brothers then asked O'Brien and LSR's Lincoln School classmate, Harmon Goldstone, then the landmarks commissioner for New York, to come up with a plan to put Sasaki's proposal into effect. This, the Four Centuries Plan, called for each of the four brothers to contribute $5 million, together with additional funds from the Rockefeller Brothers Fund, to create an endowment. The Plan also called for the Brothers to contribute the great majority of their jointly held properties within the Park and the Open Space to one or more charitable entities that would operate the properties for the benefit of the public. In June 1978, the four brothers agreed to the plan in principle, though JDR 3rd asked that one last effort be made to persuade LSR to add the Rockwood Hall parcel to the plan before it was accepted.

Two weeks later, on July 10, JDR 3rd was tragically killed in an automobile accident. Prior to his death, John had been working with O'Brien on a new will in which he would carry out his part of the Four Centuries Plan, including the $5 million bequest for the endowment of the Park. The will was virtually completed and John was awaiting Laurance's decision on Rockwood Hall when John was killed.

In December 1978, Nelson, bitterly disappointed that John had failed to endow the Park, called David and Laurance to Laurance's office at Room 5600 and informed them that he was leaving his interest in the Open Space and the Park to his second wife, Happy. Nelson advised Laurance and David that his primary interests in Pocantico Hills were making provision for Happy and preserving the Park. If Laurance and David were interested in preserving the Open Space, they could buy Nelson's share from Happy. This was a tense and dramatic moment.

Following John's death, O'Brien had made a final effort to interest the National Park Service in the Rockefeller estate, but the secretary of the interior, Cecil Andrus, was placing his primary emphasis on the Alaska Lands Bill, which he and President Jimmy Carter wished to see passed before the 1980 elections. Andrus was also direct in advising O'Brien that he did not believe Congress would support a proposal that involved public funding of the Rockefeller estate.

It was at this point that Carlisle Hummelsine, the long-time president of Colonial Williamsburg and the president of the National Trust for Historic Preservation, approached Nelson and suggested that if the Brothers were to give their interests in the Park to the National Trust, Congress would match the value of these gifts dollar for dollar. Nelson leapt at the proposal and changed his will to leave the National Trust his undivided one-quarter interest in the Park, and as he had advised Laurance and David, he left his interest in the Open Space to Happy.

On January 26, 1979, just a month after Nelson had made his decision, he died of a massive heart attack. Laurance and David were now faced with the task of pulling together the loose ends left by JDR 3rd and Nelson, and dealing with the manner in which Nelson tried to lock them in to the National Trust. The chairman of the trust, Alan Boyd, did his best to get money from Congress in accordance with Nelson and Carl Hummelsine's plan, but as Laurance and David expected, Boyd was turned down. With the option of matching funds from Congress gone, Laurance joined with David and the executors of John's and Nelson's estates in an effort to resolve the situation.

Slowly and carefully, the central argument of the Sasaki Plan was put into effect. JDR 3rd's estate traded out his interest in the Park, and his share of the Open Space, enlarged by the value of what he received for his share of the Park, was given to the state of New York as a State Park Preserve. The JDR 3rd Fund also added a $3 million endowment fund. David added key parcels of land to the State Park Preserve, and 1,600 acres were dedicated by Governor Cuomo as the first stage of the family's efforts to preserve the Open Space for public benefit. Laurance took full ownership in the Kent House, David in the Playhouse, and they divided the famous golf course on which so many dignitaries had been entertained. Kykuit, the orangery, the outdoor sculpture that Nelson had installed, and the furnishings in the house were transferred to the National Trust.

LSR faced something of a dilemma. Philosophically he continued to oppose any Rockefeller memorial, any monumentality, any public home meant to celebrate the family, but Laurance was also one of the three executors of Nelson's estate, and he believed he had a moral obligation to carry out Nelson's wishes. This sense of obligation, which was supported by his co-executors, O'Brien and J. Richardson Dilworth, overrode his personal opposition to preserving Kykuit, and with David's help, Laurance led the effort to preserve the historic property that had meant so much to Nelson.

Throughout this period Laurance was torn between his personal opposition to preserving the Park as a monument to the family and the moral obligation he felt as Nelson's executor. Although Nelson and Laurance were the closest of all the Brothers and each other's best friend, they had very different values when it came to the family estate. Laurance had worked hard to persuade the state of New York to help him develop Rockwood Hall into a riverfront park with extensive recreational facilities that could be reached from New York City by rail and water access. Thus, he was more interested in sharing Pocantico with the public than preserving the property as a monument to his family.

JDR 3rd's executors were his son, Jay, former governor of West Virginia and currently senator from his adopted state, O'Brien, and J. Richardson Dilworth. These three had worked hard to carry out John's wishes, and they succeeded. John's estate would not be involved in contributing land or funds to the Historic Trust. Instead, all of John's property would pass to New York State for the State Park Preserve, which was John's overriding interest. John's role in implementing the Sasaki Plan for Pocantico had been completed.[26]

This left Nelson's executors, Laurance, in his capacity as an executor and a property owner, and David to complete the job. Those involved in working out the specifics for the historic area knew that, when it opened to the public, Kykuit would attract substantially more annual visitation than Franklin D. Roosevelt's home at Hyde Park or the Frederick W. Vanderbilt Mansion, both National Park Service historic sites further up the Hudson. Thus all the interested parties knew that any plan to open Kykuit to the public would require great attention to issues of traffic, crowd control, and visitation levels.

From Nelson the National Trust received only one undivided interest in the

Park. This left David and Laurance with substantial leverage over the trust. When the trust submitted a study in 1985, they rejected it to await a better and more sensitive plan.

Laurance and David were concerned about the capacity of the National Trust to administer a property as large and complex as Kykuit and, most importantly, they wished the property to be used for more than public visitation. Thus, they used their leverage to work out an agreement whereby the Park would be owned by the National Trust but be leased to Historic Hudson Valley, the entity that managed the five properties formerly managed by Sleepy Hollow Restorations, Inc. Historic Hudson Valley would be responsible for visitation and interpretation. The final breakthrough came when it was agreed that the Rockefeller Brothers Fund would have use of the property for the purposes of carrying out its important philanthropic programs, including holding conferences and seminars on matters of national and international concern. In addition, the Rockefeller Brothers Fund would create a separate fund within RBF of $38 million to endow the maintenance of the historic area. Tours begin not at the house but at nearby Phillipsburg Manor, where there is parking, and only small groups, by reservation, can visit. Thus, the environment is little disturbed.

Arguably, there ought to be a Pocantico National Historical Park by which this unique estate with its attendant historical structures, its open spaces, and its association with four centuries of family life along the Hudson—as well as its significance as a place at which the Rockefeller contribution to American life could be interpreted—would join with the other units of the National Park System. The National Trust for Historic Preservation, though chartered by Congress, has a far more limited range of interests. Intelligently run, an important player in the preservation movement, and with many distinguished members on its board, the trust nonetheless strikes some historians as removed from many of the larger issues. All its properties are historic homes, largely of the wealthy (though the Casa Amesti and Cooper-Molera Adobe in Monterey, California, are clear exceptions), so that visitors to its properties gain little sense of cultural diversity, not that a Pocantico park would provide such an awareness. The trust holds only seventeen properties that are open to the public, and admission or a membership fee is charged at each. The Rockefellers have worked hard to find a solution by which Kykuit can be a winner, and the trust has been cooperative; indeed, the complex arrangement has so far proved an enormous success in the estimation of most parties, for Kykuit is both a destination point and is locally used. David and Laurance were surprised by the public interest, and this interest helped LSR as he thought about what to do at the Marsh–Billings property in Vermont. Still, he did not get the intensive-use facility along the Hudson River that he had advocated. LSR has watched closely the efforts to develop a more extensive Hudson greenway; he has remained supportive of the work of Barnabas McHenry and others at the Hudson River Valley Greenway Communities Council; and he has supported the family goal of protecting Pocantico's open spaces. Kykuit's gardens will not be seen by millions of Americans, as they might have been had Kykuit been part of a national park, but the reservation system and an admission charge of $18 per person (in 1996) has proved essential both to protect the resource and to allay local concerns about traffic and crowds. Kykuit remains in the best sense a park in transition.[27]

Throughout these years and these many projects, LSR had called himself simply "a conservationist." Infrequent references to LSR on society pages called him "the conservationist." By the 1970s he increasingly called himself "an environmentalist." For New York he had accomplished quite a lot. He had preserved his grandfather's and father's heritage at the Bronx Zoo and had helped it become a worldwide organization of great influence. He had built upon his father's initiatives at the Palisades Interstate Park, presiding over the park's commission (and eventually, serving as chair of the statewide Council on Parks), seeing its acreage dramatically increase and its use soar during his period of leadership. He had brought the state park movement into the inner city. He had most persistently, through this or that temporary or permanent, ad hoc or standing, commission, committee, or task force, helped to direct attention to the plight and the pleasures of the Hudson River, its valley and shores, from New York City to its source high on the slopes of Mount Marcy. He had provided the spark that led to strengthened protection for the Adirondacks. Through it all, he had not forgotten that the river that ran through his life also ran through the lives of millions of people, including of course his brothers, and most particularly Nelson, the vigorous and ambitious leader of New York. He had been wrong at times, once or twice significantly so, but he had never deviated from his sense that conciliation and compromise were not derisive terms, that civility was essential to the social and political fabric, and that a nation galvanized into concern for its environment, as the United States surely was, even if not sufficiently so in the judgment of many, could leave a "legacy of hope" for the generations to come. As the theologian Reinhold Niebuhr wrote, in *The Irony of American History*, "Nothing that is worth doing can be achieved in our lifetime; therefore we must be saved by hope. Nothing which is true or beautiful or good," Neibuhr concluded, "makes complete sense in any immediate context of history. . . ."[28]

X

"A Legacy of Hope"

The Navajo speak of seeking the Beautyway. The elements of one's interior life are subject to persistent disarray; calling upon a beautyway brings oneself into order with the exterior universe, so that the individual reflects the enduring relationships of the landscape. Every official resumé of Laurance Rockefeller dutifully marches through an impressive list of contributions to the environment, from the American Conservation Association to the World Wildlife Fund. But of all his conservation activities, the ones to which he referred most often in a "pre-retirement" interview late in 1993, were what he hoped he had done as a catalyst for "beauty."

Beauty, to be sure, is a subjective concept, and his progression toward a focus on natural beauty grew out of a variety of childhood influences, experiences, and assignments. Speaking of what most people would take to be a purely business enterprise, building resort hotels, he began with the premise that what people most want is "serenity, beauty, tranquility." When addressing a somewhat unlikely group, the Rod & Gun Editors Association, he said that urban people have "a right to beautiful surroundings, and a duty, a responsibility, to see that they are beautiful." Opening the White House Conference on Natural Beauty that he chaired, he declared that the "perception of beauty, and action to preserve and create it, are a fundamental test of a great society. . . ." "Beauty," he wrote in *Hawaii Business* magazine, "must be a fact of life."[1]

As we have seen, the path to these convictions lay through a thicket of influences, beginning with Laurance Rockefeller's grandfather, JDR, Sr., and his father, JDR, Jr. Reserved, rigorously moral, interested in nature and realistic about it (he once compared a park to a theater: only so many people could expect to get seats), loyal to his beliefs and persistent in his philanthropies, given to a regime (in LSR's words in 1985) of "Duty and don't," John D. Rockefeller, Jr., set his sons on the path toward an appreciation of nature, and though all walked it a little way, it was Laurance who remained on the path longest.

Thus Laurance Rockefeller became a catalyst. From apprentice to his father he became the creator of organization after organization and an activist–philanthropist in dozens more, nationally and locally. The American Conservation Association, Inc., was his creation in 1958. The National Recreation and Parks Association was formed through his initiative in 1965, by merging five smaller groups, and he served as the first president. The Conservation Foundation, of which he was co-founder, marched on from strength to strength until finally merging with the World Wildlife Fund. The National Park Foundation (which superseded the National Park Trust Fund) was, if not his creation, then much beholden to him for he gave it over a million dollars at the outset and in later years provided additional large sums on a matching basis. He was instrumental in Resources for the Future, Inc., and in the American Committee for International Wildlife Protection; he founded the Woodstock Foundation; and he stood behind Historic Hudson Valley, which succeeded Sleepy Hollow Restorations. In all, he kept to the big picture, associating protection and use, asking what the public interest was: he was not, he reminded a questioner, a "blind fish," and he seldom gave his time or his money on impulse or without adequate inquiry.

Quite amazingly, and much to Laurance Rockefeller's dismay and rare anger, these foundations and organizations, to which his commitment was public knowledge and on which individuals known to be close to him served as board members, were the subject of a remarkable report, circulated in the Department of the Interior at the height of the contentious exchanges between Nelson Rockefeller and Stewart Udall, which employed the paranoid tones of an intelligence agency to characterize LSR's relationships to them. He was found to have clear connections to thirteen conservation organizations, two of which he was said to "control" and eleven of which he had "infiltrated." Eight more organizations were "suspect" of being under his influence.[2] (Later a writer quite hostile to LSR's view of the future of the Hudson River Valley raised the total number to thirty-five.)[3] What these could have been is scarcely a mystery (see the appendix to this book) unless one believes that a routine membership in a society was tantamount to suspicious activity. Laughable as this report may have been, however, it clearly revealed how powerful Rockefeller was believed to be. Just how he might have used his membership in the Whooping Crane Conservation Association, for example, is not clear; that he openly urged The Conservation Foundation, the National Park Foundation, Resources for the Future, or the Rockefeller Brothers Fund to pursue his agendas was neither secret nor unusual.

Though Laurance Rockefeller would collect many things, his vision always was more personal, his relationship to an object or place more visual and tactile than it was abstract. Among his earliest purchases, begun on his trip west with his father, were Native-American Indian artifacts, and today his JY Ranch in Wyoming contains a small but superb array of Native American pottery and rugs. When he speaks of them to a visitor, or casually points to the placement of a figure in his office or a painting on the wall of his and Mary's home in Woodstock, he invariably emphasizes their origins and their presence. This identification with the object is allied with what some now call "post-materialistic values." Defined as a desire for personal fulfillment, self-expression, and meaning, these values emerged broadly during the nation's cultural shift in the 1960s and 1970s; holding to such values does not mean that a person lacks awareness of their capital value or wishes to lead a monastic life but, rather, that one chooses within one's own environment a form of "the simple life." Of course, one person's simple life is another person's luxury, though it is the values that are held that set the definition. When LSR wrote of the simple life in *The Reader's Digest* no doubt many thought his doing so was, at the least, peculiar; he recognized the irony, however, for his reference was to how one relates to possessions, not to the possessions themselves.[4]

One is reminded by the pottery, and by Laurance Rockefeller's frequent reference to a place, an object, even a person or a program, and certainly to a concept or accomplishment, as being "beautiful," of the Native American sense of beauty. In *Crossing Open Ground*—a metaphor for life—the nature writer Barry Lopez has described this sense as one of relating well to exterior landscapes, of being certain that what is told and done is authentic and trustworthy. It is the land that exhibits the sacred order in art, that shapes architecture, the vocabulary of landscape, even costume and ritual, all of which derive from the perceived natural order. In reading LSR's reflections on spirituality in an interview he gave early in 1994, one is struck with the way in which his thoughts tend toward this way of organizing life. Physical events become symbolic when recalled, and thus one strives to understand both "the" past and one's "own" past. Phrases like this are not usually associated with "men of affairs" or the very wealthy, and to a hard-headed pragmatist they may seem annoyingly vague. Yet they all appear in the speeches and remarks of this catalyst for conservation and they point back to his senior essay at Princeton when he tried to identify "the dropping off place of facts and values" in relation to ethics.

This lifelong interest led LSR to a unique gift to his alma mater, one which would, he hoped, bring his concerns together in a way that would be productive to higher education in general, to future generations, and to the nation at a time of considerable moral and ethical turmoil: a Center for Human Values. The goal, he told a Princeton luncheon group in 1991, was to promote "an interdisciplinary approach to enhancing consideration of ethics, values and the human spirit within the teaching process." He wished to help the next generation of students "integrate their lives philosophically and humanistically with what they were learning intellectually—and thus be better able to heal themselves as they seek to heal the world." He explored ways to move into a new area of philanthropy, to search for nature within the human spirit, to turn public attention away from "the potato race of life" by breaking down barriers between science and religion, barriers that he thought hurt the conservation movement by making it either too rationalistic or too metaphysical. If this could be done, he said in answer to a question following an address at Princeton, then through reverence for all life—through ecology—the people of this earth could become "co-creators with God of the future of this earth."[5] Here was a man who could, without embarrassment, urge a scholar to examine the evidence for the existence of extraterrestrial life, help artists explore the spiritual nature of their work, and support the view that mind, body, and spirit are all a part of the same reality.

But of course LSR was not seen by others as he saw himself. In December 1974, he appeared before the committee of the U.S. House of Representatives inquiring into the nomination of his brother, Nelson, to be vice president of the United States under President Gerald Ford. The testimony and subsequent questioning make compelling reading; most of the members of Congress professed to be concerned about how Rockefeller money was translated into what they suspected was concerted Rockefeller power. They doggedly pursued questions about the legality and magnitude of loans Nelson and Laurance had made to people who held political office, usually by appointment; why LSR had sent a telegram to President Richard Nixon in 1972 urging that he approve the acquisition of Caribbean Atlantic Airlines by Eastern Airlines; and about his investment in a hostile biography of former Justice Arthur Goldberg that appeared during Nelson's contest with him for the New York governorship in

1970. Quite naturally, virtually all the questions were about LSR as business-man, not about his philanthropy, his interest in conservation, or his values. They were legitimate questions, for members of Congress suspected that the Rockefeller brothers would, with Nelson a heartbeat away from the presidency, pool their vast resources to press a liberal Republican political agenda.

What is striking to a reader a quarter century later is that, at the outset, Lau-rance Rockefeller identified himself to the committee as "self-employed," with his primary occupation "that of a concerned environmentalist."[6] There is no doubt, even if one limits the question, "Who are you?" to the context of the hearings, that LSR profoundly and poignantly believed this to be true, but the members of Congress, with rare exception, had no interest in this subject and gave him little opportunity—though the text reveals that he was both tenacious and quick at making opportunities—to express himself on matters of conser-vation and the environment. The occupation he ascribed to himself was what he believed himself to be. When one examines a list of speeches LSR made between 1941 and 1993, one finds that he rose to speak at least five hundred times before diverse audiences and that fully half his presentations were on conservation, the environment, and recreation. Seldom did he speak on busi-ness matters, and when he did, as when he addressed the prosaic-sounding Association of Edison Illuminating Companies at their annual meeting in Boca Raton in 1966 under the dry title, "The Role of the Utility Industry in the Quality of Our Environment," he drew upon his experience in visiting Wood-side, California, for President Johnson, and told his possibly quizzical listen-ers about the relationship of the energy they supplied to the spiritual necessi-ties of beauty as revealed in nature.[7]

"Nature" is, of course, a great bag of tricks, a mother lode of resources that are inner as well as outer, spiritual as well as economic. Most people who are in the "nature business" emphasize one or the other: solitude, healing, the sense of re-creation of the spirit that comes from a place in nature that is, to the eye, unchanged (however much one may know that, in fact, the place is being shaped by artificial creations, by management principles mandated from out-side that place). Or they emphasize the ability to take a living from nature, so that it becomes a symbol for fertility, family, security, and continuity. One need only stand in a crowd in a small western town when the nation's birthday comes around and watch the "wise use" floats. Use at all may be anathema to a small group, though most realize that natural resources will, in some measure and in some way, be "used"; the debate turns upon the word "wise," which in recent years has been appropriated by those who oppose what they invariably call "locking up the land" for the benefit of nonlocals who do not contribute directly to the protection or development of the resource. The visitor from the city, hungry for an imagined rural harmony to offset urban tension, has one vision of what a Wild and Scenic River may be, while the local rancher, farmer, or professional sports fisherman and guide has quite another.

LSR has not joined the apocalyptic environmentalists who declare that, unless this or that watershed, forest, or valley is set aside immediately, all will be lost. Nor does he side with the gradual degradationists, those who feel that all is slowly decaying, that the past always is better than the present and certainly more so than the future, but who feel a solemn duty to try to stave off environmental disaster for the benefit of at least another generation or two. He clearly does not agree with those who think there is no problem: no problem because humanity will destroy itself; no problem because in the end the good Lord will provide; no problem because science and technology will, in time, find a solution to the challenges of population, food supply, the ozone layer, or pollution. Most people, having examined these possible positions, take one of two paths: they commit themselves to one solution, once having thought deeply but no longer having the will to do so, feeling that an intense and thereafter unexamined commitment to a single strategy makes them best able to act; or they abandon all positions and turn away from the question of nature and the environment, content to let someone else attempt to think through all the variables.

Yet Laurance Rockefeller appears to have kept all the variables in mind, sometimes cyclically, sometimes linearly, without a determination that only one can count above all others. He recognizes that different people have quite different ideas about what nature is for. This is the basis for his persistent search for compromise and for the charge made by some that he has never made up his mind between these environmental positions. To one person a wilderness carries high spiritual values, to another it is a source of fear, to a third it is a metaphor for economic growth and opportunity. Not one of these views is inherently wrong, though one or another may be more appropriate to humankind's needs at a given time. The only view that is quite wrong is to leave humanity out of the picture.

Shifting between these views, Rockefeller therefore frequently refers to that sense of place essential to feeling rooted in a society. He is especially fascinated by his image of Vermont.[8] Once Vermont enjoyed a golden age when it was an extended community of people who lived on and from the land, with a unifying religion and a respect for the place from which they made that living. Their humor, speech, philosophy, even their architecture was understated, direct, without waste or guile; it was simple. Then in the decades between the American Revolution and the industrial expansion that flowed through the 1880s,

Vermont was bypassed as immigrant communities and earlier Vermonters alike were attracted to the richer lands of the west and the rising factories in lower New England. Vermont was ill-suited to take part in the rapidly changing new urban world of technology: the state grew poor, underpopulated, conservative, a philosophy of sprightly hope giving way to one of unremitting endurance. This too passed, and in the last fifty years Vermont has once again expressed the earlier traits, now cast in a different light by yet another wave of transforming newcomers who are escaping from metropolitan stress, so that Vermont is seen to be a landscape of beauty, expressive of craftsmanship, individualism, regard for humanity, and a sense of community. It has again become one of the places that is spoken of as "genuine." Yet it is the external viewer who has changed as much as Vermont has changed or been "restored."

Woodstock became for LSR emblematic of his goals: of the spiritual values, creativity, and holistic vision that arises from an awareness of place. It is, in a sense, his most enduring and yet his most recent environmental interest, as it has evolved from a place where a fine nineteenth century home represented the values of Vermont to a national park that will exemplify those values to future generations. No doubt there will be other expressions of his concern for conservation, but for the moment Vermont may be taken for what he has defined as his most important gift to future generations: "a legacy of hope," as he refers to the stewardship that the park is to interpret.⁹

Commenting in 1995, Peter Dobkin Hall, a scholar who has studied the breadth of the philanthropic world, and who is not without his skepticism as to the realities of the nonprofit sector, singled the Rockefellers out for praise, for the way in which they had institutionalized giving and for working at it as a profession rather than a hobby. Laurance Rockefeller, he thought, was genuinely self-effacing and yet "very complex." He had a "true sense of privacy." It came not from shyness, from reserve, or from fear, but from a belief in "the healing and protective power of privacy." LSR had, Hall concluded, a very real respect for the intellectual process, as distinct from respect for intellectuals, and unlike many people, he could tell the difference.¹⁰ Of course his world seemed unreal to many who, in his beloved Vermont, were uncertain of where their next meal would come from. He did not think of conservation as a universal healer: the pursuit of conservation alone would not end wars, cure cancer, or resolve racial conflict. Yet, respect for nature was a preliminary to achieving such goals. "The world is big but it is comprehensible"—so said R. Buckminster Fuller, the American architect. LSR, as the American scientist Anna Botsford Comstock has written, believed that nature connected all things, and as he grew older he also believed that "love of nature counts much for sanity in later life."

Naturally enough, as LSR had carried forward the work of his father, JDR,

Jr., he continued to hope that his only son would carry on with his. He knew that his children, indeed most of the Cousins, did not have the same interest in holding the Pocantico estate together intact, and he fully understood how, as the conservation movement became the environmental movement, strategies for the future had changed, and that the next generation would pursue its own approaches to environmental matters. Still, as we have seen, he was quite delighted when Scenic Hudson, Inc., had honored both he and his son on the same occasion in 1994. This event had marked a public healing with Scenic Hudson, the organization that had opposed him over Storm King years before, though in fact this healing had long since taken place, in part through the ministrations of his advisor and friend, and Scenic Hudson's energetic member, Nash Castro. Larry had been vigorous in his defense of Scenic Hudson's goals. The event clearly suggested that there would be another Rockefeller who would carry on the family's work in conservation, though in ways that most likely would differ from the preceding generations.

Most of the time LSR remained somewhere between conservation and environmentalism in his views. The conservation movement, of which he was so much a part, emphasized efficient stewardship and use of the nation's natural resources. Conservationists believed that rationality could govern choices. They were technologically optimistic, inclined to feel that solutions could be found to problems in the environment. They supported multiple use, "conservation *and* use," though decreasingly so over the years. The leaders of the movement had been, like LSR, from prosperous, usually upper-class families who felt some sense of obligation toward the people broadly and the rich natural resources of the nation more specifically; they were well-educated and inclined to achieve their goals through voluntary associations. Conservationists eschewed partisan or ideological positions, and they seldom questioned the fundamental character of American society.

On the other hand, many environmentalists had departed from so sanguine a view of the nation's political leadership, its economic system, and its social structure. When looking to ecological goals, they questioned the applicability of technology and often saw it as an enemy. They were more fractious, divided by origins, calculations as to strategies, visions of an apocalyptic future. Some, like Paul Ehrlich, believed that the world was doomed to ultimate chaos as an ever-growing population fought for ever-decreasing resources. Others, more ideologically oriented, believed that by class or political revolution such a destructive end might be averted or, at the least, held off for a very long time. Environmentalists tended to be more urban in background; they also focused less on wilderness, on national parks and preserves, on landscape and scenic views, on historical preservation and reconstruction, all great interests of LSR and his class and generation, to take on issues that directly affected health, food supply, and inter-ethnic harmony. They concentrated on the biological structure of life—all life—and how that structure was compromised or distorted by human decisions and desires. While they put human beings onto the landscape, they also could be quite anti-humanity. As with all movements advocating fundamental change, in their methods they tended to be more shrill, fractious, physically obstructionist, and ideological than the old-line conservationists, who chose "sound argument" and "rational discourse" as their tools of persuasion. Still, the environmentalists generally argued from science, from data, even when their voices were raised.[11]

LSR's instincts were against the tactics of many of the environmentalists. He was optimistic by nature, believing that there was a divine intent in the world and that it included the creative well-being of humanity. He was nonconfrontational, seeking compromise as the most rational and least destructive of tactics. He believed that upstate New Yorkers who blocked roads and threatened state officials with physical violence when the report on the Adirondacks in the twenty-first century was released were shortsighted, ill-informed, and potentially dangerous.

But Rockefeller had also made the journey toward environmentalism, for he shared the mainstream environmentalist emphasis on getting the facts, on scientific study, and on the interrelatedness of all decisions. Though some people found it ironic or contradictory, he embraced some of the asceticism that many modern environmentalists espoused. He had turned away from Consolidated Edison's Storm King project when he realized how flawed the studies carried out by the utility company were. He had, since that time, expanded his interest in the Hudson River from Pocantico and the Hudson Highlands to embrace all of it. Though he still cherished the nation's historical heritage, he had recognized the tendency of those who put the protection of historical sites ahead of a larger planning for the whole of the environment to be rather narrowly corporate, cautious, and defensive. In the years after Storm King and especially after Nelson's death, when LSR so clearly represented the long-standing Rockefeller commitment to conservation, he had rethought where he stood. He never moved all the way to the anti-corporate, anti-government position of what he viewed as the more extreme environmentalists, for he still believed that some central planning, though increasingly through public–private partnerships, was essential, and he still believed that enlightened self-interest would lead American business to recognize the importance of a healthy, clean, and even beautiful physical environment. He wanted to help give people self-knowledge and insight so that they would see the relationship of their personal actions and their cultural beliefs to environmental health and natural beauty. He had moved with the times, not as far or as fast as some environmentalists; he had the same goals though altered strategies as the young man who joined the boards of the Palisades Interstate Park and the New York Zoological Society well over half a century before. He remained alert to change and was comfortable with it, not bitter that the world was a different place. By the 1990s he was a mainstream environmentalist who by virtue of his credibility, integrity, longevity, and strategic dominance of the centrist debate remained a vital catalyst for the movement, a player of great achievement and yet still great potential.

Even after almost six decades of leadership in the conservation field, the definitive assessment of Laurance S. Rockefeller's place in history still cannot be made, for he continues to be active. It can be said, however, that the physical impact of his work has been enormous. One cannot drive the Palisades Parkway in New York, stroll through Woodstock, Vermont, swim in the Virgin Islands, or hike the trails of the Tetons without seeing and benefiting from his work.

As important as these achievements are, however, his most lasting influence may not be on America's landscape but on its perception of public priorities. When he began, despite the efforts of Marsh, Pinchot, Muir, and the first Roosevelt, conservation was not in the first order of public issues. Over the 1950s, 1960s, and 1970s, LSR was a major force in bringing conservation to the prominent place on the public agenda it now holds. By his own works and by his patient prodding of public officials, by thousands of letters and phone calls, by hundreds of trips to Washington and Albany, by scores of well-crafted reports and recommendations, he helped ensure that conservation would become part of the national ethic and a first-order national goal.

LSR not only enhanced public understanding of conservation, he helped to shift and shape its focus. He was a key figure in the very important transition from traditional conservation to the new environmentalism. His persistence in espousing reasonable change within the system helped move concern for nature from obscurity to a full place at the cabinet table, the congressional caucuses, and the corporate board rooms without the rancor of revolution. It is this role as a champion and a catalyst for consensus rather than confrontation that may be his greatest contribution.

A Note on Sources

A full-scale biography of any living person requires an examination of the papers of all that person's correspondents and friends, of any companies and organizations with which the individual did personal business or was a member, and in this day of ubiquitous government, of extensive official collections both national and local. Clearly this is an impossible task with respect to someone like Laurance S. Rockefeller, whose interests have been deep, broad, and enduring, and which continue. I have made no effort to locate, much less examine, the major primary sources on his business career, or on his philanthropic activities outside the field of conservation. Within this field, however, I have sought to be as thorough as possible.

My research has been extensive in the Rockefeller Archive Center at North Tarrytown, New York; in relevant collections of papers at the Library of Congress (most particularly the papers of Fairfield Osborn, Eddie Rickenbacker, and Nathaniel Owings) and the National Archives; and in the Truman, Eisenhower, Kennedy, and Johnson presidential libraries. The last was especially rich in relevant collections, including those of the president himself, Stewart Udall, Liz Carpenter, and others involved in the White House Conference. The Eisenhower Library provided a treasure trove of materials on ORRRC. By correspondence I have obtained Rockefeller-related files from the Nixon Papers Project, the Ford and Carter presidential libraries, and the Southwest Pacific Regional depository of the National Archives. I have examined the records of the New York State Parks (Palisades Interstate Park and Taconic Regions), the New York Zoological Society, the National Geographic Society, the National Parks Foundation, the National Park and Conservation Association, and, as

necessary, at the Rockefeller corporate headquarters at Room 5600, 30 Rockefeller Plaza, New York City. I have consulted the Charles Lindbergh Papers in
the Yale University Library and the Robert Moses Papers, primarily at the New
York Public Library (together with a small collection held by the Yale University Library). I have searched manuscript and printed primary materials in the
New-York Historical Society, the New York State Library and Archives in
Albany, the Woodstock (VT) Historical Society, the records of Scenic Hudson, Inc., which are held by Marist College in Poughkeepsie, New York; and the
Horace M. Albright Papers at the University of California, Los Angeles. Vis-
its to the Archivo General de Puerto Rico, the Biblioteca del Universidad de
Puerto Rico, and the Fundación Luis Muñoz Marín provided less information
than I had hoped but were useful nonetheless. The librarian of the Cruz Bay
public library in St. John, Virgin Islands, made available to me relevant printed
sources and a file folder of newspaper cuttings. I was unable to gain access to
Mary Lasker interviews, held by Columbia University, or to personally visit the
Adirondack Library in Blue Mountain Lake, New York, but the latter helpfully
sent me copies of its relevant files, as did the School of American Research in
Santa Fe, New Mexico, and the Clemson University Library, which holds the
papers of George Hartzog. I was given permission to consult the papers of ex-
Governor Ronald Reagan in the Hoover Library after three requests; however,
this was too late to help me in any substantive way.

I have made no attempt to gain access to, or research, the records of most
of the conservation associations of which Laurance Rockefeller is a member
(see the appendix), with the exceptions noted above. Many of the records of
Jackson Hole Preserve, Inc., which I searched extensively, are in the Rockefeller
family archives, as are LSR's letters to and from these organizations, which led
me to believe that apart from minutes of meetings that he attended, the records
of most groups would not prove of added value, especially since his private
papers at Pocantico routinely contain agendas and other material brought back
from meetings. The family papers are rich in Save-the-Redwoods correspondence and in materials on Sleepy Hollow Restorations, and several of LSR's
other conservation-related pursuits.

Appendix

Partial List of Conservation Affiliations of Laurance S. Rockefeller*

American Committee for International Wildlife Protection, Inc.
- Board of Directors, 1971

American Conservation Association, Inc.
- Founder, President and Trustee

American Forestry Association
- Honorary President, 1968
- Honorary Vice President

American Museum of Natural History
- Life Member, 1936
- Associate Benefactor, 1941

American Scenic and Historic Preservation Society
- Recipient of Society's first Horace Albright Scenic Preservation Medal, 1957

American Society of Landscape Architects
- Honorary Member, 1968

Caneel Bay, Inc.
- Chairman, Board of Directors
- Chairman, Executive Committee

Caribbean Conservation Corporation
- Life Member

---

*I wish to thank the staff at Room 5600 for compiling this list.

Central Park Conservancy
 • Trustee, 1984–

Citizens' Advisory Committee on Environmental Quality
 • Chairman, 1969–1973
 • Member, 1973–1977
 • Chairman, Task Force on Land Utilization and Urban Growth, 1972

Citizens' Advisory Committee on Recreation and Natural Beauty
(Later the Citizens' Advisory Committee on Environmental Quality)
 • Member, 1966–1969
 • Chairman, 1968–1969

Conservation Foundation, The
 • Founding Member and Trustee, 1948–1969
 • Senior Vice President, 1962
 • Vice Chairman, 1963–1969
 • Board of Directors

Environmental Defense Fund
 • Member

First Lady's Committee for a More Beautiful Capital, The
 • Member

Grand Teton Lodge Company
 • Founder, Chairman, Member, Board of Directors, 1956–

Greenacre Foundation
 • Trustee, 1968–

Hudson River Conservation Society
 • Vice President, 1947–1948
 • Board of Directors, 1949

Hudson River Valley Commission
 • Chairman, 1965–1966

Izaak Walton League of America, Inc.
 • Honorary President, 1963–1965

Jackson Hole Preserve, Inc. (included Jackson Hole Wildlife Park)
 • President, 1940–
 • Executive Committee Member
 • Board of Trustees

Little Dix Bay Hotel Corporation
 • Chairman of the Board

Member of U.S. Delegation to the United Nations Conference on the Human
Environment, 1972
  • Lead Delegate in "Human Settlements" Subject Area

National Audubon Society
  • Life Member, 1935
  • President's Council Member, 1980–1981
  • Recipient, Audubon Medal, 1964

National Geographic Society
  • Board of Trustees, 1957–
  • Finance Committee Member, 1960–1979
  • Recipient, Audubon Medal, 1964

National Park Foundation
  • Member of Board, 1968–
  • Vice Chairman, 1975–1976
  • Board Member Emeritus, 1978–

National Recreation and Parks Association
  • Trustee, Life Trustee, 1974
  • President, 1965–1967
  • Lay Representative to Board of Trustees, 1968–1974
  • Humanitarian Award, 1973

National Trust for Historic Preservation
  • Life Member

National Wildflower Research Center
  • Charter Member of the Board
  • Honorary Trustee

National Wildlife Federation
  • Member

Nature Conservancy, The
  • Member

New York Botanical Garden
  • Life Member

New York State Conservation Council, Inc.
  • Sustaining Member

New York State Council of Parks and Outdoor Recreation
  • Vice Chairman, 1960–1963
  • Chairman, 1963–1973
  • Hudson Highlands Committee, Chairman, 1965

New York State Forestry and Park Association
- Life Member

New York State Historic Trust
- Member, 1965–

New York State Nature and Historical Preserve Trust
- Member, 1970–

New York Zoological Society
- Trustee, 1935–1986
- Second Vice President, 1939–1958
- First Vice President, 1959–1968
- President, 1969–1971
- Chairman, 1971–1985
- Honorary Chairman, 1975
- Conservation Committee Member
- International Wildlife Protection Committee Member
- Executive Committee and Advisory Board Committee Member

Outdoor Recreation Resources Review Commission
- Chairman, 1957–1962

Outdoor Recreation Review Policy Group, 1984
(New Commission created 1985)

Pacific Tropical Botanical Garden
- Member

Palisades Interstate Park Commission, 1939–1979
- Secretary, 1941–1960
- Vice President, 1960–1970
- President, 1970–1977

President's Task Force on Natural Beauty
- Member, 1964–

Resources for the Future, Inc.
- Director, 1959–1969
- Honorary Director

Rockefeller Brothers Fund
- Founder, 1940
- President, 1958–1968
- Chairman, 1968–1980
- Vice Chairman, 1980–1982

Rockefeller Family Fund
  • Founding Trustee, 1967–1977

St. Croix Landmarks Society, Inc.
  • Life Member, 1969

Save-the-Redwoods League
  • Life Member, 1941

Sleepy Hollow Restorations
  (Later Historic Hudson Valley)
  • Trustee
  • Chairman Emeritus

Society for a More Beautiful Capital, Inc.
  • Member

Task Force on Natural Beauty, 1964
  • Chairman, 1965

U.S. Public Land Law Review Commission
  • Member, 1965–1970

Westchester County Conservation Association
  • Life Member, 1937–

White House Conference on Conservation
  • Panel Moderator, 1962

White House Conference on Natural Beauty
  • Chairman, 1965

Whooping Crane Conservation Association
  • Life Member, 1969–

Wildfowl Trust (England)
  • Associate Member, 1968

Wildlife Conservation Society, The
  • Chairman

Woods Hole Oceanographic Association
  • Life Member, 1957–

World Wildlife Fund
  • Member

Notes*

Chapter I

1. The description of the scene is from a videotape of the award ceremony, "Presentation of Congressional Gold Medal to Laurance Rockefeller September 27, 1991." The text of Public Law 101–296, authorizing the medal struck, is 101st Congress, 104 Stat. 197, May 17, 1990 [S. 1853]. Though the tape provides the remarks of the president and of the recipient, it is backed up by Presidential Remarks, September 27, 1991 (draft manuscript dated September 18), and Laurance S. Rockefeller Presentation by President George Bush of the Congressional Gold Medal September 27, 1991 (manuscript), Archives, Room 5600, 30 Rockefeller Plaza. The Rockefeller Papers are in two depositories: the great bulk are in the Rockefeller Archives Center at Pocantico, in North Tarrytown, New York, while records of recent and current interest often are held at the Rockefeller corporate offices, Room 5600, 30 Rockefeller Plaza, in New York City. Hereafter references to the former will read *RAC* and to the latter *Room 5600*.
2. From Carol Lynn Yellin, MS, "Some Quotations from LSR," n.d., p. 3, Room 5600.
3. From typescript of interview with LSR by Fraser Seitel, "Conservation," Room 5600.

Chapter II

1. See the bibliography for representative examples.
2. This essay is reprinted in E.C. Kirkland, ed., *The Gospel of Wealth and Other Timely Essays* (Cambridge, MA: Harvard University Press, 1962).

---

*Quotations that are not footnoted are drawn from my interviews with Laurance Rockefeller.

3. See his "No Retreat on Abortion," *Newsweek*, June 21, 1976, p. 11.

4. There is substantial literature on the history of philanthropy in America and a rather extensive literature on the psychology and philosophy of giving. I draw here primarily on Robert H. Bremner, *American Philanthropy* (Chicago: University of Chicago Press, 1960); Peter Dobkin Hall, *Inventing the Nonprofit Sector and Other Essays on Philanthropy, Voluntarism, and Nonprofit Organizations* (Baltimore: Johns Hopkins University Press, 1992); and Cole Otnes and Richard E. Beltramini, eds., *Gift Giving: A Research Anthology* (Bowling Green, OH: Popular Press, 1996).

5. See Ida Tarbell, *The History of the Standard Oil Company* (2 vols., New York: Macmillan, 1904), first published as articles in *McClure's* magazine. This is a classic, perhaps *the* classic, of the muckraking era.

6. Many books have summarized this family history. The fullest is Allan Nevins, *A Study in Power: John D. Rockefeller, Industrialist and Philanthropist* (2 vols., New York: Scribner's, 1953). The most perceptive may be John Ensor Harr and Peter J. Johnson, *The Rockefeller Century* (New York: Scribner's, 1988). Of the hostile books the most clever is Peter Collier and David Horowitz, *The Rockefellers: An American Dynasty* (New York: Holt, Rinehart & Winston, 1976).

7. "Excerpts from Remarks by Vice President George Bush . . . ," June 24, 1986, RAC.

8. See Stephen R. Kellert and Edward O. Wilson, eds., *The Biophilia Hypothesis* (Washington: Island Press, 1993).

9. *Nature's Economy: A History of Ecological Ideas* (New York: Cambridge University Press, 1985).

Chapter III

1. See Mary Ellen Chase, *Abby Aldrich Rockefeller* (New York: Macmillan, 1950), and Bernice Kert, *Abby Aldrich Rockefeller: The Woman in the Family* (New York: Random House, 1993).

2. *The Lincoln School of Teachers College: A Descriptive Booklet* (New York: The School, 1922), p. 162.

3. See Laurance S. Rockefeller, "55th Reunion: The Lincoln School, Class of 1928," typescript (Room 5600).

4. LSR to Mama, April 10, 1921, March 18, 1928; to Papa, April 13, 17, 1921; and to Ma-Pa, October 9, 1927; LSR to Mama and Papa, [October] 13, 1928, and Father to Laurance, April 22, 1929 (Room 5600).

5. The Rockefeller family version is given in Fred Smith's unpublished manuscript biography of Laurance Rockefeller, "Exploring the West with Father—1924," and the official version appears in Barry Mackintosh, *Interpretation in the National Park Service: A Historical Perspective* (Washington: National Park Service, 1986), p. 12, and Ralph H. Lewis, *Museum Curatorship in the National Park Service, 1904–1982* (Washington: National Park Service, 1993), p. 17. Interestingly, there is no agreement on the size of this first donation. Smith says $5,000, Lewis suggests $3,000, and Horace M. Albright, as told to Robert Cahn, *The Birth of the National Park Service: The*

Founding Years, 1913–33 (Salt Lake City: Howe Brothers, 1985), says $10,000. One suspects that Smith, with access to family archives, is most likely correct.

6. On the relationship between Albright and JDR, Jr., see Joseph W. Ernst, ed., *Worthwhile Places: Correspondence of John D. Rockefeller, Jr., and Horace M. Albright* (New York: Fordham University Press, 1991), which draws upon original documents in the Rockefeller Archive Center. There is extensive correspondence in the Albright Papers in the library of the University of California, Los Angeles.

7. JDR, Jr., to LSR, n.d., quoting LSR's letter of April 2, 1929 (Room 5600).

8. See the correspondence between JDR, Jr., and Dr. Grenfell in the Sir Wilfred Thomason Grenfell Papers, Yale University Library, Record Group 254, especially boxes 3 and 9.

9. Concluding remarks from senior thesis of Laurance S. Rockefeller, Princeton University, 1932 (Room 5600).

10. Interview by unidentified interviewer (Fraser Seitel), untitled MS, on parents, family, and children, March 30, 1994, p. 14.

11. See Mary Rockefeller's preface to Marion O. Robinson, *Eight Women of the YMCA* (New York: National Board of the YMCA, 1966), and "YMCA: International Success Story," *The National Geographic* (December 1963), pp. 904–33.

12. Transcribed remarks of Laurance S. Rockefeller, Woodrow Wilson Award, Princeton University, February 16, 1991, p. 16 (Room 5600).

13. *The Reader's Digest* (February 1976), pp. 2–6.

Chapter IV

1. Laurance S. Rockefeller, "My Most Unforgettable Character," *The Reader's Digest* (October 1972), pp. 137–41.

2. (Boston: Little, Brown).

3. There have been essays about Osborn, though there is no full biography. *Seeds of the Sixties*, by Andrew Jamieson and Ron Eyerman (Berkeley: University of California Press, 1994), is particularly insightful.

4. Robert Cahn to Laurance S. Rockefeller, July 26, 1986, in Robert Cahn Papers (copies supplied to the author by Mr. Cahn). See Dwight Rettie, *Our National Park System: Caring for America's Greatest Natural and Historic Treasures* (Urbana: University of Illinois Press, 1995), pp. 196–97.

5. The Papers of Robert Moses are in the New York Public Library and the Yale University Library. There is abundant testimony in these collections to the relationship, especially with respect to New York City development and most particularly on the Upper East Side. LSR would be chosen by Moses in 1946 to be one of three commissioners of the New York Airport Authority, which would also throw them together. On Moses see Robert A. Caro, *The Power Broker: Robert Moses and The Fall of New York* (New York: Alfred A. Knopf, 1974), and on the Upper East Side, Joel Schwartz, *The New York Approach: Robert Moses, Urban Liberals, and Redevelopment of the Inner City* (Columbus: Ohio State University Press, 1993), especially pp.

220–22. Moses told some of his own story in his book, *Working for the People: Promise and Performance in Public Service* (New York: Harpers, 1956).

6. See Walter S. Ross, *The Last Hero: Charles A. Lindbergh* (rev. ed., New York: Harper & Row, 1976), p. 369.

7. Kenneth S. Davis, *The Hero: Charles A. Lindbergh and the American Dream* (Garden City, NY: Doubleday, 1959), p. 268. Later Lindbergh visited Pocantico, but it is unclear whether the Rockefeller children saw him then, despite such a claim in several books. See RAC, Record Group 33, Rockefeller Family Collection, box 185: Ruth Haupert to [George R.] Lamb, December 15, 1975.

8. William Jovanovich and Judith A. Schiff, eds., *Charles A. Lindbergh: Autobiography of Values* (New York: Harcourt Brace Jovanovich, 1978), p. 32. I am grateful to Reeve Lindbergh, daughter of Charles and Anne Morrow Lindbergh, and to Judith Schiff of the Yale University Library, for giving me permission to read the correspondence between Laurance Rockefeller and Charles Lindbergh in the Lindbergh Papers at the Yale Library. As I have not been given permission for direct quotation, all Lindbergh material in quotation marks is from other sources, particularly RAC, Record Group 33, Rockefeller Family, boxes 185 and 229.

9. (London: Chatto & Windus, 1955.) LSR was referring to a new edition, with Afterword by the author, published in 1979.

10. See Library of Congress, Edward Vernon Rickenbacker Papers, box 22: Rickenbacker to David Rockefeller, April 25, 1947, and Laurance S. Rockefeller to Rickenbacker, August 19, 1953, June 20, 1956, and February 23, 1961; box 59: Rickenbacker to Rockefeller, May 25, 1967.

11. There is no biography of Whyte. The most accessible article on his work is David Dillon, "The Sage of the City, or How a Keen Observer Solves the Mysteries of Our Streets," *Preservation: The Magazine of the National Trust for Historic Preservation*, XLVIII (October 1966), 70–75.

12. See George Seaver, *Albert Schweitzer: The Man and His Mind* (6th ed., London: Adam & Charles Black, 1969); and Deepak Chopra, *Ageless Body, Timeless Mind: The Quantum Alternative to Growing Old* (New York: Harmony Books, 1993), for influential titles. Schweitzer's *Civilization and Ethics* was of particular interest to Rockefeller. On another occasion LSR referred to two other individuals who had influenced his thinking, one about historic preservation (this was Carlisle Humelsine, one-time chairman of the National Trust for Historic Preservation) and the other about international responsibilities for the environment (Maurice Strong, a Canadian who was the first head of the United Nations' program for the environment).

13. This summary of mentors and other influences is drawn from my interviews with Laurance Rockefeller on November 9, 1994, and April 9, 1995.

Chapter V

1. See John W. Wilson, *The New Venturers: Inside the High-Stakes World of Venture Capital* (Reading, MA: Addison-Wesley, 1985), pp. 13–21, 38–40.

2. Laurance S. Rockefeller, "Business and Beauty," address in New York City, December 2, 1964, Room 5600.

3. JDR, Jr.'s gift was divided, 32,170 acres going to Grand Teton National Park and the remainder to the National Elk Refuge. On LSR's view of how his father managed to get Secretary of the Interior Harold Ickes to persuade President Roosevelt to use the Antiquities Act to declare a national monument see Columbia University, Oral History Project Files: Ed Edwin, "Interview with Laurance Rockefeller," January 10, 1967, pp. 33–35. See also RAC, Record Group III 2 E, 92: Albright to LSR, May 7, and Kenneth Chorley to LSR, February 5 and July 15, 1947. Slightly different figures are given for the acreage in JDR, Jr.'s gift depending on the source.

4. On the problems of creating the park see Robert W. Righter, *Crucible for Conservation: The Creation of Grand Teton National Park* (Boulder: Colorado Associated University Press, 1982).

5. The words are Michael Frome's in *Regreening the National Parks* (Tucson: University of Arizona Press, 1992), p. 134.

6. This remark is quoted in many works. It is given its most aggressive context in Don Hummel, *Stealing the National Parks* (Bellevue, WA: Free Enterprise Press, 1987), pp. 25–26. Having studied Grand Teton park administration reasonably carefully for another purpose, I conclude that there have been only three truly unwise management decisions: allowing off-road use of snowmobiles in winter, overuse of pesticides, especially in the Jenny Lake area, and failing to recognize the historical value of the built structures in Jackson Hole.

7. See RAC, Record Group 33, Rockefeller Family General Files, box 181: "Extracts from Oral Interviews with Laurance S. Rockefeller and Horace M. Albright," MS, p. 12.

8. Jackson Hole Preserve, Inc., which would run the Rockefeller hotels in the national park, was a concessionaire, so it is not surprising that National Park Service policy on concessions would be a consistent Rockefeller concern. He took a particular interest in the report of the Concessions Advisory Group to the secretary of the interior in 1948 and, in 1961, through the American Conservation Association, sponsored a study by the National Planning Association on private enterprise and visitor services in public outdoor recreation areas.

9. On Chapman see Harry S. Truman Presidential Library, Oscar Chapman Papers, Correspondence File 1949-53, ROA-ROG: LSR to Chapman, June 1 and July 27, 1951.

10. People who have not been to Jackson Hole—the portion in the national park—confuse it with Jackson, the town, and sometimes give the impression that what they call the "theme park ambience" of Jackson is also present in the park. In fact, it is because of JHPI that this is not so. For one such ambiguous reading see Jim Robbins, *Last Refuge: The Environmental Showdown in Yellowstone and the American West* (New York: William Morrow, 1993).

11. RAC, Record Group III 2 E, Office of the Messrs. Rockefeller, Box 92, folder 845: William Voigt, Jr., to Harold P. Fabian, November 3, Arthur H. Carhart to Fabian, November 1, Murie to Osborn, October 21, all 1948, and Murie to LSR, May 24, 1947.

12. With the exception of the Dorado Beach Resort in Puerto Rico, where with reluctance LSR permitted a small casino that, to his pleasure, was virtually unnoticed and little used.

13. See transcription of "Interview on Resorts," conducted by Fraser Seitel, November 18, 1993, p. 96.

14. This summary is taken from Alvin Moscow, *The Rockefeller Inheritance* (New York: Doubleday, 1977), pp. 195–96, 299–311, and from "Interview on Resorts," *seriatim.*

15. RAC, Record Group 2, Office of the Messrs. Rockefeller, Series III 2E, box 86, folder 800: "Remarks by Mr. Laurance S. Rockefeller, Chairman of the Board of Jackson Hole Preserve, on the Transfer of Lands on St. John Island to the United States."

16. There is general agreement among historians of the National Park System that Conrad Wirth's Mission 66 did more harm than good, and it is unfortunate that the new national park was the focus of some of the untested initiatives that proved hurtful elsewhere. To be sure, Wirth would not agree. See his *Parks, Politics and the People* (Norman: University of Oklahoma Press, 1980). For a representative example of a negative judgment on Mission 66 at the time see Devereux Butcher, a former executive secretary of the National Parks Association, writing in the *Atlantic Monthly:* "Resorts or Wilderness?" (February 1961), pp. 45–51. With hindsight, historians were no less negative: consult Alfred Runte, *National Parks: The American Experience* (2nd ed., Lincoln: University of Nebraska Press, 1987). My own judgment is less severe, although on balance I too conclude that Mission 66 diverted the Park Service from its basic purpose.

17. Memorandum, LSR to writer, March 30, 1995.

18. See Ismaro Velazquez Net, *Muñoz y Sanchez Vilella* (Puerto Rico: Universidad de Puerto Rico, 1974); R. Elfren Bernier, *Luis Muñoz Marín, Lider y Maestro* (Coamo, PR: Anecdotario Mumarino, 1988); Rexford G. Tugwell, *The Art of Politics as Practiced by Three Great Americans: Franklin Delano Roosevelt, Luis Muñoz Marín, and Fiorello H. La Guardia* (Garden City, NY: Doubleday, 1958); Thomas Aitken, Jr., *Poet in the Fortress: The Story of Luis Muñoz Marín* (New York: New American Library, 1964); and Raymond Carr, *Puerto Rico: A Colonial Experiment* (New York: Oxford University Press, 1984).

19. Comment from Clayton W. Frye, Jr., to author, February 7, 1995. For years Frye was president of the Olohana Corporation, which owned most of the land at Mauna Kea, and was Director and vice chairman of Rockresorts.

20. Don Aanavi, *The Art of Mauna Kea: Asian and Oceanic Art at Mauna Kea Beach Hotel* (Honolulu: East-West Center, 1990), pp. 10, 15–25, 156; RAC, Record Group 33,

Rockefeller Family Collection, box 229, "Remarks," MS, p. 3; Interview, "Resorts," pp. 58, 89–92.

21. Much of this detail is from the transcript of Fraser Seitel's "Resorts" interview with LSR on November 18, 1993. This text has added elements of interest, for Seitel clearly had read Alvin Moscow's *The Rockefeller Inheritance*, and at two points LSR contradicted Moscow's 1977 book; Seitel persisted in each case to the point of it being quite clear that LSR's memory was accurate and, thus, that the Moscow book had at times slightly embroidered a story.

22. West Lebanon, NH, *Valley News*, January 14, 1983.

Chapter VI

1. Stephen Fox, *The American Conservation Movement: John Muir and His Legacy* (Madison: University of Wisconsin Press, 1985), p. 219.

2. See C.J. Taylor, *Negotiating the Past* (Montreal: McGill-Queen's University Press, 1990), p. 81.

3. Accounts differ on how much JDR, Jr., actually spent at Williamsburg: I accept the figure of $60 million given by Moscow in *The Rockefeller Inheritance*, p. 211. The highest figure I have seen is $90 million, in Ary J. Lamme III, *America's Historic Landscapes: Community Power and the Preservation of Four National Historic Sites* (Knoxville: University of Tennessee Press, 1989), p. 85. The situation is further confused by the fact that JDR, Jr., purchased Moore House, which is within Yorktown, and gave it to the National Park Service. Further, not all of Jamestown is within the NPS unit, for the upper end of the island is an affiliated unit owned by the Association for the Preservation of Virginia Antiquities. For the Rockefeller impact on Virginia, see Donald J. Gonzales, *The Rockefellers at Williamsburg: Backstage with the Founders, Restorers and World-Renowned Guests* (McLean, VA: EPM Publications, 1991). LSR's main contribution was in persuading Lila and DeWitt Wallace, owners of *The Reader's Digest*, to give $17 million to Colonial Williamsburg, largely for a gallery of the decorative arts.

4. For general background see Susan R. Schrepfer, *The Fight to Save the Redwoods: A History of Environmental Reform, 1917–1978* (Madison: University of Wisconsin Press, 1983), and Schrepfer, "Conflict in Preservation: The Sierra Club, Save-the-Redwoods League and Redwood National Park," *Journal of Forest History*, XXIV (April 1980), 60–77. See also Thomas J. Crabtree, "The Redwoods: To Preserve and Protect," *Environmental Law*, V (Winter 1975), 283–310. LSR's comment on the park's significance appears in "A Conversation with Laurance Spelman Rockefeller," a video tape made on February 20, 1992 (Room 5600).

5. The National Geographic Society first told the public of the discovery of "the world's tallest tree" in its issue of July 1964, and it outlined its park proposal two years later. See three articles in *The National Geographic*: Melville Bell Grosvenor, "World's Tallest Tree Discovered," July 1964, pp. 1–9; Grosvenor, "A Park to Save

the Tallest Trees," July 1966, pp. 62–64; and Paul Z. Zahl, "Finding the Mt. Everest of All Living Things," July 1964, pp. 10–51. *The National Geographic* frequently returns to the national park scene and seldom fails to mention the redwood park. For a recent instance see the thoughtful summary of the problems the park system faces, "Our National Parks" (October 1994), pp. 3–55, by John G. Mitchell.

6. The "seen them all" statement is quoted in Frome, *Regreening the National Parks*, p. 39. For the more likely statement, see Lou Cannon, *Reagan* (New York: G.P. Putnam's, 1982), p. 351.

7. Those who feel there are not enough as well as those who feel there are too many redwood parks in California tend to play a numbers game, so that the total number of parks differs depending upon the source consulted. There are some important distinctions that do change the numbers: the parks that contain virgin redwoods, those that focus on the coastal redwood, those that preserve the giant sequoia of the interior, and those that quite incidentally protect a small stand of trees though the park was created for other purposes. Thus the figures range from a low of eighteen to a maximum of thirty-two. The lower figure is more accurate with respect to the goals of the movement to create a Redwood National Park, while the higher more appropriately reflects the achievements of the Save-the-Redwoods League. The best figure is twenty-eight. One state park, Calaveras Big Trees, had once been considered for national park status.

8. The figure often given for Johnson's administration is 35 parks. See, for example, Joseph A. Califano, Jr., *The Triumph and Tragedy of Lyndon Johnson: The White House Years* (New York: Simon & Schuster, 1991), p. 338 n. But Barry Mackintosh, *The National Parks: Shaping the System* (Washington: Department of the Interior, 1991), pp. 81–83, makes it clear that the higher figure is correct.

9. The details of LSR's activities on behalf of Redwood National Park are pieced together from the following sources in the Lyndon B. Johnson Presidential Library (hereafter, LBJ Library): Papers of Lyndon Baines Johnson, Confidential File/Name File R, box 150 *seriatim*; box 220: Laurance S. Rockefeller file, memorandum, Orren Beaty, assistant to the secretary of the interior, to Lee C. White, White House staff, December 29, 1964, with Stewart Udall to LSR, December 7, and to Clinton Anderson, December 18 attached; *ibid.*: LSR to LBJ, June 11, July 7, 20, 1965, October 28, 1966, March 7 and October 17, 1967; *ibid.*, LBJ to LSR, February 24, 1967, and Joseph Califano to LBJ, April 17, 1967; *ibid.*, Executive LE/PA: Marvin Watson to LBJ, October 4, and LSR to LBJ, October 17 and reply, November 20, 1967, and October 2, 1968; Records of the Executive Departments, Interior, microfilm roll 7: Redwood Park Controversy; *ibid.*, Oral History, Sharon Francis (interviewed by Dorothy Pierce McSweeney, June 4, 1969), pp. 3–6; *ibid.*, Oral History: George B. Hartzog, Jr. (interviewed by Joe B. Frantz, December 20, 1968), p. 28; and *ibid.*, Oral History, Laurance S. Rockefeller (interviewed by Joe B. Frantz, August 5, 1969), pp. 15–16, 38. For LSR's opposition to

outright land exchanges see Hoover Institution, Stanford, CA, Ronald Reagan collection, box 119: Paul Beck to Phil Battaglia, April 19, 1967.

10. Johnson Papers, *op cit.*, Office Files of John Macy [chief of the Civil Service]: LSR file and Louis Schwatz, Jr., to LBJ, May 1, 1967; and Oral History, Sharon Francis (interviewed by Dorothy Pierce McSweeney, June 27, 1969), p. 57.

11. LSR's relations with the Save-the-Redwoods League are amply documented in RAC, Record Group 33, General Files, especially box 41. I also draw upon my own interview with LSR on November 9, 1994. The search for a compromise was written of by William V. Shannon in the *New York Times*, August 27, 1967.

12. Bill Boyarsky, *The Rise of Ronald Reagan* (New York: Random House, 1968), pp. 212, 215.

13. See LBJ Library, White House Central File, PA (Parks and Monuments), boxes 5, 15, 16, 17, 18 for this opposition. See also *Different Drummer*, II (Winter 1995), 38–39.

14. See LBJ Library, Department of Interior, Secretary, Subject File 82: September 27, 1968—January 24, 1969, and file 59 *seriatim.*

15. On this story, see Frank Graham, Jr., *The Adirondack Park* (New York: Alfred A. Knopf, 1978), ch. 24. There is no evidence of any Rockefeller intention to expand any existing hotels or resorts, though since this was a time of growth in Rockresort projects, Mauna Kea having opened in 1965 and the Woodstock Inn slated for 1969, such a concern was not unreasonable. There was a Rockefeller property at Upper Saranac Lake, called The Point, that had originated as a summer camp in the 1930s, built by William Avery Rockefeller, a nephew of John D. Rockefeller, Sr. It would be sold to Edward G.L. Carter in 1979, and only then did it become a luxury resort. There would also be an ambitious attempt by Larry Rockefeller to create a significant resort property at Beaver Kill, into which LSR would put quite substantial sums, but this was later and in the southwest corner of the Catskill State Park.

16. See Peter Marsh Modley, "Human Problems and Recreational Development: The Proposed Adirondack Mountains National Park," unpublished M.A. thesis, Syracuse University, 1969.

17. See Richard A. Liroff and G. Gordon Davis, *Protecting Open Space: Land Use Control in the Adirondack Park* (Cambridge, MA: Ballinger, 1981).

18. There is a substantial literature on the Adirondack Park and the national park proposal, listed in the bibliography. My conclusion, based on an examination of the primary sources, is basically favorable to the idea of a national park, though I have some doubts on the grounds of standards. For the hostile argument, see in particular Anthony N. D'Elia, *The Adirondack Rebellion* (Loon Lake, NY: Ochiota Books, 1979).

19. Bill McKibben, "A Second Chance," *Land and People*, VIII (Spring 1996), 26–27.

20. See, in particular, Roderick Frazier Nash, *The Rights of Nature: A History of Environ-*

mental Ethics (Madison: University of Wisconsin Press, 1989), pp. 96–97; Donald Fleming, "Roots of the New Conservation Movement," *Perspectives in American History*, VI (1972), 34–39; and René Dubos, "Conservation, Stewardship and the Human Heart," *Audubon Magazine*, LXXIV (September 1972), 20–28.

21. See Russell Train's tribute to Laurance S. Rockefeller, read at the Conservation Stewardship Workshop, Marsh–Billings National Historical Park, Woodstock, Vermont, November 19–21, 1993 (November 20, pp. 1–2).

22. Aldo Leopold, *A Sand County Almanac, and Sketches Here and There* (New York: Oxford University Press, 1987), pp. 203–4.

23. See draft Introduction, General Management Plan, Marsh–Billings National Historical Park, November 18, 1996, Room 5600. On Marsh and the Adirondacks, see Jane Eblen Keller, *Adirondack Wilderness: A Story of Man and Nature* (Syracuse: Syracuse University Press, 1980), p. 157.

24. See John H. McDill, *The Billings Farm* (Woodstock: n.p., 1948), and revised edition, 1971; *Billings Farm & Museum News* (1987–ongoing); Scott E. Hastings, Jr., and Geraldine S. Ames, *The Vermont Farm Year in 1890* (Woodstock: Billings Farm & Museum, 1983); and on the adjacent mansion, Janet Houghton McIntyre, "The Billings Mansion: A History of Its Design and Furnishing, 1869–1900: A Summary Report Derived from the Records of the Collections Cataloging Project, 1975–1977," unpublished typescript in the Marsh–Billings Mansion archives, Woodstock. All of the Brothers contributed to another historical activity, the Rockefeller Family Archive, creating what Peter Dobkin Hall has called a form of historical counter discourse. Consult Hall's insightful chapter in his and George E. Marcus's, *Lives in Trust: The Fortunes of Dynastic Families in Late Twentieth-Century America* (Boulder: Westview Press, 1992), pp. 255–348.

25. Robert Shankland, *Steve Mather of the National Parks* (New York: Alfred A. Knopf, 1951), p. 297; Ronald A. Foresta, *America's National Parks and Their Keepers* (Washington: Resources for the Future, 1984), p. 23.

26. George B. Hartzog Papers, Strom Thurmond Institute, Clemson University: Folder 1038, Hartzog to all assistant directors, August 5, 1969; Douglass Hubbard to Hartzog, July 24, 1970; and Hartzog to LSR, draft, July 28, 1970.

27. See *National Parks for the 21st Century: The Vail Agenda* (Post Mills, VT: Chelsea Green Publishing, n.d.).

28. William J. Briggle, "The Vail Agenda: A Foundation for Change," unpubl. MS, January 25, 1994.

29. Frome, *Regreening*, p. 216.

30. Quoted in James MacGregor Burns, ed., *To Heal and To Build: The Programs of President Lyndon B. Johnson* (New York: McGraw-Hill, 1968), p. 293.

31. See John C. Miles, *Guardians of the Parks: A History of the National Parks and Conservation Association* (Washington: Taylor & Francis, 1995), pp. 310–12. This study led to a significant publication, *Investing in Park Futures: A Blueprint for Tomorrow* (Washing-

ton: The Association, 1988). Volume VIII of the project was on *New Parks: New Promise*, and it presented 221 mini-studies on possible new NPS units.

32. National Park Foundation, *1988 Annual Report* (Washington), p. 6.

33. "LR Remarks at Scenic Hudson Dinner Honoring Four Generations of the Rockefeller Family," MS, LSR to Klara B. Sauer, February 28, 1994, and copies provided by Nash Castro; Castro to author, March 18 and November 1, 1994.

Chapter VII

1. The following summary draws in part upon Fred Smith's unpublished manuscript, "The Other Brother," pp. 420 ff.

2. See Outdoor Recreation Resources Review Commission (hereafter ORRRC), Report 27, p. 119, for a slightly different version of the Penfold story.

3. See Galen Cranz, *The Politics of Park Design: A History of Urban Parks in America* (Cambridge, MA: MIT Press, 1982), p. 105.

4. Interview of LSR conducted by Fraser Seitel, "Conservation," December 16, 1993, pp. 51, 56.

5. The process by which members of the commission and the advisory council were chosen can be traced through the following sources, all in the Dwight D. Eisenhower Library in Abilene, Kansas: Central Files OF 143-I, box 735: William H. Bates to Eisenhower, May 23, 27, 1958, Thor C. Tollefson to Eisenhower, July 17, 1958, Joseph W. Martin to Eisenhower, July 21, 1958, and Robert E. Hampton to Sherman Adams, September 15, 1958; *ibid.*, 143-L: LSR to Gerald Morgan, November 14, 1958, and Hampton Memorandum, September 17, 1958; *ibid.*, 143-I-2: Richard E. McArdle to Adams, July 11, 1958; Official File: Cross Reference Sheets, 143-145-N, box 123: ORRRC file; *ibid.*, 132-L-1, Personal-Confidential file, Advisory Council-Outdoor Recreation Resources Review Board (*sic*): David W. Peyton to Hampton, September 17, 1958, Gustafson to Hampton, February 17, 1959, with enclosures; *ibid.*, Endorsements 134-J-2, box 1056, *passim*; Hatfield Chilson Papers, A76-23: speeches by Fred A. Seaton, December 1956, May 14, 1958; Elmer F. Bennett Papers, A70-21, box 19, ORRRC folder, *passim*.

6. Full sets of the ORRRC report, released in 1962 in twenty-seven volumes, are difficult to find today. I have used the set held by the Yale University Library.

7. Smith speaking to the present writer, March 17, 1994. The quotation is from LSR's letter to his father, April 2, 1931.

8. Thomas R. Cox, *The Park Builders: A History of State Parks in the Pacific Northwest* (Seattle: University of Washington Press, 1988), p. 116.

9. I draw here upon my own unpublished manuscript, "The Rise of the National Park Ethic." A perhaps unintended result, and one that I conclude was ultimately harmful to the national park concept, was that the National Park Service felt it had been chastised for not more aggressively using the mandate given to it by the Parks, Parkway, and Recreation Act of 1936 to develop a federal plan for recre-

ation and rushed much too quickly into accepting units as National Recreation
Areas, some of which were worthy and some not. The Park Service understood
that its primary purpose was not recreational but it was ineffective in defending
its position during this time.

10. Foresta, *America's National Parks*, p. 226. As the ORRRC report was released, Alfred
A. Knopf, a member of the National Park Service Advisory Board, published a
superb new book by the dean of American interpreters, Freeman Tilden. *The State
Parks: Their Meaning in American Life* (New York, 1962) surveyed state parks around
the country chosen from recommendations made by National Park Service
regional directors. Tilden singled out 74 for extended treatment, with thumbnail
sketches of another 111, and discussed the place the state park movement had in
the overall recreational and conservation scheme. (Within thirty years six of the
seventy-four parks would come in to the national park system, nine others would
be unsuccessfully proposed for national park status, and thirteen would be designated National Historic or National Natural Landmarks. The figures for the 111
parks were four, six, and eight respectively.) This path-breaking study was financed
by Laurance Rockefeller and Jackson Hole Preserve, Inc.

11. Memorandum, Henry L. Diamond to author, October 14, 1994, with encl.

12. John Fitzgerald Kennedy Library, Boston, White House Name File, box 2361:
LSR to Kennedy, February 14, and reply, April 11, 1963. There is a substantial file
of routine correspondence in this file and elsewhere.

Chapter VIII

1. See Fred Smith's MS biography of LSR, from which this and the preceding para-
graph are paraphrased. See also LBJ Library, White House Social Files, Alpha
File, box 1779: Mrs. Johnson to "Mr. Rockefeller," August 31, and reply, September 17, 1964.

2. LBJ Library, box 220, LSR file: Commission, February 6, 1965; Seitel interview
with LSR, "Conservation," p. 56.

3. See LBJ Library, box 220, LSR file: LBJ to LSR, January 28, 1965; president's
charge to the conference, *Beauty for America: Proceedings of the White House Conference on
Natural Beauty* (Washington: Government Printing Office, 1965), and *seriatim*.

4. See Vaughn Davis Bornet, *The Presidency of Lyndon B. Johnson* (Lawrence: University
Press of Kansas, 1983), pp. 117, 136–37, on the above paragraphs.

5. Elizabeth Simpson Smith, *Five First Ladies: A Look into the Lives of Nancy Reagan, Ros-
alyn Carter, Betty Ford, Pat Nixon, and Lady Bird Johnson* (New York: Walker, 1986), p.
115.

6. On the relationship between LSR and Mrs. Johnson, see "A Conversation with
Laurance Spelman Rockefeller," a videotape of an interview on February 20, 1992;
the many entries in Mrs. Johnson's *A White House Diary* (New York: Holt, Rinehart
and Winston, 1970); and my interview with Mrs. Johnson, April 13, 1995.

7. This subject is a rich one, and there is much interesting material in the records. I

am brief here because there is an excellent study that covers a good bit of the ground: Lewis L. Gould, *Lady Bird Johnson and the Environment* (Lawrence: University Press of Kansas, 1988). One should also consult Liz Carpenter's lively memoir, *Ruffles and Flourishes: The Warm and Tender Story of a Simple Girl Who Found Adventure in the White House* (Garden City, NY: Doubleday, 1970); Stewart L. Udall, *The Quiet Crisis* (New York: Discus Books, 1964); Gordon Langley Hall, *Lady Bird and Her Daughters* (Philadelphia: Macrae Smith, 1967); and Paul F. Boller, Jr., *Presidential Wives* (New York: Oxford University Press, 1988). The initial *Report to The President from The First Lady's Committee for a More Beautiful Capital* (Washington: The Committee, n.d.) is invaluable and hard to find. I am grateful to Nash Castro for supplying me with a copy.

At the Lyndon B. Johnson Library in Austin there are many informative primary sources. I have drawn on several Oral Histories in particular: Sharon Francis (interviewed by Dorothy Pierce McSweeney, May 20, June 4, 27, August 20, 1969); Elizabeth Rowe (interviewed by Michael L. Gillette, June 6, 16, 1975); Laurance S. Rockefeller (interviewed by Joe B. Frantz, August 5, 1969); Stewart Udall (interviewed by Joe B. Frantz, May 19, July 29, October 31, December 16, 1969); Nash Castro (interviewed by Joe B. Frantz, February 25, March 4, 20, 1969—with additional interviews currently embargoed); Elizabeth Carpenter (interviewed by Joe B. Frantz, April 6, 1969); Bess Abell (interviewed by T.H. Baker, May 28, June 13, July 1, 1969); Conrad L. Wirth (interviewed by Joe B. Frantz, August 5, 1969), John W. Gardner (interviewed by David G. McComb, December 20, 1971); Alan S. Boyd (interviewed by David G. McComb, May 15, 1969); Lowell K. Bridwell (interviewed by David G. McComb, October 17, 1969); Claudia T. (Mrs. Lady Bird) Johnson (interviewed by Nancy Smith, January 23, 1987); and my interview with Mrs. Johnson, April 13, 1995. There also is valuable material in the White House Social File, Alpha, 664, 1779, and 319 (the latter opened October 27, 1994); *ibid.*, box 1340: Mrs. Albert (Mary) Lasker, a particularly full file; *ibid.*, Beautification, box 1: Formation of Committee, and boxes 2–4; *ibid.*, box 220, LSR file; and *ibid.*, Department of the Interior, Secretary, Subject File 76: Annual Reports, Citizens' Advisory Committee on Recreation and Natural Beauty; and Library of Congress, Nathaniel A. Owings Papers, boxes 1–6, especially on Pennsylvania Avenue.

8. On the memorial grove, see the booklet released in 1977 at the dedication of a new foot bridge across Boundary Channel to the site, *The Lyndon Baines Johnson Memorial Grove on the Potomac* (Washington: The Eastern National Park & Monument Association, 1977), with essays by Nash Castro and Lonnelle Aikman. LSR also took an interest in the LBJ State Park in Texas (not to be confused with the LBJ National Historic Site or later National Historical Park). See John Barnett, "LBJ State Park," *Parks & Recreation*, V (December 1970), 32–34, 54. See also *Life* (August 13, 1965).

9. Yale University, Charles Lindbergh Papers, MG 325, Ser. IV, box 148: Citizens'

Advisory Committee on Environmental Quality, 1970 file, *passim*, especially LSR
to Lindbergh, April 30. Almost all accounts of LSR's telephone call to Lindbergh,
ferreted out in the Philippines, asking him to return to the States to accept
appointment to the commission, say that Lindbergh was working with the Tasa-
day people. But as they were not discovered until June 1971, after which he made
them his special concern, this cannot have been the case in 1970. Rather, at the
time Lindbergh was an outside director of Panamin, the Private Association for
National Minorities in the Philippines, having been drawn into awareness of the
genocidal tendencies of civilization and some governments by Tom Harrisson, a
British anthropologist and expert on Borneo and Mindoro, and he was working
to protect the Tboli. See Joyce Milton, *Loss of Eden: A Biography of Charles and Anne
Morrow Lindbergh* (New York: HarperCollins, 1993), pp. 443 *et seq.*

10. *Community Action for Environmental Quality* (Washington: Government Printing
Office, 1970). There were various earlier reports on targeted subjects such as the
disposal of liquid waste.

11. (New York: Thomas Y. Crowell, 1973); Citizens' Advisory Committee on Environmental Quality, *Report to the President and to the Council on Environmental Quality*
(April 1971), pp. 47–54.

12. Lindbergh Papers, box 148: Diamond to Lindbergh, June 11, 1973.

13. The Nixon presidential papers are not yet available. On the relationship between
Nixon and LSR prior to the presidency, see National Archives Pacific Southwest
Region, Laguna Niguel, CA, Richard M. Nixon Pre-Presidential Papers, series
320: Rockefeller Brothers Fund, Inc., box 560.

Chapter IX

1. Palisades Interstate Park Commission, Bear Mountain headquarters, LSR file:
"Remarks of Laurance S. Rockefeller at the Dedication of the Rockefeller State
Park Preserve, Pocantico Hills, New York, May 2, 1986."

2. See David H. Haney, "The Pursuit of the Scenic and the Creation of Acadia
National Park," unpubl. MS, Thesis Review, Yale University, November 7, 1994.
I wish to thank Mr. Haney for sharing his manuscript with me.

3. RAC, Record Group 33, General Files, box 181: "Extracts from Oral Interviews
with Laurance S. Rockefeller and Horace M. Albright."

4. On the history of the park, see Palisades Interstate Park Commission, *60 Years of
Park Cooperation, N.Y.–N.J.: A History 1900–1960* (Bear Mountain: The Commission,
1960). The words comprise the NHL citation.

5. On the building of aesthetic parkways, see the excellent collection of papers in
the Proceedings of the Second Biennial Linear Parks Conference, 1987, *Parkways:
Past, Present, and Future* (Boone, NC: Appalachian Consortium Press, 1989).

6. Palisades Interstate Park Commission, Bear Mountain Park headquarters, minutes: December 18, 1978.

7. Michael P. Cohen, *The History of the Sierra Club, 1892–1970* (San Francisco: Sierra Club Books, 1988), pp. 279–80.
8. See Frances F. Dunwell, *The Hudson River Highlands* (New York: Columbia University Press, 1991), p. 202.
9. See report of [Arthur D. Little, Inc.], "Industrial Trends in the Hudson Valley: Report to the Hudson River Valley Commission, January 1966," RAC.
10. For a balanced account see Joseph L. Sax, *Defending the Environment: A Strategy for Citizen Action* (New York: Knopf, 1971), pp. 73–83. For views in strong opposition to the expressway, see the books by Myer Kutz, Helen Leavitt, Alan Q. Mowbray, and William Rodgers listed in the bibliography. See also Stewart Udall, Oral History transcript, LBJ Library.
11. There is a considerable literature on this controversy. The quotations here are from Laurence Pringle, "Storm Over Storm King," *Audubon*, LXX (August 1968), 60–73.
12. Palisades Interstate Park Commission, minutes: January 27, May 20, June 17, September 16, 1974, January 27, December 15, 1975; *ibid.*, LSR file: [Draft remarks by Nash Castro on the dedication of the Rockefeller Plaque in 1981], with Isabelle K. Savell to Castro, October 18, 1981. Castro left the National Park Service, where he had worked with LSR as regional director for the Capital Parks, to become the executive director of the Palisades Interstate Park Commission from 1969 to 1990. See also Palisades Interstate Park Commission, *Second Century Plan* (N.p.: [The Commission], 1990). The Interstate Park System included restored historic sites as well: Senate House in Kingston, Washington's Headquarters at Newburgh, Knox's Headquarters, the New Windsor Cantonment, Stony Point Battlefield, and Fort Lee.
13. University of California, Los Angeles, Horace Albright Papers, box 7: Albright to LSR, May 18, 1964.
14. Henry L. Diamond, "Nelson A. Rockefeller and the Environment: The Improbable Tree Hugger," unpubl. MS. I wish to thank Mr. Diamond for supplying me with a copy of this paper.
15. James E. Underwood and William J. Daniels, *Governor Rockefeller in New York: The Apex of Pragmatic Liberalism in the United States* (Westport, CT: Greenwood Press, 1982), pp. 98–102, 109–15.
16. Robert H. Connery and Gerald Benjamin, *Rockefeller of New York: Executive Power in the Statehouse* (Ithaca: Cornell University Press, 1979), pp. 19–23.
17. Hudson River Valley Greenway Council, *A Greenway for the Hudson River Valley: A New Strategy for Preserving an American Treasure* (New York: Historic Hudson Valley, 1989), *passim;* Greenway Conservancy for the Hudson River Valley, *Draft Progress Report* (Albany: The Council and Conservancy, 1995).
18. Though never invoked, the report did suggest some of the arguments to be found in the literature of the 1980s on how "gritty cities" such as Troy, New York, Lowell, Massachusetts, and Bethlehem, Pennsylvania, might create tourist amenities.

See The Urban Land Institute, *Environmental Comment*, whole number (January 1981), "Cultural Tourism and Industrial Cities." Trenton and Paterson, New Jersey, and Waterbury, Connecticut, were also singled out. So far only Lowell has had any real success.

19. The instruments by which such areas might receive federal designation and forms of protection have changed across the years. At an earlier date, the Hudson Valley might have been designated a "cultural landscape" and/or a "rural historic district." See Robert Z. Melnick, *Cultural Landscapes: Rural Historic Districts in the National Park System* (Washington: U.S. Department of the Interior, 1984). LSR and his advisors had been working along a different path, which is more closely reflected in the now-preferred approach, a National Heritage Area. Such areas may include linear corridors. See National Coalition for Heritage Areas, *Heritage Links*, I (January 1994), 1. National heritage areas are a proposal coming through the Park Service for coordinating preservation and conservation efforts within a carefully defined landscape and then incorporating the area or not into the system, or designating it as an affiliated area.

20. See especially Peter Canning, *American Dreamers: The Wallaces and Reader's Digest, An Insider's Story* (New York: Simon & Schuster, 1996).

21. Interview with William Conway, February 2, 1995. For a history of the zoo, see William Bridges, *Gatherings of Animals: An Unconventional History of the New York Zoological Society* (2nd ed., New York: The Society, 1995), and the Wildlife Conservation Society's 1995 Centennial Meeting "Historical Film."

22. "A Century of Saving Wildlife," *Wildlife Conservation*, XCVIII (April 1995), whole no., 73. On the zoo, see its successive *Annual Reports*. I am grateful to William Conway for making these available to me. See also Wildlife Conservation Society, *Saving Wildlife since 1895* (New York: The Society, 1994), which summarizes the society's many programs.

23. Caro, *Power Broker*, pp. 678–88. See also Yale University Library, Robert Moses Papers, Manuscript Group 360, box 1, on the aquarium and, in 1963, the New York World's Fair.

24. Transcript of interview conducted by Fraser Seitel, December 16, 1993, pp. 19–22.

25. These complexities are explained in Harr and Johnson, *Rockefeller Conscience*, pp. 493–99.

26. Sasaki Associates, Inc., *Master Plan Draft Environmental Impact Statement, Proposed State Park, Rockefeller Property, Pocantico Hills, New York* (Albany: New York State Office of Parks, Recreation and Historic Preservation, October 1, 1982), Appendix V, "Recreational and Visitation Patterns in the Hudson River Valley," pp. 2, 36. Sasaki Associates had prepared an earlier plan, in 1975, as had the Boyce Thompson Institute. Initially 800 acres were transferred to the state. See "Remarks— Laurance S. Rockefeller Press Conference, Proposed State Park Pocantico Hills, New York, Wednesday, July 28, 1982," p. 3, Room 5600; and *Remarks of Laurance S. Rockefeller at the Dedication of the Rockefeller State Park Preserve* (printed brochure, n.p.),

May 2, 1986. There is a file of correspondence on the proposed State Park Preserve at the New York State Office of Parks, Recreation, and Historic Preservation Taconic Region in Staatsburg, New York. I wish to thank John R. Middle-
brooks, regional program specialist, and Nash Castro for making this file, and the
Sasaki Associates study, available to me. On the inability of the state to maintain
the historic structures, and thus the need to transfer buildings that were on the
National Register of Historic Places to the National Trust for Historic Preservation, see in particular Orin Lehman, Commissioner of Parks and Recreation for
the State of New York, to Governor Hugh Carey, April 19, 1979, copy.

27. See *New York Times*, May 6, 1994; Henry Joyce, "Preservation and the Philanthropic
Vision: The Rockefeller Family Legacy in the Hudson River Valley," *Historic Hudson Valley Magazine* (1994), pp. 24–28, 30, 33, 35; *Kykuit*, an undated and unpaginated
guide to the house and its galleries; and Joyce, *Kykuit: The House and Gardens of the
Rockefeller Family* (N.p: Historic Hudson Valley Press, 1994).

28. Reinhold Niebuhr, *The Irony of American History* (New York: Scribner's, 1952), p. 63.

Chapter X

1. These quotations are drawn from "Some Quotations from LSR: Verbatim and
Condensed," compiled by Carol Lynn Yellin, pp. 6, 9, 13, 14, 17.

2. Alan Talbot, *Power Along the Hudson: The Storm King Case and the Birth of Environmentalism* (New York: E.P. Dutton, 1972), p. 143.

3. Michael K. Heiman, *The Quiet Evolution: Power, Planning, and Profits in New York State*
(New York: Praeger, 1988), pp. 201, 204, 259 n. 18.

4. These paragraphs draw upon the transcript of Fraser Seitel's interview with LSR
December 16, 1993; Carol Lynn Yellin's compilation, "Some Quotations from
LSR"; LSR's remarks and speeches, *seriatim*; and my own conversations with him.

5. "Remarks of Laurance S. Rockefeller Woodrow Wilson Award Princeton University—February 16, 1991: Luncheon Remarks," MS, pp. 5, 20 (Room 5600); and
transcribed "Remarks, February 16, 1991," from the question and answer session
that followed, p. 6, *ibid.*

6. See "Nomination of Nelson A. Rockefeller to be Vice President of the United
States," *Congressional Record*, Senate, November 5, and House, December 4, 1974:
Senate, 885–905, 1397–98; House, 871–947.

7. Omitting speeches that were to celebrate an occasion, such as a retirement at 5600
or the annual Christmas tree lighting at Rockefeller Center, in which the contents
might touch upon any of a variety of subjects, LSR spoke at 209 environment-
specific gatherings. See Memorandum, June 9, 1987 (with undated added pages
bringing the record to January 1993), Joe Ernst to Carol LeBrecht, "Chronologi-
cal Listing of Speeches Given by LSR."

8. For an interesting exploration of how an individual responds to different places,
see Winifred Gallagher, *The Power of Place* (New York: HarperCollins, 1993).

9. Interview #6, "MS-K & Spirituality," January 24, 1994, p. 64, by Fraser Seitel; Yellin, "Some Quotations," p. 3.

10. Interview with Peter Dobkin Hall, Associate Director, Program on Nonprofit Organizations, Institution for Social and Policy Studies, Yale University, May 5, 1995.

11. Robert C. Paehlke, *Environmentalism and the Future of Progressive Politics* (New Haven: Yale University Press, 1989), pp. 20–22.

Bibliography

Printed Primary Sources*

Adams, Arthur G., ed. *The Hudson River in Literature: An Anthology*. Albany: State University of New York Press, 1980.

The Adirondack Council. *2020 Vision: Fulfilling the Promise of the Adirondack Park, Volume 2: Completing the Adirondack Wilderness System*. N.p.: The Adirondack Council, 1990.

Adirondack Land Trust. *Developing a Land Conservation Strategy: A Handbook for Land Trusts*. N.p.: Adirondack Land Trust, 1987.

Adirondack Mountain Club. *The Forest Preserve of New York*. Schenectady: Adirondack Mountain Club, 1964.

Adirondack Park Agency. *Adirondack Park Land Use and Development Plan*. Rye Brook, NY: Adirondack Park Agency, 1973.

Adirondack Park Agency. *Adirondack Park State Land Master Plan*. Albany: Adirondack Park Agency, 1972.

Adirondack Park Agency. *Annual Reports* (through 1994). Rye Brook, NY: The Agency, generally published year following date of report.

Albright, Horace M., as told to Robert Cahn. *The Birth of the National Park Service: The Founding Years, 1913–33*. Salt Lake City: Howe Brothers, 1985.

Albright, Horace M. "John D. Rockefeller, Jr.," *National Parks Magazine*, XXXV (April 1961), 8–10.

Argis, Emily, Clare Novak, and Christine Piwonka, comps. *Hudson River Valley Greenway Historic Sites Directory*. Albany: Hudson River Valley Greenway, 1966.

Artz, Robert M., ed. *Guide to New Approaches to Financing Parks & Recreation*. Washington: Acropolis Books, 1970.

---

*Official government reports, if cited in full in the notes, are omitted here.

Association for the Protection of the Adirondacks. *Annual Reports of the President*. Variously, from New York City, Schenectady, etc., 1902–present.

Brant, Irving. *Adventures in Conservation with Franklin D. Roosevelt*. Flagstaff, AZ: Northland Publishing, 1988.

Buckley, William F., Jr. *The Governor Listeth: A Book of Inspired Political Revelations*. New York: G.P. Putnam's, 1970.

Burns, James MacGregor, ed. *To Heal and to Build: The Programs of President Lyndon B. Johnson*. New York: McGraw-Hill, 1968.

Califano, Joseph A., Jr. *The Triumph & Tragedy of Lyndon Johnson: The White House Years*. New York: Simon & Schuster, 1991.

Carpenter, Liz. *Ruffles and Flourishes: The Warm and Tender Story of a Simple Girl Who Found Adventure in the White House*. Garden City, NY: Doubleday, 1970.

Castro, Nash. *Remarks . . . June 15, 1989*. N.p.: 1989.

Chorley, Kenneth. *"Only Tomorrow": An Address*. Newport, RI: Remington Ward, 1947.

Citizens' Committee for the ORRRC Report. *Action for Outdoor Recreation for America*, Rev. ed. Washington: The Committee, 1964.

Clawson, Marion, and Jack L. Knetsch. *Economics of Outdoor Recreation*. Baltimore: Johns Hopkins University Press, 1966.

The Commission on the Adirondacks in the Twenty-First Century. *The Adirondack Park in the Twenty-First Century*, 3 vols. Albany: State of New York, 1990.

Davis, George B. *Developing a Land Conservation Strategy*. N.p.: Adirondack Land Trust, 1987.

Diamond, Henry L., and Patrick F. Noonan. *Land Use in America*. Washington: Island Press, 1996.

Dilsaver, Lary M., ed. *America's National Park System: The Critical Documents*. Lanham, MD: Rowman & Littlefield, 1994.

Dubos, René. "Conservation, Stewardship and the Human Heart," *Audubon Magazine*, LXXIV (September 1972), pp. 20–28.

Elmer, Isabel Lincoln. *Cinderella Rockefeller: A Wealth Beyond All Knowing*. New York: Freundlich, 1987.

Ernst, Joseph W., ed. *"Dear Father"/"Dear Son": Correspondence of John D. Rockefeller and John D. Rockefeller, Jr.* New York: Fordham University Press, 1994.

Ernst, Joseph W., ed. *Worthwhile Places: Correspondence of John D. Rockefeller, Jr. and Horace M. Albright*. New York: Fordham University Press, 1991.

Fosdick, Harry Emerson. *The Living of Those Days*. New York: Harper & Brothers, 1956.

Gates, Frederick W. *Chapters in My Life*. New York: Free Press, 1977.

Getty, J. Paul. *As I See It: The Autobiography of J. Paul Getty*. Englewood Cliffs: Prentice-Hall, 1976.

Goddard, Donald, ed. *Saving Wildlife: A Century of Conservation*. New York: Harry N. Abrams, 1995.

Goldman, Eric F. *The Tragedy of Lyndon Johnson*. New York: Knopf, 1974.

Hartzog, George B., Jr. *Battling for the National Parks*. Mt. Kisco, NY: Moyer Bell, 1988.

Hopkins, L. Thomas, and James E. Mendenhall. *Achievement at Lincoln School: A Study of Academic Test Results in an Experimental School*. New York: Lincoln School of Teachers College, 1934.

Horowitz, David. *Radical Son: A Journey Through Our Times*. New York: Free Press, 1997.

Hubbard, Barbara Marx. *The Hunger of Eve: A Woman's Odyssey Toward the Future*. Harrisburg: Stackpole Books, 1976.

Hummel, Don. *Stealing the National Parks*. Bellevue, WA: Free Enterprise Press, 1987.

Ickes, Harold L. *The Autobiography of a Curmudgeon*. New York: Reynal & Hitchcock, 1943.

Ickes, Harold L. *The Secret Diary of Harold L. Ickes*, 3 vols. New York: Simon and Schuster, 1953–54.

Ives, Susan. "A Conversation with Bill McKibben." *Land and People* (The Trust for Public Land), VIII (Spring 1996), 22–27.

Jamieson, Paul, ed. *The Adirondack Reader*. Glens Falls: The Adirondack Mountain Club, 1982.

Johnson, Lady Bird. *A White House Diary*. New York: Holt, Rinehart and Winston, 1970.

Kristol, Irving, and Paul H. Weaver, eds. *Critical Choices for Americans: Volume II, The Americans: 1976*. Lexington, MA: Lexington Books, 1976.

Lasky, Victor. *Arthur J. Goldberg: The Old and the New*. New Rochelle: Arlington House, 1970.

The Lincoln School of Teachers College, 1926–1927. New York: The School, n.d.

The Lincoln School of Teachers College: A Descriptive Booklet. New York: The School, 1922.

Lindbergh, Charles A. *Autobiography of Values*. New York: Harcourt Brace Jovanovich, 1978.

Leopold, Aldo. *A Sand County Almanac, and Sketches Here and There*. New York: Oxford University Press, 1967.

Lourie, Peter. *River of Mountains*. Syracuse: Syracuse University Press, 1995.

Marsh, George Perkins. *Man and Nature: Physical Geography as Modified by Human Action* (subsequently *Human Geography as Modified by Human Action*, rev. ed., 1874). New York: Charles Scribner, 1864.

McKibben, Bill. *Hope, Human and Wild: True Stories of Living Lightly on the Earth*. Boston: Little, Brown, 1995.

McPherson, Harry. *A Political Education*. Boston: Little, Brown, 1972.

Moses, Robert. *Working for the People: Promise and Performance in Public Service*. New York: Harper & Brothers, 1956.

Muñoz Marín, Luis. *Historia del Partido Popular Democratico*. San Juan: El Batey, 1984.

Murie, Margaret E., and J. Olaus. *Wapiti Wilderness*. New York: Alfred A. Knopf, 1966.

New York, State of. *Report of the Joint Legislative Committee on Appraisal and Assessment of Publicly Owned Lands*. Albany: Legislative Document No. 23, 1965.

New York State Department of Environmental Conservation. *Environmental Plan for New York State: Preliminary Edition*. Albany: The Department, 1975.

New York (State) Temporary Study Commission on the Future of the Adirondacks. *The Future of the Adirondack Park.* Albany: The State, 1970.

New York World's Fair. *Official Guide Book of the New York World's Fair 1939,* 3rd ed. New York: Exposition Publications, 1939.

O'Donnell, Frank. "Conservation, Inc.," *Nature Conservancy Annual Report,* XLIII (February 1993).

Osborn, Fairfield. *Our Plundered Planet.* Boston: Little, Brown, 1948.

Otnes, Cele, and Richard F. Beltramini, et al. *Gift Giving: A Research Anthology.* Bowling Green: Popular Press, 1996.

Palisades Interstate Park Commission. *60 Years of Park Cooperation, N.Y.–N.J.: A History 1900–1960.* Bear Mountain: The Commission, 1960.

Ridenour, James M. *The National Parks Compromised: Pork Barrel Politics and America's Treasures.* Merrillville, IN: ICS Books, 1994.

Righter, Robert W. *A Teton Country Anthology.* Boulder: Roberts Rinehart, 1990.

Robinson, Marion O. *Eight Women of the YMCA.* New York: National Board of the YMCA, 1966.

Rockefeller, Mary French. "YWCA: International Success Story," *The National Geographic* (December 1963), pp. 904–33.

Rockefeller, Mary and Laurance. "Parks, Plans, and People," *The National Geographic* (January 1967), pp. 74–119.

Rockefeller, Nelson A. *Our Environment Can Be Saved.* Garden City, NY: Doubleday, 1970.

Rosario Natal, Carmelo, ed. *Luis Muñoz Marín: Juicios Sobre Su Significado Historico.* San Juan: Fundación de Luis Muñoz Marín, 1990.

Sasaki Associates, Inc. *Master Plan and Draft Environmental Impact Statement, Proposed State Park, Rockefeller Property, Pocantico Hills, New York.* Albany: New York State Office of Parks, Recreation, and Historic Preservation, 1982.

Sax, Joseph L. *Defending the Environment: A Strategy for Citizen Action.* New York: Knopf, 1971.

Schullery, Paul. *The National Park Service: A Seventy-Fifth Anniversary Album.* Boulder: Roberts Rinehart, 1991.

Smith, Fred. Unpublished manuscript biographies of LSR, one largely illustrated, and referred to in house as "the short manuscript," the other full, often attractively anecdotal, and referred to as "the long manuscript." There may be a third manuscript called "Notes on the Life and Times of John D. Rockefeller's 3rd Grandson," as a title page and contents, as by M. Frederik Smith, is cited by Alvin Moscow, though I have been unable to locate it. All references are to the "long" manuscript.

Thompson, Ben, Roger Thompson, and Conrad Wirth. *A Report on a Proposed Adirondack Mountains National Park* (New York: Rockefeller Center, 1967).

Tugwell, Rexford G. *The Art of Politics as Practiced by Three Great Americans: Franklin Delano*

Roosevelt, Luis Muñoz Marín, and Fiorello H. LaGuardia. Garden City, NY: Doubleday, 1958.

Udall, Stewart L. "To Elevate the Life of the People." *In* James MacGregor Burns, ed., *To Heal and to Build: The Programs of President Lyndon B. Johnson.* New York: McGraw-Hill, 1968, pp. 289–94.

Udall, Stewart L. *The Quiet Crisis.* New York: Discus Books, 1964.

U.S. Senate. *Nomination of Nelson A. Rockefeller to be Vice President of the United States.* Washington: Government Printing Office, 1974.

West, J. B., with Mary Lynn Kotz. *Upstairs at the White House: My Life with the First Ladies.* New York: Coward, McCann & Geoghegan, 1973.

White House Conference on Natural Beauty. *Beauty for America: Proceedings of the White House Conference on Natural Beauty.* Washington: Government Printing Office, 1965.

White, Theodore H. *The Making of the President, 1964.* New York: Atheneum, 1965.

White, Theodore H. *The Making of the President, 1968.* New York: Atheneum, 1969.

Wilson, Malcolm. "My Years with Nelson Rockefeller." *In* Colby, Peter W., ed., *New York State Today: Politics, Government, Public Policy* (Albany: State University of New York Press, 1985), pp. 139–45.

Wirth, Conrad L. *Parks, Politics, and the People.* Norman: University of Oklahoma Press, 1980.

Zahniser, Ed, ed. *Where Wilderness Preservation Began: Adirondack Writings of Howard Zahniser.* Utica: North Country Books, 1992.

Zeckendorf, William. *Zeckendorf: The Autobiography of William Zeckendorf.* New York: Holt, Rinehart and Winston, 1970.

Secondary Accounts

Aanavi, Don. *The Art of Mauna Kea: Asian and Oceanic Art at Mauna Kea Beach Hotel.* Honolulu: East-West Center, 1990.

Abels, Jules. *The Rockefeller Billions: The Story of the World's Most Stupendous Fortune.* New York: Macmillan, 1965.

Adams, Arthur G. *The Hudson: A Guidebook to the River.* Albany: State University of New York Press, 1981. Reprinted by Fordham University Press, New York, 1996.

Adams, Arthur G. *The Hudson through the Years.* Bronx: Fordham University Press, 1996.

Aguiar, Michael. "In the Spotlight: The Hudson River," *Kaatskill Life,* X (Spring 1995), pp. 26–29.

Aitken, Thomas, Jr. *Poet in the Fortress: The Story of Luis Muñoz Marín.* New York: New American Library, 1964.

Alderson, William T., and Shirley Payne Low. *Interpretation of Historic Sites,* 2nd rev. ed. Nashville: American Association for State and Local History, 1985.

Aldrich, Nelson W., Jr. *Old Money: The Mythology of America's Upper Class.* New York: Knopf, 1988.

Allen, Gary. *The Rockefeller File.* Seal Beach, CA: '76 Press, 1976.

Allen, Thomas B., and others. *America's Outdoor Wonders: State Parks and Sanctuaries.* Washington: National Geographic Society, 1987.

Allen, William H. *Rockefeller: Giant, Dwarf, Symbol.* New York: Institute for Public Service, 1930.

Amir, Shaul. *Research on Conflict in Locational Decisions: Conservation Kills a Highway: The Hudson River Expressway Controversy.* Discussion Paper IV, University of Pennsylvania, Wharton School of Finance and Commerce, September 1970.

Barnett, John. "LBJ State Park." *Parks & Recreation,* V (December 1970), pp. 32–34, 54.

Baxter, Gordon, and Finlay Weir. "Baxters and Its Visitor Centre." *In* J.M. Fladmark, ed., *Heritage: Conservation, Interpretation and Enterprises*: Papers presented at The Robert Gordon University Heritage Convention 1993. London: Donhead, 1993, pp. 251–58.

Baxter, Raymond J. *Railroad Ferries of the Hudson: And Stories of a Deckhand.* Woodcliff Lake, NY: Lind, 1987.

Beamish, Richard. "An Embattled Wilderness." *National Parks,* LXVI (September 1992), pp. 36–41.

Beauvais, Joel. "Planning, Property, and Power: A Political Post-Mortem of the Commission for the Adirondacks in the Twenty-First Century," unpubl. B.A. thesis, Yale University, 1995.

Benson, Susan Porter, ed. *Preserving the Past: Essays on History and the Public.* Philadelphia: Temple University Press, 1986.

Bernier, R. Elfren. *Luis Muñoz Marín, Lider y Maestro.* Coamo: Ramallo Brothers, 1988.

Bethke, Robert D. *Adirondack Voices: Woodsmen and Woods Lore.* Urbana: University of Illinois Press, 1981.

Betts, Robert B. *Along the Ramparts of the Tetons: The Saga of Jackson Hole, Wyoming.* Boulder: Colorado Associated University Press, 1978.

Boller, Paul F., Jr. *Presidential Wives.* New York: Oxford University Press, 1988.

Bornet, Vaughn Davis. *The Presidency of Lyndon B. Johnson.* Lawrence: University Press of Kansas, 1983.

Boyarsky, Bill. *The Rise of Ronald Reagan.* New York: Random House, 1968.

Boyle, Robert H. *The Hudson River: A Natural and Unnatural History.* New York: W.W. Norton, 1969.

Bremner, Robert H. *American Philanthropy.* Chicago: University of Chicago Press, 1960.

Bremner, Robert H. *Giving: Charity and Philanthropy in History.* New Brunswick, NJ: Transactions Publishers, 1994.

Brown, Dona. *Inventing New England: Regional Tourism in the Nineteenth Century.* Washington: Smithsonian Institution Press, 1995.

Brown, E. Richard. *Rockefeller Medicine Men: Medicine and Capitalism in America.* Berkeley: University of California Press, 1979.

Burgess, Larry E. *Daniel Smiley of Molonk: A Naturalist's Life.* Fleischmanns, NY: Purple Mountain Press, 1996.

Buschman, Charles G. "Preserving Scenic Areas: The Adirondack Land Use Program," *Yale Law Journal*, LXXXIV, no. 8 (1975), pp. 1705–21.

Cahn, Matthew Alan. *Environmental Deceptions: The Tensions between Liberalism and Environmental Policymaking in the United States*. Albany: State University of New York Press, 1995.

Campbell, Carlos C. *Birth of a National Park in the Great Smoky Mountains*, rev. ed., Knoxville: University of Tennessee Press, 1969.

Canning, Peter. *American Dreamers: The Wallaces and Reader's Digest: An Insider's Story*. New York: Simon & Schuster, 1996.

Cannon, Lou. *Reagan*. New York: Putnam's, 1982.

Carmer, Carl. *The Hudson*. New York: Rinehart, 1974.

Caro, Robert A. *The Power Broker: Robert Moses and the Fall of New York*. New York: Knopf, 1974.

Carr, Albert Z. *John D. Rockefeller's Secret Weapon*. New York: McGraw-Hill, 1962.

Carr, Raymond. *Puerto Rico: A Colonial Experiment*. New York: New York University Press, 1984.

"A Century of Saving Wildlife," *Wildlife Conservation*, XCVIII (April 1995), whole number.

Chambers, Andrea. *Dream Resorts*. New York: Clarkson N. Potter, 1983.

Chase, Alston. *Playing God in Yellowstone: The Destruction of America's First National Park*. Boston: Atlantic Monthly Press, 1986.

Chase, Mary Ellen. *Abby Aldrich Rockefeller*. New York: Macmillan, 1950.

Clinton, Susan Maloney. *First Ladies*. Chicago: Children's Press, n.d.

Cobb, Thomas L. "An Overview of National Park, National Forest and Other Protected Area Management Systems with Selected Institutional Examples." *In* The Commission on the Adirondacks in the Twenty-First Century, *The Adirondack Park in the Twenty-First Century, Technical Reports*. Albany: State of New York, 1990, I, pp. 288–325.

Cohen, Michael P. *The History of the Sierra Club, 1892–1970*. San Francisco: Sierra Club Books, 1988.

Colby, Gerard, with Charlotte Dennett. *Thy Will Be Done: The Conquest of the Amazon— Nelson Rockefeller and Evangelism in the Age of Oil*. New York: HarperCollins, 1995.

Colby, P. W., and J. K. White, eds. *New York State Today: Politics, Government, Public Policy*. Albany: State University of New York Press, 1989.

Colihan, Jane. "Out of the Woods," *American Heritage*, XLVIII (April 1997), pp. 68–77.

Collier, Peter, and David Horowitz. *The Rockefellers: An American Dynasty*. New York: Holt, Rinehart & Winston, 1976.

Collier, Sargent F. *Mt. Desert Island and Acadia National Park: An Informal History*. Camden, ME: Down East Books, 1978.

Connery, Robert H., and Gerald Benjamin. *Rockefeller of New York: Executive Power in the Statehouse*. Ithaca: Cornell University Press, 1979.

BIBLIOGRAPHY

Cormier, Frank. *LBJ: The Way He Was.* New York: Doubleday, 1977.

Corner, George W. *A History of the Rockefeller Institute, 1901–1953.* New York: Rockefeller Institute Press, 1964.

Cox, Thomas R. *The Park Builders: A History of State Parks in the Pacific Northwest.* Seattle: University of Washington Press, 1988.

Crabtree, Thomas J. "The Redwoods: To Preserve and Protect." *Environmental Law,* V (Winter 1975), pp. 283–310.

Cranz, Galen. *The Politics of Park Design: A History of Urban Parks in America.* Cambridge, MA: MIT Press, 1982.

Creekmore, Betsey Beeler. *Knoxville,* 3rd ed. University of Tennessee Press, 1976.

Cronon, William, ed. *Uncommon Ground: Toward Reinventing Nature.* New York: W.W. Norton, 1995.

Crosby, Alfred W. "The Past and Present of Environmental History." *American Historical Review,* C (October 1995), pp. 1177–89.

Curti, Merle, and Roderick Nash. *Philanthropy in the Shaping of American Higher Education.* New Brunswick, NJ: Rutgers University Press, 1965.

Curtis, Jane, Peter Jennison, and Frank Lieberman. *Frederick Billings: Vermonter, Pioneer Lawyer, Business Man, Conservationist.* Woodstock, VT: The Woodstock Foundation, 1986.

Curtis, Jane and Will, and Frank Lieberman. *The World of George Perkins Marsh, America's First Conservationist and Environmentalist.* Woodstock, VT: Countryman Press, 1982.

Daley, Robert. *An American Saga: Juan Trippe and His Pan Am Empire.* New York: Random House, 1980.

Davies III, J. Clarence, and Barbara S. Davies. *The Politics of Pollution,* 2nd ed. Indianapolis: Pegasus, 1975.

Davis, Kenneth S. *The Hero: Charles A. Lindbergh and the American Dream.* Garden City, NY: Doubleday, 1959.

DeLaughter, Jerry. *Mountain Roads & Quiet Places,* rev. ed. Gatlinburg: Great Smoky Mountains Natural History Association, 1993.

D'Elia, Anthony N. *The Adirondack Rebellion.* Loon Lake, NY: Ochiota Books, 1979.

Dillard, Tom W. "Winthrop Rockefeller, 1967–1971." *In* Timothy P. Donovan and Willard B. Gatewood, Jr., eds., *The Governors of Arkansas: Essays in Political Biography.* Fayetteville: University of Arkansas Press, 1981.

Dillon, David. "Sage of the City, or How a Keen Observer Solves the Mysteries of Our Street," *Preservation: The Magazine of the National Trust for Historic Preservation,* XLVIII (October 1996), pp. 71–75.

Divine, Robert A., ed. *Exploring the Johnson Years.* Austin: University of Texas Press, 1981.

Divine, Robert A. *The Johnson Years:* Volume Three, *LBJ at Home and Abroad.* Lawrence: University Press of Kansas, 1994.

Dixon, John A., and Tom van't Hof. "Conservation Pays Big Dividends in Caribbean," *Forum for Applied Research and Public Policy,* XII (Spring 1997), pp. 43–48.

Dunn, Durwood. *Cades Cove: The Life and Death of a Southern Appalachian Community.* Knoxville: University of Tennessee Press, 1988.

Dunwell, Frances F. *The Hudson River Highlands.* New York: Columbia University Press, 1991.

Elliott, Melinda. *Exploring Human Worlds,* rev. ed. Santa Fe: School of American Research, 1991.

Engbeck, Joseph H., Jr. *State Parks of California from 1864 to the Present.* Portland, OR: Charles H. Belding, 1980.

Ettling, John. *The Germ of Laziness: Rockefeller Philanthropy and Public Health in the New South.* Cambridge, MA: Harvard University Press, 1981.

Everhart, William C. *The National Park Service.* New York: Praeger, 1972.

Farr, Finis. *Rickenbacker's Luck: An American Life.* Boston: Houghton Mifflin, 1979.

Fisher, Ron. *Our Threatened Inheritances: Natural Treasures of the United States.* Washington: National Geographic Society, 1984.

Fitch, Edwin M., and John F. Shanklin. *The Bureau of Outdoor Recreation.* New York: Praeger, 1970.

Fleming, Donald. "Roots of the New Conservation Movement." *Perspectives in American History,* VI (1972), pp. 7–94.

Flynn, Jean. *Lady: A Biography of Claudia Alta (Lady Bird) Johnson, Texas' First Lady.* Austin: Eakin Press, 1992.

Folwell, Elizabeth. *The Adirondack Book,* 2nd ed. Lee, MA: Berkshire House, 1996.

Fosdick, Raymond B. *Adventures in Giving: The Story of the General Education Board.* New York: Harper & Row, 1962.

Fosdick, Raymond B. *John D. Rockefeller, Jr.: A Portrait.* New York: Harper & Brothers, 1956.

Fosdick, Raymond B. *The Story of the Rockefeller Foundation.* New York: Harper & Brothers, 1952.

Fowler, Robert Booth. *The Greening of Protestant Thought.* Chapel Hill: University of North Carolina Press, 1955.

Fox, Stephen. *John Muir and His Legacy: The American Conservation Movement.* Boston: Little, Brown, 1981.

Francis, Austin M. "Lure of the Beaverkill," *Countryside,* I (Summer 1990).

Frantz, Joe B. *Aspects of the American West: Three Essays.* College Station: Texas A&M University Press, 1976.

Frome, Michael. *Battle for the Wilderness.* New York: Praeger, 1974.

Frome, Michael. *Regreening the National Parks.* Tucson: University of Arizona Press, 1992.

Frome, Michael. *Strangers in High Places: The Story of the Great Smoky Mountains,* expanded ed. Knoxville: University of Tennessee Press, 1966.

Fursenko, A.A. *Die Dynastie Rockefeller.* Berlin: VEB Deutscher Verlag der Wissenschaften, 1972.

Gallagher, Winifred. *The Power of Place.* New York: HarperCollins, 1993.

Gatewood, Willard Badgette, Jr. "North Carolina's Role in the Establishment of the

Great Smoky Mountains National Park." *The North Carolina Historical Review*, XXXVII (April 1960), pp. 165–84.

Gelernter, David. *1939: The Lost World of the Fair*. New York: Free Press, 1995.

Gervasi, Frank. *The Real Rockefeller*. New York: Atheneum, 1964.

Gilborn, Craig. *Durant: The Fortunes and Woodland Camps of a Family in the Adirondacks*. Blue Mountain Lake: Adirondack Museum, 1981.

Gill, Brendan. *Lindbergh Alone*. New York: Harcourt Brace Jovanovich, 1977.

Gitelman, H.M. *Legacy of the Ludlow Massacre: A Chapter in American Industrial Relations*. Philadelphia: University of Pennsylvania Press, 1988.

Gonzales, Donald J. *The Rockefellers at Williamsburg: Backstage with the Founders, Restorers and World-Renowned Guests*. McLean, VA: EPM Publications, 1991.

Goodale, Thomas L., and Geoffrey C. Godbey. *The Evolution of Leisure: Historical and Philosophical Perspectives*. State College, PA: Venture Publishing, 1988.

Gore, Peter H., and Mark B. Lapping. "Environmental Quality and Social Equality: Wilderness Preservation in a Repressed Region, New York State's Adirondacks." *The American Journal of Economics and Sociology*, XXXV (October 1976), pp. 349–590.

Gould, Lewis L. "Lady Bird Johnson and Beautification." *In* Robert A. Divine, ed., *The Johnson Years: Vietnam, the Environment, and Science*. Lawrence: University of Kansas Press, 1987, II, pp. 150–80.

Gould, Lewis L. *Lady Bird Johnson and the Environment*. Lawrence: University Press of Kansas, 1988.

Gould, Lewis L. *1968: The Election that Changed America*. Chicago: Ivan R. Dee, 1993.

Goulder, Grace. *John D. Rockefeller: The Cleveland Years*. Cleveland: Western Reserve Historical Society, 1972.

Graham, Frank, Jr. *The Adirondack Park: A Political History*. New York: Alfred A. Knopf, 1978.

Grimes, Richard. *Jay Rockefeller: Old Money, New Politics*. Parsons, WV: McClain Printing, 1984.

Gunther, John. *Taken at the Flood: The Story of Albert D. Lasker*. New York: Harper & Brothers, 1960.

Hahn, Emily. *Animal Gardens*. Garden City, NY: Doubleday, 1967.

Hall, Gordon Langley. *Lady Bird and Her Daughters*. Philadelphia: Macrae Smith, 1967.

Hall, Peter Dobkin. *Inventing the Nonprofit Sector and Other Essays on Philanthropy, Voluntarism, and Nonprofit Organizations*. Baltimore: Johns Hopkins University Press, 1992.

Haney, David H. "The Pursuit of the Scenic at the Creation of Acadia National Park." Unpubl. MS, Thesis Review, Yale University, November 7, 1994.

Harr, John Ensor, and Peter J. Johnson. *The Rockefeller Century*. New York: Scribner's, 1988.

Harr, John Ensor, and Peter J. Johnson. *The Rockefeller Conscience: An American Family in Public and in Private*. New York: Scribner's, 1991.

Harris, David. *The Last Stand: The War Between Wall Street and Main Street Over California's Ancient Redwoods*. New York: Times Books, 1995.

Hartmann, Susan M. "Women's Issues and the Johnson Administration." *In* Robert A. Divine, *The Johnson Years: Volume Three, LBJ at Home and Abroad.* Lawrence: University Press of Kansas, 1994, pp. 53–81.

Harvey, Mark W. T. *A Symbol of Wilderness: Echo Park and the American Conservation Movement.* Albuquerque: University of New Mexico Press, 1994.

Hatch, Charles E. *Virgin Islands National Park.* Washington: National Park Service, 1972.

Hawke, David Freeman. *John D.: The Founding Father of the Rockefellers.* New York: Harper & Row, 1980.

Hays, Samuel P. *Beauty, Health, and Permanence: Environmental Politics in the United States, 1955–1985.* New York: Cambridge University Press, 1987.

Heckscher, August, and Phyllis Robinson. *Open Spaces: The Life of American Cities.* New York: Harper & Row, 1977.

Heidenry, John. *Theirs Was the Kingdom: Lila and DeWitt Wallace and the Story of the Reader's Digest.* New York: W.W. Norton, 1993.

Heiman, Michael K. *The Quiet Evolution: Power, Planning, and Profits in New York State.* New York: Praeger, 1988.

Holbrook, Sabra. *The American West Indies: Puerto Rico and the Virgin Islands.* New York: Meredith Press, 1969.

Hosmer, Charles B., Jr. *Preservation Comes of Age: From Williamsburg to the National Trust, 1926–1949,* 2 vols. Charlottesville: University Press of Virginia, 1981.

Hungerford, Edward. *Men and Iron: The History of New York Central.* New York: Thomas Y. Crowell, 1938.

Ise, John. *Our National Park Policy: A Critical History.* Baltimore: Johns Hopkins University Press, 1961.

Jackson, John Brinckerhoff. *A Sense of Place, A Sense of Time.* New Haven: Yale University Press, 1994

Jadan, Doris. *A Guide to the Natural History of St. John.* Charlotte Amalie: Environmental Studies Program, 1979.

Jakle, John A. *The Tourist: Travel in Twentieth-Century North America.* Lincoln: University of Nebraska, 1985.

James, Estelle, ed. *The Nonprofit Sector in International Perspective: Studies in Comparative Culture and Policy.* New York: Oxford University Press, 1989.

Jamieson, Andrew, and Ron Eyerman. *Seeds of the Sixties.* Berkeley: University of California Press, 1994.

Jennison, Peter S. *The History of Woodstock, Vermont, 1890–1983.* Woodstock: Countryman Press, 1985.

Johnson, Roberta. *Puerto Rico: Commonwealth or Colony?* New York: Praeger, 1980.

Jolley, Harley E. *The Blue Ridge Parkway.* Knoxville: University of Tennessee Press, 1969.

Jolley, Harley E. *Blue Ridge Parkway: The First 50 Years.* N.p.: Appalachian Consortium Press, 1985.

Jonas, Gerald. *The Circuit Riders: Rockefeller Money and the Rise of Modern Science.* New York: Norton, 1989.

242

BIBLIOGRAPHY

Josephson, Emanuel M. *The Strange Death of Franklin D. Roosevelt: History of the Roosevelt–Delano Dynasty, America's Royal Family.* New York: Chedney Press, 1948.

Josephson, Emanuel M. *The Truth About Rockefeller: "Public Enemy No. 1"— Studies in Criminal Psychopathy.* New York: Chedney Press, 1964.

Joyce, Henry. "Preservation and the Philanthropic Vision: The Rockefeller Family Legacy in the Hudson River Valley." *Historic Hudson Valley Magazine* (1994), pp. 24–28, 30, 33, 35.

Joyce, Henry. *Tour of Kykuit: The House and Gardens of the Rockefeller Family.* N.p.: Historic Hudson Valley Press, 1994.

Kaiser, Harvey. *The Great Camps of the Adirondacks.* Boston: Godine, 1982.

Kasson, John F. *Amusing the Millions: Coney Island at the Turn of the Century.* New York: Hill & Wang, 1978.

Kaufman, Polly Welts. *National Parks and the Woman's Voice: A History.* Albuquerque: University of New Mexico Press, 1996.

Kearns, Doris. *Lyndon Johnson and the American Dream.* New York: Harper & Row, 1976.

Keller, Jane Eblen. *Adirondack Wilderness: A Story of Man and Nature.* Syracuse: Syracuse University Press, 1980.

Kellert, Stephen R. and Edward O. Wilson, eds. *The Biophilia Hypothesis.* Washington: Island Press, 1993.

Kert, Bernice. *Abby Aldrich Rockefeller: The Woman in the Family.* New York: Random House, 1993.

Klapthor, Margaret Brown. *The First Ladies,* 7th ed. Washington: White House Historical Association, 1994.

Koebner, Linda. *Zoo Book: The Evolution of Wildlife Conservation Centers.* New York: Forge, 1994.

Kramer, Michael, and Sam Roberts. *"I Never Wanted to be Vice-President of Anything": An Investigative Biography of Nelson Rockefeller.* New York: Basic Books, 1976.

Kreuzer, Terese Loeb. "A Balancing Act." *Caribbean Travel and Life,* XII (April 1997), pp. 50, 52–55.

Krinsky, Carol Herselle. *Rockefeller Center.* New York: Oxford University Press, 1978.

Kutz, Myer. *Rockefeller Power.* New York: Simon & Schuster, 1974.

Lambert, Darwin. *The Undying Past of Shenandoah National Park.* Boulder: Roberts Rinehart, Inc., 1989.

Lamme, Ary J. III. *American's Historic Landscapes: Community Power and the Preservation of Four National Historic Sites.* Knoxville: University of Tennessee Press, 1987.

Landy, Marc K., Marc J. Roberts, and Stephen R. Thomas. *The Environmental Protection Agency: Asking the Wrong Questions, From Nixon to Clinton,* expanded ed. New York: Oxford University Press, 1994.

Lankford, Nelson D. *The Last American Aristocrat: The Biography of Ambassador David K.E. Bruce, 1898–1977.* Boston: Little, Brown, 1996.

Lear, Linda J. *Harold L. Ickes: The Aggressive Progressive, 1874–1933.* New York: Garland, 1981.

Leavitt, Helen. *Superhighway—Superhoax*. Garden City, NY: Doubleday, 1970.

Lee, Martha F. *Earth First: Environmental Apocalypse*. Syracuse: Syracuse University Press, 1995.

Leed, Eric J. *The Mind of the Traveler: From Gilgamesh to Global Tourism*. New York: Basic Books, 1991.

Lewis, Gordon K. *Notes on the Puerto Rican Revolution*. New York: Monthly Review, 1974.

Lewis, Ralph H. *Museum Curatorship in the National Park Service, 1904–1982*. Washington: National Park Service, 1993.

Limburg, K.E., M.A. Moran, and W.T. McDowell. *The Hudson River Ecosystem*. New York: Springer Verlag, 1986.

Lindbergh, Anne Morrow. *Gift from the Sea*. London: Chatto & Windus, 1979.

Linear Parks Conference. *Second Biennial Parkways Conference: Past, Present, and Future*. Boone, NC: Appalachian Consortium Press, 1989.

Liroff, Richard A., and G. Gordon Davis. *Protecting Open Space: Land Use Control in the Adirondack Park*. Cambridge, MA: Ballinger, 1981.

Lowenthal, David. *Possessed by the Past: The Heritage Crusade and the Spoils of History*. New York: Free Press, 1997.

Lowry, William R. *The Capacity for Winter: Preserving National Parks*. Washington: Brookings Institution, 1994.

Luckett, Perry D. *Charles A. Lindbergh: A Bio-Bibliography*. New York: Greenwood Press, 1986.

Lundberg, Ferdinand. *The Rich and the Super-Rich*. New York: Lyle Stuart, 1968.

Lundberg, Ferdinand. *The Rockefeller Syndrome*. Secaucus, NJ: Lyle Stuart, 1975.

Macauley, David, ed. *Minding Nature: The Philosophers of Ecology*. New York: Guildford Press, 1996.

Machlis, Gary E., ed. *Interpretive Views*. Washington: National Parks and Conservation Association, 1986.

Machlis, Gary E., and Donald R. Field, eds. *On Interpretation: Sociology for Interpreters of Natural and Cultural History*. Corvallis: Oregon State University Press, 1984.

Mack, Arthur C. *The Palisades of the Hudson*. Edgewater, NJ: Palisade Press, 1909.

Mackintosh, Barry. *Interpretation in the National Park Service: A Historical Perspective*. Washington: National Park Service, 1986.

Magat, Richard, ed. *Philanthropic Giving: Studies in Varieties and Goals*. New York: Oxford University Press, 1989.

Manchester, William. *A Rockefeller Family Portrait, from John D. to Nelson*. Boston: Little, Brown, 1959.

Marcus, George E., and Peter Dobkin Hall. *Lives in Trust: The Fortune of Dynastic Families in Late Twentieth-Century America*. Boulder: Westview Press, 1992.

Marquis, Alice Goldfarb. *Art Lessons: Learning from the Rise and Fall of Public Arts Funding*. New York: Basic Books, 1995.

Marquis, Alice G. *Hopes and Ashes: The Birth of Modern Times, 1929–1939*. New York: Free Press, 1986.

Marshall, Anthony D. *Zoo.* New York: Random House, 1994.

Marshall, Anthony D. "Zoo Story," *Wildlife Conservation,* XCVIII (June 1994), 78 ff.

Mason, Jeffrey Moussaieff, and Susan McCarthy. *When Elephants Weep: The Emotional Lives of Animals.* New York: Delacorte Press, 1995.

McElvaine, Robert S. *Mario Cuomo: A Biography.* New York: Scribner's, 1988.

McKibben, Bill. "The Once and Future Wilderness," *Natural History* (no. 5, 1992), pp. 58–63.

McKibben, Bill. "A Second Chance," *Land and People,* VIII (Spring 1996), pp. 26–27.

McMahon, Felicia Faye. "Forging 'The Adirondacker.'" *Western Folklore,* L (July 1991), pp. 277–95.

McMartin, Barbara. *The Great Forest of the Adirondacks.* Utica, NY: North Country Books, 1994.

Means, Marianne. *The Woman in the White House.* New York: Random House, 1963.

Melnick, Robert Z. *Cultural Landscapes: Rural Historic Districts in the National Park System.* Washington: U.S. Department of the Interior, 1984.

Melosi, Martin V. "Lyndon Johnson and Environmental Policy." *In* Robert A. Divine, ed., *The Johnson Years: Vietnam, the Environment, and Science.* Lawrence: University of Kansas Press, 1987, II, pp. 113–49.

Michaels, Joanne, and Mary-Margaret Barile. *The Hudson Valley and Catskill Mountains,* 2nd ed. Woodstock, VT: Countryman Press, 1993.

Middleton, Harry. *LBJ: The White House Years.* New York: Harry N. Abrams, 1990.

Miles, John C. *Guardian of the National Parks: A History of The National Parks and Conservation Association.* Washington: Taylor & Francis, 1995.

Miller, Merle. *Lyndon: An Oral Biography.* New York: Ballantine, 1980.

Milton, Joyce. *Loss of Eden: A Biography of Charles and Anne Morrow Lindbergh.* New York: HarperCollins, 1993.

Modley, Peter Marsh. "Human Problems and Recreational Development: The Proposed Adirondack Mountains National Park." Unpubl. M.A. thesis, Syracuse University, 1969.

Moffett, Mark W. "Tree Giants of North America: Climbing an Ecological Frontier." *The National Geographic,* CXCI (January 1997), pp. 44–61.

Morán Arce, Lucas. *Historia de Puerto Rico,* rev. ed. San Juan: Librotex, 1987.

Morris, Charles R. *The Cost of Good Intentions: New York City and the Liberal Experiment, 1960–1975.* New York: W.W. Norton, 1980.

Morris, Joe Alex. *Nelson Rockefeller: A Biography.* New York: Harper & Row, 1960.

Morris, Joe Alex. *Those Rockefeller Brothers: An Informal Biography of Five Extraordinary Young Men.* New York: Harper & Brothers, 1953.

Moscow, Alvin. *The Rockefeller Inheritance.* New York: Doubleday, 1977.

Mosley, Leonard. *Lindbergh: A Biography.* Garden City, NY: Doubleday, 1976.

Mowbray, Alan Q. *Road to Ruin.* New York: Lippincott, 1969.

Mulligan, Tim. *The Traveler's Guide to the Hudson River Valley,* 3rd ed. New York: Random House, 1995.

Myers, Norman. *Ultimate Security: The Environmental Basis of Political Stability.* New York: W.W. Norton, 1993.

Mylod, John. *Biography of a River: The People and Legends of the Hudson Valley.* New York: Hawthorne, 1969.

Nash, Roderick Frazier. *The Rights of Nature: A History of Environmental Ethics.* Madison: University of Wisconsin Press, 1989.

Nash, Roderick Frazier. *Wilderness and the American Mind.* New Haven: Yale University Press, 1967.

Nathan, Gary Paul, and Stephen Trimble. *The Geography of Childhood: Why Children Need Wild Places.* Boston: Beacon Press, 1994.

National Geographic's Guide to the National Parks of the United States, rev. ed. Washington: National Geographic, 1992.

Nevins, Allan. *John D. Rockefeller: The Heroic Age of American Enterprise,* 2 vols. New York: Scribner's, 1940.

Nevins, Allan. *John D. Rockefeller, Industrialist and Philanthropist: A Study in Power,* 2 vols. New York: Scribner's, 1953.

Newhall, Nancy. *A Contribution to the Heritage of Every American: The Conservation Activities of John D. Rockefeller, Jr.* New York: Alfred A. Knopf, 1957. With Prologue by Fairfield Osborn and Epilogue by Horace M. Albright.

Niebuhr, Reinhold. *The Irony of American History.* New York: Scribner's, 1952.

Nielsen, Waldemar A. *The Big Foundations.* New York: Columbia University Press, 1972.

Nielsen, Waldemar A. *The Golden Donors: A New Anatomy of the Great Foundations.* New York: Dutton, 1985.

Nixon, Stuart. *Redwood Empire.* New York: E.P. Dutton, 1966.

Nyhuis, Allen W. *The Zoo Book.* Albany, CA: Carousel Press, 1994.

Nyhuis, Allen W. *The Zoo Book: A Guide to America's Best.* New York: N.p., 1994.

O'Brien, Raymond J. *American Sublime: Landscape and Scenery of the Lower Hudson Valley.* New York: Columbia University Press, 1981.

Odendahl, Teresa, ed. *America's Wealthy and the Future of Foundations.* New York: The Foundation Center, 1987.

Olwig, Karen Fog. "National Parks, Tourism and Local Development, A West India Case," *Human Organization,* XXXIX (Spring 1980), pp. 22–31.

O'Neill, Edward A. *Rape of the American Virgins.* New York: Praeger, 1972.

Ostrower, Francis. *Why the Wealthy Give.* Princeton: Princeton University Press, 1996.

Owens, W.A. *Pocantico Hills, 1609–1959.* Tarrytown: Sleepy Hollow Restorations, 1960.

Packard, Vance. *The Ultra Rich.* Boston: Little, Brown, 1989.

Paehlke, Robert, ed. *Conservation and Environmentalism: An Encyclopedia.* New York: Garland, 1995.

Paehlke, Robert C. *Environmentalism and the Future of Progressive Politics.* New Haven: Yale University Press, 1989.

Persico, Joseph E. *The Imperial Rockefeller: A Biography of Nelson A. Rockefeller.* New York: Simon and Schuster, 1982.

Popper, Frank J. *The Politics of Land-Use Reform.* Madison: University of Wisconsin Press, 1981.

Powell, Wolter W., ed. *The Nonprofit Sector: A Research Handbook.* New Haven: Yale University Press, 1987.

Pringle, Laurence. "Storm Over Storm King," *Audubon,* CXX (August 1968), pp. 60–73.

Pyke, Tom, and Beth Day. *Pocantico: Fifty Years in the Rockefeller Domain.* New York: Duell, Sloan and Pearce, 1964.

Reich, Cary. *The Life of Nelson A. Rockefeller: Worlds to Conquer, 1908–1958.* New York: Doubleday, 1996.

Reiger, John P. *American Sportsmen and the Origins of Conservation,* rev. ed. Norman: University of Oklahoma Press, 1986.

Reilly, William K. *The Use of Land: A Citizen's Guide to Urban Growth.* New York: Crowell, 1973.

Righter, Robert W. "The Brief, Hectic Life of Jackson Hole National Monument." *The American West,* XIII (December 1976), pp. 30–33, 57–62.

Righter, Robert W. *Crucible for Conservation: The Creation of Grand Teton National Park.* Boulder: Colorado Associated University Press, 1982.

Robbins, Jim. *Last Refuge: The Environmental Showdown in Yellowstone and the American West.* New York: William Morrow, 1993.

Robbins, Roy M. *Our Landed Heritage: The Public Domain, 1776–1936.* Princeton: Princeton University Press, 1942.

Robinson, Alan H. *Virgin Islands National Park: The Story Behind the Scenery.* Las Vegas, NV: KC Publications, 1974.

Roberts, Ann Rockefeller. *Mr. Rockefeller's Roads: The Untold Story of Acadia's Carriage Roads & Their Creator.* Camden, ME: Down East Books, 1990.

Rodgers, William. *Rockefeller's Follies: An Unauthorized View of Nelson A. Rockefeller.* New York: Stein and Day, 1966.

Rosario Natal, Carmelo. *Luis Muñoz Marín y la Independencia de Puerto Rico (1907–1946).* San Juan: Producciones Historicas, 1994.

Rose-Ackerman, Susan, ed. *The Economics of Nonprofit Institutions: Studies in Structure and Policy.* New York: Oxford University Press, 1986.

Ross, Walter S. *The Last Hero: Charles Lindbergh,* rev. ed. New York: Harper & Row, 1976.

Rothman, Hal. *Preserving Different Pasts: The American National Monuments.* Urbana: University of Illinois Press, 1989.

Rulon, Philip Reed. *The Compassionate Samaritan: The Life of Lyndon Baines Johnson.* Chicago: Nelson-Hall, 1981.

Runte, Alfred. *National Parks: The American Experience,* 2nd ed., revised. Lincoln: University of Nebraska Press, 1987.

Sale, Kirkpatrick. *The Green Revolution: The American Environmental Movement, 1962–1992.* New York: Hill and Wang, 1993.

Samuel, Raphael. *Theatres of Memory: Volume 1—Past and Present in Contemporary Culture.* London: Verso, 1994.

Saarinen, Aline B. *The Proud Possessors*. New York: Random House, 1958.

Sax, Joseph L. *Mountains Without Handrails: Reflections on the National Parks*. Ann Arbor: University of Michigan Press, 1980.

Saylor, David J. *Jackson Hole, Wyoming: In the Shadow of the Tetons*. Norman: University of Oklahoma Press, 1970.

Schaller, George B. *The Last Panda*. Chicago: University of Chicago Press, 1993.

Schenkel, Albert F. *The Rich Man and the Kingdom: John D. Rockefeller, Jr., and the Protestant Establishment*. Minneapolis: Fortress Press, 1995.

Schneider, Paul. *The Adirondacks: A History of America's First Wilderness*. New York: Henry Holt, 1997.

Schrepfer, Susan R. "Conflict in Preservation: The Sierra Club, Save-the-Redwoods League and Redwood National Park." *Journal of Forest History*, XXIV (April 1980), pp. 60–77.

Schrepfer, Susan R. *The Fight to Save the Redwoods: A History of Environmental Reform, 1917–1978*. Madison: University of Wisconsin Press, 1983.

Schwartz, Joel. *The New York Approach: Robert Moses, Urban Liberals, and Redevelopment of the Inner City*. Columbus: Ohio State University Press, 1993.

Seaver, George. *Albert Schweitzer: The Man and His Mind*, 6th ed. London: Adam & Charles Black, 1969.

Seely, Bruce E. *Building the American Highway System: Engineers and Policy Makers*. Philadelphia: Temple University Press, 1987.

Shankland, Robert. *Steve Mather of the National Parks*. New York: Knopf, 1951.

Shenkman, Richard. *Legends, Lies, and Cherished Myths of American History*, New York: William Morrow, 1988.

Shortridge, James R. *The Middle West: Its Meaning in American Culture*. Lawrence: University Press of Kansas, 1989.

Sidey, Hugh. *A Very Personal Presidency: Lyndon Johnson in the White House*. New York: Athenaeum, 1968.

Silverman, Michael R. "The Impact of Competing Pressure Groups on the Passage of the N.Y.S. Adirondack Park Land Use Bill of 1973." Unpubl. Ph.D. diss., New York University, 1976.

Sleicher, Charles Albert. *The Adirondacks: American Playground*. New York: Exposition Press, 1960.

Smith, Charles Dennis. "The Appalachian National Park Movement, 1885–1901." *The North Carolina Historical Review*, XXXVII (January 1960), pp. 38–65.

Smith, Elizabeth Simpson. *Five First Ladies: A Look into the Lives of Nancy Reagan, Rosalynn Carter, Betty Ford, Pat Nixon, and Lady Bird Johnson*. New York: Walker, 1986.

Snow, Donald. *Inside the Environmental Movement: Meeting the Leadership Challenge*. Washington: Island Press, 1992.

Snyder, Opal. "History of the Great Smoky Mountain National Park." Unpubl. M.A. thesis, George Peabody College of Teachers, 1935.

Spirn, Anne Whisten. *The Granite Garden: Urban Nature and Human Design*. New York: Basic Books, 1984.

Stanne, Stephen P., Robert G. Panetta, and Brian E. Forist. *The Hudson: An Illustrated Guide to the Living River*. New Brunswick, NJ: Rutgers University Press, 1996.

Stasz, Clarice. *The Rockefeller Women: Dynasty of Piety, Privacy, and Service*. New York: St. Martin's Press, 1995.

Stebenne, David L. *Arthur J. Goldberg: New Deal Liberal*. New York: Oxford University Press, 1996.

Steinberg, Michael. *Our Wilderness: How the People of New York Found, Changed and Preserved the Adirondacks*. Lake George, NY: Adirondack Mountains Club, 1992.

Stonecash, Jeffrey M., John Kenneth White, and Peter W. Colby. *Governing New York State*, 3rd ed. Albany: State University of New York Press, 1994.

Straetz, Ralph A., and Frank J. Munger. *New York Politics*. New York: New York University Press, 1960.

Strong, Douglas E. *Dreamers & Defenders: American Conservationists*. Lincoln: University of Nebraska Press, 1988.

Swain, Donald C. *Wilderness Defender: Horace M. Albright and Conservation*. Chicago: University of Chicago Press, 1970.

Talbot, Allan. *Power Along the Hudson: The Storm King Case and the Birth of Environmentalism*. New York: E.P. Dutton, 1972.

Talbot, Allan. *Settling Things: Six Case Studies in Environmental Mediation*. Washington: Conservation Foundation, 1983.

Tanner, Ogden. *Gardens of the Hudson River Valley: An Illustrated Guide*. New York: H.N. Abrams, 1996.

"Tarnished Jewels: The Case for Reforming the Park Service." *Different Drummer*, whole number (Winter 1995), pp. 1–48.

Taylor, C.J. *Negotiating the Past*. Montreal: McGill-Queen's University Press, 1990.

Terrie, Philip G. "The Adirondack Forest Preserve: The Irony of Forever Wild," *New York History*, LXII (July 1981), pp. 261–88.

Terrie, Phillip G. *Contested Terrain: A New History of Nature and People in the Adirondacks*. Syracuse: Syracuse University Press, 1997.

Terrie, Philip G. *Forever Wild: Environmental Aesthetics and the Adirondack Forest Preserve*. Philadelphia: Temple University Press, 1985.

Terrie, Phillip G. "A Hard Place to Live." *Adirondack Life*. XXVIII (April 1997), pp. 54–59, 72–73.

Terrie, Philip G. "Urban Man Confronts the Wilderness: The Nineteenth-Century Sportsman in the Adirondacks." *Journal of Sport History*, V (Winter 1978), pp. 7–20.

Thompson, George F., ed. *Landscape in America*. Austin: University of Texas Press, 1995.

Thompson, Roger C. "The Doctrine of Wilderness: A Study of the Policy and Politics of the Adirondack Preserve/Park." Unpubl. Ph.D. diss., Syracuse University, 1962.

Tilden, Freeman. *Interpreting Our Heritage*, 3rd ed. Chapel Hill: University of North Carolina Press, 1977.

Tilden, Freeman. *The National Parks: What They Mean to You and Me*. New York: Alfred A. Knopf, 1951.

Tilden, Freeman. *The State Parks: Their Meaning in American Life*. New York: Alfred A. Knopf, 1962.

Toops, Connie. *Great Smoky Mountains*. Stillwater, MN: Voyageur Press, 1992.

Troy, Gil. *Affairs of State*. New York: Free Press, 1997.

Truman, Margaret. *First Ladies*. New York: Random House, 1995.

Tucker, William. *Progress and Privilege: America in the Age of Environmentalism*. Garden City, NY: Anchor Press/Doubleday, 1982.

Tudge, Colin. *Last Animals at the Zoo: How Mass Extinction Can Be Stopped*. Washington: Island Press, 1992.

Turner, Michael. *The Vice President as Policy Maker: Rockefeller in the Ford White House*. Westport, CT: Greenwood Press, 1982.

Underwood, James E., and William J. Daniels. *Governor Rockefeller in New York: The Apex of Pragmatic Liberalism in the United States*. Westport, CT: Greenwood Press, 1982.

Unger, Irwin and Debi. *Turning Point, 1968*. New York: Scribner's, 1988.

Urwin, Cathy Kunzinger. *Agenda for Reform: Winthrop Rockefeller as Governor of Arkansas, 1967–71*. Fayetteville: University of Arkansas, 1991.

Van Tassel, David D., and John J. Grabowski, eds. *The Encyclopedia of Cleveland History*. Bloomington: Indiana University Press, 1987.

Van Til, Jon, ed. *Critical Issues in American Philanthropy: Strengthening Theory and Practice*. San Francisco: Jossey-Bass, 1990.

Van Valkenburgh, Norman J. *The Adirondack Forest Preserve: A Narrative of the Evolution of the Adirondack Forest Preserve of New York State*. Blue Mountain Lake, NY: The Adirondack Museum, 1979. Re-issued by University Microfilms, Ann Arbor, 1995.

Van Valkenburgh, Norman J. *The Forest Preserve of New York State in the Adirondack and Catskill Mountains: A Short History*. Schenectady: Adirondack Research Center, 1983.

Velazquez Net, Ismaro. *Muñoz y Sanchez Vilella*. San Juan: Universidad de Puerto Rico, 1974.

Walth, Brent. *Fire at Eden's Gate: Tom McCall & the Oregon Story*. Portland: Oregon Historical Society Press, 1994.

Ward, John A. *The Arkansas Rockefeller*. Baton Rouge: Louisiana State University Press, 1978.

Watkins, T.H. *Righteous Pilgrim: The Life and Times of Harold L. Ickes, 1874–1952*. New York: Henry Holt, 1990.

Welsh, Peter C. *Jacks, Jobbers and Kings: Logging the Adirondacks, 1850–1950*. Utica: North Country Books, 1995.

West, Carroll Van. *Tennessee's Historic Landscapes*. Knoxville: University of Tennessee Press, 1995.

Westermann, J.H. *Nature Preservation in the Caribbean*. Utrecht: Publications of the Foundation for Scientific Research in Surinam and the Netherlands Antilles, no. 9, 1953.

Whaley, John Thomas. "A Timely Idea at an Ideal Time: Knoxville's Role in Establishing the Great Smoky Mountains National Park." Unpubl. M.A. thesis. University of Tennessee, 1984.

White House Historical Association. *The White House: An Historic Guide*. 18th ed., Washington: The Association, 1994.

White, William Chapman. *Adirondack Country*. Syracuse: Syracuse University Press, 1985.

Wild, Peter. *Pioneer Conservationists of Western America*. Missoula: Mountain Press, 1979.

Williams, Deborah. *Natural Wonders of New York: A Guide to Parks, Preserves & Wild Places*. Castine, ME: Country Roads Press, 1995.

Wilson, Alexander. *The Culture of Nature: North American Landscape from Disney to the Exxon Valdez*. Cambridge, MA: Blackwell, 1992.

Wilson, John W. *The New Venturers: Inside the High-Stakes World of Venture Capital*. Reading, MA: Addison-Wesley, 1985.

Wilson, Richard Guy, Dianne H. Pilgrim, and Dickran Tashjian. *The Machine Age in America, 1918–1941*. New York: Harry B. Abrams, 1986.

Winkelman, B.F. *John D. Rockefeller: The Authentic and Dramatic Story of the World's Greatest Money Maker and Money Giver*. Chicago: John C. Winston Co., 1937.

Winkler, John K. *John D.: A Portrait in Oils*. New York: Vanguard Press, 1929.

Winks, Robin W. *Frederick Billings: A Life*. New York: Oxford University Press, 1990.

Winks, Robin W. "The National Park Service Act of 1916: 'A Contradictory Mandate'?" *Denver University Law Review*, LXXIV (1997).

Wood, Joseph S. *The New England Village*. Baltimore: John Hopkins University Press, 1997.

Woodard, Charles L., ed. *Ancestral Voice: Conversations with N. Scott Momaday*. Lincoln: University of Nebraska Press, 1989.

Worster, Donald. *Nature's Economy: A History of Ecological Ideas*. New York: Cambridge University Press, 1985.

Yergin, Daniel. *The Prize: The Epic Quest of Oil, Money, and Power*. New York: Simon & Schuster, 1993.

Zimmerman, Joseph F. *The Government and Politics of New York State*. New York: New York University Press, 1981.

Zinser, Charles I. *The Economic Impact of the Adirondack Park Private Land Use and Development Plan*. Albany: State University of New York Press, 1980.

Zinser, Charles I. *Outdoor Recreation: United States National Parks, Forest, and Public Lands*. New York: John Wiley, 1995.

Zinsser, William. *American Places*. New York: HarperCollins, 1992.

Index